alan cooper

THE INMATES ARE RUNNING THE ASYLUM

SAMS

A Division of Pearson Education
800 East 96th Street, Indianapolis, Indiana 46240

The Inmates Are Running the Asylum

Copyright © 2004 by Sams Publishing

International Standard Book Number: 0-672-32614-0

Library of Congress Catalog Card Number: 2003116997

Printed in the United States of America

First Printing: March 2004

07   06   05   04   4   3   2

Trademarks

Warning and Disclaimer

Bulk Sales

Sams Publishing offers excellent discounts on this book when ordered in quantity for bulk purchases or special sales. For more information, please contact

U.S. Corporate and Government Sales
1-800-382-3419
corpsales@pearsontechgroup.com

For sales outside of the U.S., please contact

International Sales
1-317-428-3341
international@pearsontechgroup.com

Publisher
Paul Boger

Executive Editor
Candace Hall

Managing Editor
Charlotte Clapp

Project Editor
Dan Knott

Copy Editor
Eileen Cohen

Indexer
Ken Johnson

Proofreader
Juli Cook

Publishing Coordinator
Cindy Teeters

Interior Designer
Karen Ruggles

Cover Designer
Alan Clements

Page Layout
Eric S. Miller

DEDICATION

For Sue, Scott and Marty, with love.

ACKNOWLEDGMENTS

I could not have written this book without the care and help of many wonderful friends and colleagues. In particular, several people performed the demanding and difficult job of reading and commenting on the manuscript, sometimes more than once. Their comments made me answer tough questions, introduce my topics, sum up my points, quench my flames, and corral my wild fits of indignation. The book is far better because of the contributions of Kim Goodwin, Lane Halley, Kelly Bowman, Scott McGregor, David West, Mike Nelson, Mark Dziersk, Alan Karp, Terry Swack, Louie Weitzman, Wayne Greenwood, Ryan Olshavsky, John Meyer, Lisa Saunders, Winnie Shows, Kevin Wandryk, Glenn Halstead, Bryan O'Sullivan, Chuck Owen, Mike Swaine, and Skip Walter. I really appreciate your time, care, and wisdom. In particular, Jonathan Korman's comments and counsel were invaluable in helping me to distill my themes. I must also thank all the talented and hard-working people at Cooper Interaction Design who did my job for me while I was busy writing. Deserving of special thanks is Design Director Wayne Greenwood, who did a great job under pressure keeping our design quality and morale high.

Getting the illustrations done turned out to be one of the more interesting production challenges. Chad Kubo, the masterful creator of the images, did a remarkable job of interpreting my vague ideas into crisp and memorable images. They add a lot to the book. The illustrations could not have been done at all without the tireless art direction work of Penny Bayless and David Hale. Still others helped with the many production tasks. Thanks to Brit Katzen for fact checking and research and Mike Henry for copy editing.

Writing a book is a business, and for making it a successful one I also owe sincere thanks to my team of technology-savvy businesspersons, headed by my agent Jim Levine, and including Glenn Halstead, Lynne Bowman, Kelly Bowman, and Sue Cooper. At Pearson, Brad Jones supported this project throughout, but the most credit goes to Chris Webb, whose tenacity, focus, and hard work really made *The Inmates* happen.

I really appreciate the many people who provided moral support, anecdotes, advice, and time. Thanks very much to Daniel Appleman, Todd Basche, Chris Bauer, Jeff Bezos, Alice Blair, Michel Bourque, Po Bronson, Steve Calde, David Carlick, Jeff Carlick, Carol Christie, Clay Collier, Kendall Cosby, Dan Crane, Robert X. Cringely, Troy Daniels, Lisa Powers, Philip Englehardt, Karen Evensen, Ridgely Evers, Royal Farros, Pat Fleck, David Fore, Ed Forman, Ed Fredkin, Jean-Louis Gassee, Jim Gay, Russ Goldin, Vlad Gorelik, Marcia Gregory, Garrett Gruener, Chuck Hartledge, Ted Harwood, Will Hearst, Tamra Heathershaw-Hart, J.D. Hildebrand, Laurie Hills, Peter Hirshberg, Larry Keeley, Gary Kratkin, Deborah Kurata, Tom Lafleur, Paul Laughton, Ellen Levy, Steven List, T.C. Mangan, David Maister, Robert May, Don McKinney, Kathryn Meadows, Lisa Mitchell, Geoffrey Moore, Bruce Mowery, Nate Myers, Ed Niehaus, Constance Petersen, Keith Pleas, Robert Reimann, John Rivlin, Howard Rheingold, Heidi Roizen, Neil Rubenking, Paul Saffo, Josh Seiden, Russ Siegelman, Donna Slote, Linda Stone, Toni Walker, Kevin Weeks, Kevin Welch, Dan Willis, Heather Winkle, Stephen Wildstrom, Terry Winograd, John Zicker, and Pierluigi Zappacosta.

This "year long" project took 20 months, and my family showed great patience with me. I owe the greatest debt of love and thanks to my wife, Sue Cooper, and to my handsome young sons, Scott and Marty. I love you with all of my heart.

TABLE OF CONTENTS

INTRODUCTION

Run for your lives—the computers are invading. Awesomely powerful computers tackling ever more important tasks with awkward, old-fashioned interfaces. As these machines leak into every corner of our lives, they will annoy us, infuriate us, and even kill a few of us. In turn, we will be tempted to kill our computers, but we won't dare because we are already utterly, irreversibly dependent on these hopeful monsters that make modern life possible.

Fortunately, we have another option. We need to fundamentally rethink how humans and machines interact. And rethink the relationship in deep and novel ways, for the fault for our burgeoning problems lies not with our machines, but with us. Humans designed the interfaces we hate; humans continue to use dysfunctional machines even as the awkward interfaces strain their eyes, ache their backs, and ruin their wrist tendons. We all are, as the title of this book suggests, the inmates running the techno-asylum of our own creation.

This book is a guide to our escape. Or rather, Alan Cooper reveals that the door to the asylum lies wide open. We are free to leave any time we want, but mad as we have all become, we never noticed until now. The secret lies in redefining the way we interact with our computers in a larger context.

Alan Cooper is not merely a fellow inmate; he is also a heretic whose ideas will likely infuriate those who would want to keep us locked up. These are the engineers who built the systems we hate and who still believe the way out of this mess is to build better interfaces. But the very notion of *interface* is itself an artifact of an age when computers were scarce and puny, and barely able to interact with their human masters. *Interface* made sense when the entire interaction took place across the glass-thin no-man land of a computer screen. Now it is an utterly dangerous notion in a world where computers are slipping into every corner of our lives. Computers no longer interface with humans—they interact, and the interaction will become steadily deeper, more subtle, and more crucial to our collective sanity and ultimate survival.

Alan Cooper understands the shift from interface to interaction better than anyone I know. His ideas come from years of experience in helping design products that slip elegantly and unobtrusively into our lives. He has walked his talk for years, and now he has finally found the time to turn his practice into a lucid description of the challenge we face, and a methodology for escaping the asylum we have so lovingly built. Read on and you will find your freedom.

Paul Saffo
Director
Institute for the Future

Foreword to the Original Edition

The Business-Case Book

I intended to write a very different book from this one: a how-to book about the interaction-design process. Instead, in May 1997 on a family visit to Tuscany, my friends Don McKinney and Dave Carlick talked me into this one. They convinced me that I needed to address a business audience first.

They knew I wanted to write a how-to design book, and—although they were encouraging—they expressed their doubts about the need for interaction design, and they wanted me to write a book to convince them of its value. Their argument was intriguing, but I was unsure that I could write the book they wanted.

Late one night on the veranda of our shared ochre villa overlooking Firenze, I was having an earnest conversation with Dave and Don. Several empty bottles of Chianti stood on the table, along with the remains of some bread, cheese, and olives. The stars shone brightly, the fireflies danced over the lawn, and the lights on the ancient domes of the Tuscan capital twinkled in the distance. Once again, Dave suggested that I postpone the idea of a how-to book on design and instead "make the business case for interaction design."

I protested vigorously, "But Dave, I don't know how to write that book." I ticked off the reasons on my fingertips. "It means that I'd have to explain things like how the current development process is messed up, how companies waste money on inefficient software construction, how unsatisfied customers are fickle, and how a better design process can solve that."

Dave interrupted me to say simply, "They're called chapters, Alan."

His remark stopped me dead in my tracks. I realized that I was reciting an old script, and that Dave was right. A book that made "the business case" *was* necessary—and more timely—than a book that explained "how to." And both Dave and Don convinced me that I really could write such a book.

Business-Savvy Technologist/Technology-Savvy Businessperson

The successful professional for the twenty-first century is either a *business-savvy technologist* or a *technology-savvy businessperson*, and I am writing for this person.

The technology-savvy businessperson knows that his success is dependent on the quality of the information available to him and the sophistication with which he uses it. The business-savvy technologist, on the other hand, is an entrepreneurial engineer or scientist trained for technology, but possessing a keen business sense and an awareness of the power of information. Both of these new archetypes are coming to dominate contemporary business.

You can divide all businesspeople into two categories: those who will master high technology and those who will soon be going out of business. No longer can an executive delegate information processing to specialists. Business *is* information processing. You differentiate yourself today with the quality of your information-handling systems, not your manufacturing systems. If you manufacture anything, chances are it has a microchip in it. If you offer a service, odds are that you offer it with computerized tools. Attempting to identify businesses that depend on high technology is as futile as trying to identify businesses that depend on the telephone. The high-tech revolution has invaded every business, and digital information is the beating heart of your workday.

It's been said, "To err is human; to really screw up, you need a computer." Inefficient mechanical systems can waste a couple of cents on every widget you build, but you can lose your entire company to bad information processes. The leverage that software-based products—and the engineers that build them—have on your company is enormous.

Sadly, our digital tools are extremely hard to learn, use, and understand, and they often cause us to fall short of our goals. This wastes money, time, and opportunity. As a business-savvy technologist/technology-savvy businessperson, you produce software-based products or consume them—probably both. Having better, easier-to-learn, easier-to-use high-tech products is in your personal and professional best interest. Better products don't take longer to create, nor do they cost more to build. The irony is that they don't have to be difficult, but are so only because our process for making them is old-fashioned and needs fixing. Only long-standing traditions rooted in misconceptions keep us from having better products today. This book will show you how you can demand—and get—the better products that you deserve.

The point of this book is uncomplicated: We can create powerful and pleasurable software-based products by the simple expedient of *designing* our computer-based products *before* we build them. Contrary to the popular belief, we are not already doing so. Designing interactive, software-based products is a specialty as demanding as constructing them.

⌘

Having made my choice to write the business-case book rather than the how-to design book, I beg forgiveness from any interaction designers reading this book. In deference to the business audience, it has only the briefest treatment of the actual nuts and bolts of interaction-design methodology (found primarily in Part IV, "Interaction Design Is Good Business"). I included only enough to show that such methodology exists, that it is applicable to any subject matter, and that its benefits are readily apparent to anyone, regardless of their technical expertise.

Alan Cooper
Palo Alto, California
http://www.cooper.com
inmates@cooper.com

Foreword

I recently met with a senior executive at one of the world's largest technology companies. His official title is Vice President for Ease of Use, and he is responsible for a great number of software products, large and small. He is a brilliant and accomplished fellow with roots in the formal Human-Computer Interaction community. He is steeped in the ways of "usability"—of testing and observing behind one-way mirrors—as is his company. But he came to talk about design, not testing, and about personas, not users. He said that his company has completely ceased all postdevelopment usability testing and has instead committed to predevelopment design efforts. He further asserted that all of his staffers trained in the art of *in vitro* user observation were being retrained to do *in situ* ethnographic research.

This executive and his company are emblematic of the sea of change that has occurred in the industry in the five short years since *The Inmates* was first published. The book has served as both a manifesto for a revolution and a handbook for a discipline. Countless midlevel product managers have sent me email describing why—after reading *The Inmates*—they purchased a copy of the book for each of their departments' senior executives. Meanwhile, software builders and universities alike have used the three chapters in Part IV, "Interaction Design Is Good Business," as a rudimentary how-to manual for implementing Goal-Directed® design using personas.

I am deeply grateful to all of the managers, programmers, executives, and usability practitioners who have used the ideas in this book to help bring usability out of the laboratory and into the field and changed its focus from testing to design. Because of their efforts, the entire landscape of the usability profession has changed. Today, most of the organizations I have contact with have one or more interaction-design professionals on their payrolls, who have an ever-increasing influence over the quality and behavior of the software products and services being created. It's gratifying to know that this book has contributed to their success.

I recall giving a keynote presentation at a programmer's conference in 1999, shortly after this book was first published. That talk had the same title as the book, and I opened by asserting that "inmates are running the asylum, and *you* are the inmates." You could hear a pin drop as the more than 2,500 engineers in the audience grappled with that accusation. In the silence that engulfed the auditorium, I went on to present the basic premise of this book, and an hour later, that crowd of *Homo logicus* was so sufficiently convinced that they honored me with a standing ovation. Surprisingly, most programmers have become enthusiastic supporters of design and designers. They know that they need help on the human side of software construction, and they are very happy to be finally receiving some useful guidance. They recognize that any practice that improves the quality and acceptance of their programs doesn't threaten them.

In the past, executives assumed that interaction design was a programming problem and delegated it to programmers, who diligently tried to solve the problem even though their skills, training, mindset, and work schedule prevented them from succeeding. In the spirit of problem diagnosis, this book takes pains to describe this failure, which is necessarily a story of the programmer's failure. Some of them took offense at my descriptions, imagining that I was maligning or blaming programmers for bad software. They are certainly the *agents* by which bad software is created, but they are by no means culpable. I do not blame programmers for hard-to-use software, and I'm very sorry to have given any programmer a contrary impression. With few exceptions, the programmers I know are diligent and conscientious in their desire to please end users and are unceasing in their efforts to improve their programs' quality. Just like users, programmers are simply another victim of a flawed process that leaves them too little time, too many conflicting orders, and utterly insufficient guidance. I am very sorry to have given any programmers the impression that I fault them.

The intractability of the software-construction process—particularly the high cost of programming and the low quality of interaction—is simply not a technical problem. It is the result of business practices imposed on a discipline—software programming—for which they are obsolete. With pure hearts, the best of intentions, and the blessing of upper management, programmers attempt to fix this problem by engineering even harder. But more or better engineering cannot solve these problems. Programmers sense the growing futility of their efforts, and their frustration mounts.

In my recent travels I have noticed a growing malaise in the community of programmers. Sadly, it is the best and most experienced of them who are afflicted the worst. They reflect cynicism and ennui about their efforts because they know that their skills are being wasted. They may not know exactly how they are misapplied, but they cannot overlook the evidence. Many of the best programmers have actually stopped programming because they find the work frustrating. They have retreated into training, evangelism, writing, and consulting because it does-n't feel so wasteful and counterproductive. This is a tragic and entirely avoidable loss. (The open-source movement is arguably a haven for these frustrated programmers—a place where they can write code according to their own stan-dards and be judged solely by their peers, without the advice or intervention of marketers or managers.)

Programmers are not given sufficient time, clear enough direction, or adequate designs to enable them to succeed. These three things are the responsibility of business executives, and they fail to deliver them for preventable reasons, not because they are stupid or evil. They are simply not armed with adequate tools for solving the complex and unique problems that confront them in the infor-mation age. Now here I am sounding like I'm slamming people again, only this time businesspeople are in my sights instead of programmers. Once again, to solve the problem one must deconstruct it. I'm questing after solutions, not scapegoats.

Management sage Peter Drucker can see the problem from his unique view-point, having both observed and guided executives for the majority of his 92 years. In a recent interview in CIO magazine, he commented on the wide-eyed optimism of executives in the 1950s and 1960s as digital computers first nudged their way into their businesses. Those executives imagined that computers "would have an enormous impact on how the business was run," but Drucker exclaims, "This isn't what happened. Very few senior executives have asked the question, 'What information do I need to do my job?'" Although digital comput-ers have given executives unprecedented quantities of data, few have asked whether this data is appropriate for guiding the corporation. Operations have changed dramatically, but management has not followed suit. Drucker accuses our obsolete accounting systems, born in mercantilism, come of age in an era of steam and iron, and doddering into senility in the dawning twenty-first century information age. Drucker asserts, "The information you need the most is about the outside world, and there is absolutely none."

During the last few years of the twentieth century, as the dot-com bubble inflat-ed, truckloads of ink were used to sell the idea that there was a "new economy" on the Internet. The pundits said that selling things on the World Wide Web, where stores were made of clicks instead of bricks, was a fundamentally different way of doing business, and that the "old economy" was as good as dead. Of course, almost all of those new-economy companies are dead and gone, the ven-ture capitalists who backed them are in shock, and the pundits who pitched the new economy have now recanted, claiming it was all a hopeless dream. The new, new thinking says we must still be in the old, old economy.

Actually, I believe that we really *are* in a new economy. What's more, I think that the dot-coms never even participated in it. Instead, the dot-coms were the last gasp of the *old* economy: the economy of manufacturing.

In the industrial age, before software, products were *manufactured* from solid material—from atoms. The money it took to mine, smelt, purchase, transport, heat, form, weld, paint, and transport dominated all other expenditures. Accountants call these "variable costs" because that expense varies directly with each product built. "Fixed costs," as you might expect, don't vary directly and include things such as corporate administration and the initial cost of the factory.

The classic rules of business management are rooted in the manufacturing traditions of the industrial age. Unfortunately, they have yet to address the new realities of the information age, in which products are no longer made from atoms but are mostly software, made only from the arrangements of bits. And bits don't follow the same economic rules that atoms do.

Some fundamental truths hold for both the old and the new economies. The goal of all business is to make a sustainable profit, and there is only one legal way to do so: Sell some goods or services for more money than it costs you to make or acquire them. It follows that there are two ways to increase your profitability: Either reduce your costs or increase your revenues. In the old economy, reducing your costs worked best. In the new economy, increasing your revenue works much, much better.

Today's most vital and expensive products are made largely or completely of software. They consume no raw materials. They have no manufacturing cost. They have no transportation cost. There is no welding, hammering, or painting. This is the real difference between the industrial-age economy and the information-age economy: In the information age, there is little or no variable cost, whereas in the late industrial age, variable cost was the dominant factor. Indeed, the absence of variable cost is what *makes* this a new economy.

Is the salary you pay the programmers on your staff a fixed cost or a variable cost? One hour of programming is definitely not directly related to one product sale; you can sell that same code over and over again. An investment in programming can be leveraged across millions of salable items, just as an investment in a factory is leveraged across all the products built within it.

Writing software is not a variable cost, but it's not really a fixed cost either. Writing software is an ongoing, revenue-generating operation of the company, and it is not the same as constructing a factory. The expensive craftsmen who build the factory leave and go to work on some other job after the building is erected. Programmers are far more expensive than carpenters or ironworkers, and they never go away because their work is apparently never completed. Some might suggest that programming is research and development, and there are similarities. However, R & D is the thinking and experimenting done to establish the theoretical viability of a product and is not performed the same way that products are built in a production environment. Fittingly, traditional accounting separates R & D expenditures from the daily operations that generate revenue. Writing software doesn't work well in any of those old business-accounting categories.

Now, you might discount this little terminology mismatch as a minor quibble for bean-counters with green eyeshades to debate over beers, but it actually has a huge effect on how software is funded, managed, and—most significantly— regarded by senior executives.

Programmers create software, and business executives create revenue streams and profit centers. Programmers measure their success by the quality of the product, and business executives measure their success by the profitability of their investments. They measure this profitability by applying the language of business mathematics, which recognizes fixed costs, variable costs, corporate overhead, and research and development, but, unfortunately, it has no model appropriate for software or programming. Accounting is the basic language of business, and these categories are so fundamental to all business measurement and communication that contemporary executives have completely internalized them. They see programming as simply another corporate expense to be fitted into an already existing category. In practice, most executives simply treat programming as a manufacturing effort—a variable cost. (For tax purposes, most software companies account for programming as R & D, but it is regarded as a variable cost in every other respect.) This is the worst possible choice because it hopelessly prejudices their business decision making.

The key advantage of the industrial age was that products could be mass-produced, which means they could be made available to the masses at affordable prices. The advantage to customers was the availability of functions that were previously unavailable or only expensively hand built for the wealthy. Companies competed on the basis of their sales prices, which were directly related to their variable costs: the cost of manufacturing and shipping. In the information age, it is taken for granted that products are available at affordable prices to everyone. After all, software can be downloaded and distributed to any number of customers for essentially no cost and with little or no human effort.

Remember, businesses can grow profits by increasing revenue or reducing costs. That is, a business can increase its fixed-cost investment, improving its product's quality, which increases its pricing strength, or it can reduce its variable cost, which means decreasing the cost of manufacturing. In the old manufacturing economy of atoms, reducing costs was simple and effective, and it was the preferred tactic. When today's executives regard programming the same as manufacturing, they imagine that reducing the cost of programming is similarly simple and effective. Unfortunately, those rules don't apply anymore.

Because software has relatively insignificant variable costs, there is little business advantage to be had in reducing them. Programmers' salaries appear to be a variable cost from an accountant's point of view, but they are much more like a long-term investment—a fixed cost. Reducing the cost of programming is not the same as reducing the cost of manufacturing. It's more like giving cheap tools to your workers than it is like giving the workers smaller paychecks. The companies that are shipping programming jobs overseas in order to pay reduced salaries are missing the point entirely.

What's more, the only available economic upside comes from making your product or service more desirable by improving its quality, and you can't do that by reducing the money you spend designing or programming it. In fact, you need to invest *more* time and money on the research, thinking, planning, and designing phase to make your results better suited to your customers' needs.

Of course, this requires a mode of thinking that is quite unfamiliar to twenty-first century businesspeople. Instead of *reducing* what they spend to build *each* object, they need to *increase* what they spend to build *all* objects. This is the essence of the real new economy and precisely what Peter Drucker was talking about.

Modern pharmaceutical companies inventing high-tech drugs share some similarities to the new software economy. The actual manufacturing cost of a single pill is miniscule, but the development costs can run to billions of dollars over a decade or more. The upside of shipping a new miracle drug can be boundless, but there is only a catastrophic downside in shipping that drug before it has been developed completely. Pharmaceuticals know that reducing development costs is not a viable business strategy.

Like inventing medicine, building software isn't the same as building a factory. The factory is a physical asset that a company owns, and the factory workers are largely interchangeable. The intangible but extremely complicated patterns of thought that is software has value only when accompanied by the programmers who wrote it. No company can treat programmers the same as a factory. Programmers demand continuous attention and support well above that of any factory.

Architecture—the human design part of programming, in which users are studied, use scenarios are defined, interaction is designed, form is determined, and behavior is described—is the part of the software-construction process that is most frequently dispensed with as a cost-saving measure. It is certainly possible to do too much design, but there is no advantage in reducing it. Every dollar or hour spent on architecture will yield tenfold savings during programming. Additionally, when you invest a sufficient amount of competent design, your product becomes very desirable, which means that it will make more money for you. Its desirability will establish your brand, increase your ability to raise prices, generate customer loyalty, and give your product a longer, stronger lifespan. Although there's no advantage in cost reduction, there is big advantage in quality enhancement. Ironically, the best way to increase profitability in the information age is to spend more.

Unfortunately, most executives have an almost irresistible desire to reduce the time and money invested in programming. They see, incorrectly, the obsolete advantage in reducing costs. What they don't see is that reduction in investment in programming has strong negative effects on a product's long-term quality, desirability, and therefore profitability. Of course, simply spending more money doesn't guarantee improvement, and it can often make things worse when additional money is unaccompanied by wisdom, analysis, and guidance. My first mentor, Dan Joaquin, used to say that the old maxim "You get what you pay for" should properly be inverted to "You *don't* get what you *don't* pay for." Proceeding without proper planning risks spending *way* too much. The trick is to spend the correct amount, and that demands significant expertise in software-construction management. It also demands process tools that provide managers with the insight and information they need to make the correct decisions. Providing those tools is this book's goal.

The dot-com boom was populated with companies whose entire business model consisted of the reduction of variable costs. Although many dot-coms claimed various online advantages, their Web sites were sufficiently ponderous and unhelpful to be far less satisfying than simply driving to the mall. Dot-com founders swooned with ecstasy (as did the press) because they could establish a retail enterprise for a remarkably lower variable cost. Their complete and spectacular failure demonstrated beyond doubt that the economic rules of the information age are different from those of the industrial age.

In the old economy, lower variable costs meant wider distribution and lower retail costs. Those twin advantages directly benefited the consumer, and they are the foundation for the economic success of the industrial revolution. In the new economy, business success depends on adding something new and better for the consumer. The actual quality of every part of the transaction, from browsing to comparison shopping to comprehensiveness, must be noticeably better for the end user. Wading through 11 screens only to have to telephone the company anyway is far less satisfying than making the purchase conventionally. Entering your name, address, and credit card information three or four times, only to find that the site can't sell you everything you need and a trip to the atom-based store is necessary anyway, has the unfortunate effect of making the entire online sale completely unnecessary and undesirable. Today, simply lowering costs for the vendor doesn't guarantee success.

When Pets.com sold dog food over the Internet, it didn't offer better dog food, and it didn't offer a customer experience better than you could get at the local brick-and-mortar pet store; it didn't offer any better information, intelligence, or confidence. All it offered was cheaper shipping, stocking, and selling—variable costs all—for Pets.com. It was a classic industrial-age-economy tactic of cost reduction that ignored the fundamental principles of the new economy. Far from being the first breath of a new economy, it was the last gasp of the old.

I am absolutely convinced that you can sell *anything* on the Internet profitably and successfully. The trick is that your online store must offer a measurably greater degree of shopper satisfaction than any competing retail medium, and price is only one small component of satisfaction. There is only one way to accomplish this: You must architect your system to deliver the highest possible end-user satisfaction. Treating any aspect of software design and construction as if it were a manufacturing process courts failure. The design and programming of software is simply not a viable target for conventional cost-reduction methods. It's certainly possible to spend too much time and money on building software, but the danger of spending too little is far greater.

Such danger is probably not shocking or unfamiliar to you, but it is nearly inconceivable to most senior business executives who are responsible for running big companies. Those execs are still using accounting models popular in the age of steam, yet every aspect of their companies is fully dependent on software for operations, decision making, communications, and finance. The terms and concepts those executives use are simply not cognizant of the unique nature of doing business in an era when the tools and products of commerce are intangible arrangements of bits instead of railroad carloads of iron. The sock puppets were cool, though.

Even though corporations are hiring interaction designers and applying goal-directed methods, the quality of our software products hasn't actually improved that much. What's more, the high cost of programming and the basic intractability of the software-construction process remain ever-present. Why?

Change is impossible until senior business executives realize that software problems are not technical issues, but are significant business issues. Our problems will remain unsolved until we change our *process* and our *organization*.

Not only do companies follow obsolete financial models, but they also follow an inappropriate organizational model. This model is copied directly from academia, where the act of creating software is entangled with the planning and engineering of that software. Such is the nature of research. Tragically, and apparently without notice, this paradigm has been carried over intact into the world of business, where it does not belong.

All modern manufacturing disciplines have roots in preindustry except software, whose unique medium appeared well after industrialization was a fait accompli. Only programming comes directly from academia, where there are no time limits on research, student power is dirt cheap, profit is against the rules, and a failing program can be considered a very successful experiment. It's not a coincidence that Microsoft, IBM, Oracle, and other leading software companies reside in "campuses." Universities never have to make money, hit deadlines, or build desirable, useful products.

All nonsoftware businesses begin with research and end with mass production and distribution of their products or services. They plan carefully in between, cognizant of the dangers to both bank account and reputation if they attempt premature production of an ill-conceived product. They know that time, thought, and money invested in planning will pay big dividends in the smoothness and speed of manufacturing and the popularity and profitability of their end products.

In all other construction disciplines, engineers plan a construction strategy that craftsmen execute. Engineers don't build bridges; ironworkers do. Only in software is the engineer tasked with actually building the product. Only in software is the "ironworker" tasked with determining how the product will be constructed. Only in software are these two tasks performed concurrently instead of sequentially. But companies that build software seem totally unaware of the anomaly. Engineering and construction are so crossbred as to be inseparable and apparently indistinguishable by practitioners or executives. Planning of all sorts is either omitted or delayed until far too late. Profoundly complex technical engineering problems are habitually left unsolved until construction of code intended for public release is well underway, when it is too economically embarrassing to back up.

Architecture must be integrated into early-stage engineering planning. In fact, it should drive early-stage engineering, but because such engineering is typically deferred until construction has begun and is corrupted by intermingling with production coding, the architectural design lacks an entry point into the construction process. Despite the fact that companies are hiring interaction designers and retraining their usability testers to create personas, their work has little effect on either the cost of construction or the quality of the finished product.

The solution lies in the hands of corporate presidents and chief executive officers. When these execs delegate the solution to their chief technology officers or vice presidents of engineering they miss the point. Those worthy officers are technicians, and the problem is not a technical one. As Drucker pointed out, the accounting tools CEOs depend on simply do not represent the true state of their organizations. It's like saying that because the speedometer is accurate the car is headed in the right direction. In a business world dominated by digital technology, that is simply no longer true.

One of the biggest problems of applying incorrect accounting and organizational methods to software construction is that executives don't realize how much of their programming dollar is wasted. An accurate system would show that at least one half of every dollar is misspent and that it takes another two or three dollars to fix the problems caused by the initial bad investment. In any other business, such statistics would be cause for revolution, but in software we remain in a state of blissful ignorance.

Over the past 13 years my company, Cooper, has consulted with hundreds of companies. My talented designers have provided most of them with blueprints for products that would help them enormously, yet only a handful have been able to take full advantage of them. Most of them treat interaction design and software architecture as advice, and their programmers and engineers *always* have the last word. None of those companies' CEOs has any clue as to what is really going on in the engineers' cubicles, so they squeeze the schedule without reason. The programmers are always working in an environment of scarcity, primarily lacking time to program well, but also lacking the time to determine what should be programmed at all. They are forced to protect themselves by rejecting advice and prevaricating to their managers.

I believe that there are two kinds of executives: those who are engineers, and those who are terrified of engineers. The former propagate the familiar problems because their viewpoint is hopelessly blinkered by a conflict of interest. The latter propagate them because they cannot speak the language of programmers. I don't mean Java or C#. I mean that business people and programmers lack common tools and common goals. *Homo sapiens* delegate human problems to *Homo logicus* and are unaware that the solution could be so much better if they applied—at the executive level—appropriate financial and organizational models instead.

There is a colossal opportunity for companies to break this logjam and organize around customer satisfaction instead of around software, around personas instead of around technology, around profit instead of around programmers. I eagerly await the enlightened executive who seizes this chance and forever alters the way software is built by providing the industry with a bold and successful example.

Alan Cooper
Menlo Park, California
October 2003
http://www.cooper.com
inmates@cooper.com

Part I

COMPUTER OBLITERACY

1

What Do You Get When You Cross a Computer with an Airplane?

In December 1995, American Airlines Flight 965 departed from Miami on a regularly scheduled trip to Cali, Columbia. On the landing approach, the pilot of the 757 needed to select the next radio-navigation fix, named "ROZO." He entered an "R" into his navigation computer. The computer returned a list of nearby navigation fixes starting with "R," and the pilot selected the first of these, whose latitude and longitude appeared to be correct. Unfortunately, instead of "ROZO," the pilot selected "ROMEO," 132 miles to the northeast. The jet was southbound, descending into a valley that runs north–south, and any lateral deviation was dangerous. Following indications on the flight computer, the pilot began an easterly turn and slammed into a granite peak at 10,000 feet. One hundred and fifty-two passengers and all eight crewmembers aboard perished. Four passengers survived with serious injuries. The National Transportation Safety Board investigated, and—as usual—declared the problem human error. The navigational aid the pilot was following was valid, but not for the landing procedure at Cali. In the literal definition of the phrase, this was indeed human error, because the pilot selected the wrong fix. However, in the larger picture, it wasn't the pilot's fault at all.

The front panel of the airplane's navigation computer showed the currently selected navigation fix and a course-deviation indicator. When the plane is on course, the needle is centered, but the needle gives no indication whatsoever about the correctness of the selected radio beacon. The gauge looks pretty much the same just before landing as it does just before crashing. The computer told the pilot he was tracking precisely to the beacon he had selected. Unfortunately, it neglected to tell him the beacon he selected was a fatal choice.

⌘

Communications can be precise and exacting while still being tragically wrong. This happens all too frequently when we communicate with computers, and computers are invading every aspect of our modern lives. From the planes we fly to just about every consumer product and service, computers are ubiquitous, and so is their characteristically poor way of communicating and behaving.

There is a widely told joke in the computer industry that goes like this: A man is flying in a small airplane and is lost in the clouds. He descends until he spots an office building and yells to a man in an open window, "Where am I?" The man replies, "You are in an airplane about 100 feet above the ground." The pilot immediately turns to the proper course, spots the airport, and lands. His astonished passenger asks how the pilot figured out which way to go. The pilot replies, "The answer the man gave me was completely correct and factual, yet it was no help whatsoever, so I knew immediately he was a software engineer who worked for Microsoft, and I know where Microsoft's building is in relation to the airport."

When seen in the light of the tragedy of Flight 965, the humor of the joke is macabre, yet professionals in the digital world tell it gleefully and frequently because it highlights a fundamental truth about computers: They may tell us facts, but they don't inform us. They may guide us with precision, but they don't guide us where we want to go. The flight computer on Flight 965 could easily have told the pilots that "ROMEO" was not an appropriate fix for their approach to Cali. Even a simple hint that it was "unusual" or "unfamiliar" could have saved the airplane. Instead, it seemed as though the computer was utterly unconcerned with the actual flight and its passengers. It cared only about its own internal computations.

Hard-to-use computers affect us all, sometimes fatally. Software-based products are not *inherently* hard to use; they are that way because we use the wrong process for creating them. In this book, I intend to reveal this bad process by showing its effect and describing its cause. I'll then show how to change the process so that our software-based products become friendly, powerful, and desirable. First, I'll use this chapter to show how serious this problem really is.

What Do You Get When You Cross a Computer with a Camera?

Here is a riddle for the information age: What do you get when you cross a computer with a camera? Answer: A computer! Thirty years ago, my first camera, a 35mm Pentax Model H, had a small battery in it that powered the light meter. I merely swapped in a new one every couple of years, as I would a wristwatch battery.

Fifteen years ago, my first electronic camera, a 35mm Canon T70, used two AA batteries to power its rather simple exposure computer and its automatic film drive. It had a simple on/off switch so that the batteries wouldn't wear down needlessly.

Five years ago, my filmless Logitech, a first-generation digital camera, had a similar on/off switch, but it also had the smarts of a rudimentary computer inside it. If I forgot to turn it off, it automatically shut down after one minute of inactivity. Neat.

One year ago, my second-generation digital camera, a Panasonic PalmCam, had an even smarter computer chip inside it. It was so smart that its on/off switch had evolved into an "Off/Rec/Play" switch. It had modes: I had to put it into Rec mode to take pictures and Play mode to view them on its small video display.

My newest camera, a Nikon COOLPIX 900, is a third-generation digital camera and the smartest yet. In fact, it has a full-blown computer that displays a Windows-like hourglass while it "boots up." Like some mutant fish with extra heads, its on/off switch has *four* settings: Off/ARec/MRec/Play. "ARec" means "automatic record" and "MRec" means "manual record." As far as I can tell, there is no difference. There is no "On" setting, and none of my friends can figure out how to turn it on without a lengthy explanation.

The new camera is very power-hungry, and its engineers thoughtfully provided it with a sophisticated computer program that manages the consumption of battery power. A typical scenario goes like this: I turn the evil Off/etc. switch to "MRec," wait about seven long seconds for the camera to boot up, then point it at my subject. I aim the camera and zoom in to properly frame the image. Just as I'm about to press the shutter button, the camera suddenly realizes that simultaneously running the zoom, charging the flash, and energizing the display has caused it to run out of power. In self-defense, it suspends its capability to actually take pictures. But I don't know that because I'm looking through the viewfinder, waving my arms, saying "smile," and pressing the shutter button. The computer detects the button press, but it simply cannot obey. In a misguided effort to help out, the power-management program instantly takes over and makes an executive decision: Shed load. It shuts down the power-greedy LCD video display. I look at the camera quizzically, wondering why it didn't take the picture, shrug my shoulders, and let my arm holding the camera drop to my side. But as soon as the LCD is turned off, more battery power is available for other systems. The power-management program senses this increase and realizes that it *now* has enough electricity to take pictures. It returns control to the camera program, which is waiting patiently to process the command it received when I pressed the shutter button, and it takes a nicely auto-focused, well-exposed, high-resolution digital picture of my kneecap.

That old mechanical Pentax had manual focusing, manual exposure, and manual shutter speed, yet it was far less frustrating to use than the fully computerized, modern Nikon COOLPIX 900, which has automatic focusing, exposure, and shutter speed. The camera may still take pictures, but it *behaves* like a computer instead of a camera.

⌘

A frog that's slipped into a pot of cold water never recognizes the deadly rising temperature as the stove heats the pot. Instead, the heat anesthetizes the frog's senses. I was unaware, like the frog, of my cameras' slow march from easy to hard to use as they slowly became computerized. We are all experiencing this same, slow, anesthetizing encroachment of computer behavior in our everyday lives.

What Do You Get When You Cross a Computer with an Alarm Clock?

A computer! I just purchased an expensive new clock-radio for my bedroom, a JVC FS-2000. It has a very sophisticated computer brain and offers high fidelity, digital sound, and lots of features. It wakes me up at a preset time by playing a CD, and it has the delicacy and intelligence to slowly fade up the volume when it begins to play at 6:00 a.m. This feature is really pleasant and quite unique, and it compensates for the fact that I want to hurl the infuriating machine out the window.

It's very hard to tell when the alarm is armed, so it occasionally fails to wake me up on a Monday and rousts me out of bed early on a Saturday. Sure, it has an indicator to show the alarm is set, but that doesn't mean it's useful. The clock has a sophisticated alphanumeric LCD that displays all of its many functions. The presence of a small clock symbol in the upper-left corner of the LCD indicates the alarm is armed, but in a dimly lit bedroom the clock symbol cannot be seen. The LCD has a built-in backlight that makes the clock symbol visible, but the backlight only comes on when the CD or radio is explicitly turned on. There's a gotcha, however: The alarm simply won't ever sound while the CD is explicitly left on, regardless of the setting of the alarm. It is this paradoxical operation that frequently catches me unawares.

It is simple to disarm the alarm: Simply press the "Alarm" button once, and the clock symbol disappears from the display. However, to arm it, I must press the "Alarm" button exactly five times. The first time I press it, the display shows me the time of the alarm. On press two, it shows the time when it will turn the sound off. On press three, it shows me whether it will play the radio or the CD. On press four, it shows me the preset volume. On press five, it returns to the normal view, but with the alarm now armed. But with just one additional press, it *disarms* the alarm. Sleepy, in a dark bedroom, I find it difficult to perform this little digital ballet correctly.

Being a nerdy gizmologist, I continue to fiddle with the device in the hope that I will master it. My wife, however, long ago gave up on the diabolical machine. She loves the look of the sleek, modern design and the fidelity of the sound it produces, but it failed to pass the alarm-clock test weeks ago because it is simply too hard to make work. The alarm clock may still wake me up, but it *behaves* like a computer.

By contrast, my old $11 noncomputerized alarm clock woke me up with a sudden, unholy buzzing. When it was armed, a single red light glowed. When it was not armed, the red light was dark. I didn't like this old alarm clock for many reasons, but at least I could tell when it was going to wake me up.

⌘

Because it is far cheaper for manufacturers to use computers to control the internal functioning of devices than it is to use older, mechanical methods, it is economically inevitable that computers will insinuate themselves into every product and service in our lives. This means all of our products will soon behave the same as most obnoxious computers, unless we try something different.

⌘

This phenomenon is not restricted to consumer products. Just about every computerized device or service has more features and options than its manual counterpart. Yet, in practice, we often wield the manual devices with more flexibility, subtlety, and awareness than we do the modern versions driven by silicon-chip technology.

High-tech companies—in an effort to improve their products—are merely adding complicating and unwanted features to them. Because the broken process cannot solve the problem of bad products, but can only add new functions, that is what vendors do. Later in this book I'll show how a better development process makes users happier without the extra work of adding unwanted features.

What Do You Get When You Cross a Computer with a Car?

A computer! Porsche's beautiful high-tech sports car, the Boxster, has seven computers in it to help manage its complex systems. One of them is dedicated to managing the engine. It has special procedures built into it to deal with abnormal situations. Unfortunately, these sometimes backfire. In some early models, if the fuel level in the gas tank got very low—only a gallon or so remaining—the centrifugal force of a sharp turn could cause the fuel to collect in the side of the tank, allowing air to enter the fuel lines. The computer sensed this as a dramatic change in the incoming fuel mixture and interpreted it as a catastrophic failure of the injection system. To prevent damage, the computer would shut down the ignition and stop the car. Also to prevent damage, the computer wouldn't let the driver restart the engine until the car had been towed to a shop and serviced.

When owners of early Boxsters first discovered this problem, the only solution Porsche could devise was to tell them to open the engine compartment and disconnect the battery for at least five minutes, giving the computer time to forget all knowledge of the hiccup. The sports car may still speed down those two-lane blacktop roads, but now, in those tight turns, it *behaves* like a computer.

⌘

In a laudable effort to protect Boxster owners, the programmers turned them into humiliated victims. Every performance-car aficionado knows that the Porsche company is dedicated to lavishing respect and privilege on its clientele. That something like this slipped through shows that the software inside the car is not coming from the same Porsche that makes the rest of the car. It comes from a company within a company: the programmers, not the legendary German automobile engineers. Somehow, the introduction of a new technology surprised an older, well-established company into letting some of its core values slip away. Acceptable levels of quality for software engineers are far lower than those for more traditional engineering disciplines.

What Do You Get When You Cross a Computer with a Bank?

A computer! Whenever I withdraw cash from an automatic teller machine (ATM), I encounter the same sullen and difficult behavior so universal with computers. If I make the slightest mistake, it rejects the entire transaction and kicks me out of the process. I have to pull my card out, reinsert it, reenter my PIN code, and then reassert my request. Typically, it wasn't my mistake, either, but the ATM computer finesses me into a misstep. It always asks me whether I want to withdraw money from my checking, savings, or money-market account, even though I have only a checking account. Subsequently, I always forget which type it is, and the question confuses me. About once a month I inadvertently select "savings," and the infernal machine summarily boots me out of the entire transaction to start over from the beginning. To reject "savings," the machine has to know that I don't have a savings account, yet it still offers it to me as a choice. The only difference between me selecting "savings" and the pilot of Flight 965 selecting "ROMEO" is the magnitude of the penalty.

The ATM also restricts me to a $200 "daily withdrawal limit." If I go through all of the steps—identifying myself, choosing the account, selecting the amount—and then ask for $220, the computer unceremoniously rejects the entire transaction, informing me rudely that I have exceeded my daily withdrawal limit. It doesn't tell me what that amount is, inform me how much money is in my account, or give me the opportunity to key in a new, lower amount. Instead, it spits out my card and leaves me to try the whole process again from scratch, no wiser than I was a moment ago, as the line of people growing behind me shifts, shuffles, and sighs. The ATM is correct and factual, but it is no help whatsoever.

The ATM has rules that must be followed, and I am quite willing to follow them, but it is unreasonably computer-like to fail to inform me of them, give me contradictory indications, and then summarily punish me for innocently transgressing them. This behavior—so typical of computers—is not intrinsic to them. Actually, nothing is intrinsic to computers: They merely act on behalf of their software, the program. And programs are as malleable as human speech. A person can speak rudely or politely, helpfully or sullenly. It is as simple for a computer to behave with respect and courtesy as it is for a human to speak that way. All it takes is for someone to describe how. Unfortunately, programmers aren't very good at teaching that to computers.

Computers Make It Easy to Get into Trouble

Computers that sit on a desk simply behave in the same, irritating way computers always have, and they don't have to be crossed with anything. My friend Jane used to work in public relations as an account coordinator. She ran Windows 95 on her desktop PC, using Microsoft Word to write memos and contracts. The core of Windows 95 is the hierarchical file system. All of Jane's documents were stored in little folders, which were stored in other little folders. Jane didn't understand this or see the advantage to storing things that way. Actually, Jane didn't give it a lot of thought but merely took the path of least resistance.

Jane had just finished drafting the new PR contract for a Silicon Valley startup company. She selected Close from the File menu. Instead of simply doing as she directed and closing the document, Word popped up a dialog box. It was, of course, the all-too-familiar Do You Want to Save the Changes? confirmation box. She responded—as always—by pressing the Enter key. She responded this way so consistently and often that she no longer even looked at the dialog box.

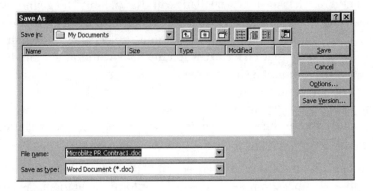

The first dialog box was followed immediately by another one, the equally familiar Save As box. It presented Jane with lots of confusing buttons, icons, and text fields. The only one that Jane understood and used was the text-entry field for File Name. She typed in a likely name and then clicked the Save button. The program then saved the PR contract in the My Documents folder. Jane was so used to this unnecessary drill that she gave it no thought.

At lunchtime, while Jane was out of her office, Sunil, the company's computer tech, installed a new version of VirusKiller 2.1 on her computer. While working on Jane's PC, Sunil used Word to view a VirusKiller Readme file. After viewing the file, Sunil closed it and returned Jane's computer to exactly the way it was before lunch. At least, he thought he did.

After lunch, Jane needed to reopen the PR contract and get a printout to show to her boss. Jane selected Open from the File menu, and the Open dialog box appeared. Jane expected the Open dialog box to show her, in neat alphabetic order, all of her contracts and documents. Instead, it showed her a bunch of file-names that she had never seen before and didn't recognize. One of them was named Readme.doc.

Of course, when Sunil used Word to view the Readme file, he instructed Jane's copy of Word to look in an obscure folder six levels deep and inadvertently steered it away from Jane's normal setting of My Documents.

Jane was now quite bewildered. Her first, unavoidable thought was that all of her hard work had somehow been erased, and she got very worried. She called over René, her friend and co-worker, but René was just as confused as Jane was. Finally, in a state approaching panic, Jane telephoned Sunil to ask for his help. Sunil was not at his desk, and it wasn't until Monday morning that he had a chance to stop by and set things right. Jane, René, Sunil—and the PR company— each lost a half-day's productivity.

Although computer operating systems need hierarchical file systems, the people who use them don't. It's not surprising that computer programmers like to see the underlying hierarchical file systems, but it is equally unremarkable that normal users like Jane don't. Unremarkable to everyone, that is, except the programmers who create the software that we all use. They create the behavior and information presentation that they like best, which is very different from the behavior and information presentation that is best for Jane. Jane's frustration and inefficiency is blamed on Jane, and not on the programmers who torpedoed her.

At least Jane has a job. Many people are considered insufficiently "computer literate" and are thus not employable. As more and more jobs demand interaction with computers, the rift between the employable and the unemployable becomes wider and more difficult to cross. Politicians may demand jobs for the underprivileged, but if the underprivileged don't know how to use computers, no company can afford to let them put their untrained hands on the company's computers. There is too much training involved, and too much exposure to the destruction of data and the bollixing up of priceless databases.

The obnoxious behavior and obscure interaction that software-based products exhibit is institutionalizing what I call "software apartheid": Otherwise-normal people are forbidden from entering the job market and participating in society because they cannot use computers effectively. In our enlightened society, social activists are working hard to break down race and class barriers while technologists are hard at work inadvertently erecting new, bigger ones. By purposefully designing our software-based products to be more human and forgiving, we can automatically make them more inclusive, more class- and color-blind.

Commercial Software Suffers, Too

Not only are computers taking over the cockpits of jet airliners, but they are also taking over the passenger cabin, behaving in that same obstinate, perverse way that is so easy to recognize and so hard to use. Modern jet planes have in-flight entertainment (IFE) systems that deliver movies and music to passengers. IFE systems are merely computers connected with LANs, just like the computers in your office. Advanced IFE systems are generally installed only on larger airplanes flying transoceanic routes.

One airline's IFE system was so frustrating for the flight attendants to use that many of them were bidding to fly shorter, local routes to avoid having to learn and use the difficult systems. This is remarkable, considering that the time-honored airline route-bidding process is based on seniority, and that those same long-distance routes have always been considered the most desirable plums because of their lengthy layovers in exotic locales such as Singapore or Paris. For flight attendants to bid for unglamorous, unromantic yo-yo flights from Denver to Dallas or from Los Angeles to San Francisco just to avoid the IFE system indicated a serious morale problem. Any airline that inflicted bad tools on its most prized employees—the ones who spent the most time with the customer—was making a foolish decision and profligately discarding money, customer loyalty, and staff loyalty.

The computer IFE system that another large airline created was even worse. It linked movie delivery with the cash-collection function. In a sealed jet airplane flying at 37,000 feet, cash-collection procedures had typically been quite laissez-faire; after all, nobody was going to sneak out the back door. Flight attendants delivered goods and services when it was convenient and collected later when their hands weren't full and other passengers weren't waiting for something. This kept them from running unnecessarily up and down the narrow aisles. Sure, there were occasional errors, but never more than a few dollars were involved, and the system was quite human and forgiving; everyone was happy and the work was not oppressive.

With cash collection connected to content delivery by computer, the flight attendant had to first get the cash from the passenger, then walk all the way to the head end of the cabin, where the attendant's console was, enter an attendant password, then perform a cash-register-like transaction. Only when that transaction was completed could the passenger actually view a movie or listen to music. This inane product design forced the flight attendants to walk up and down those narrow aisles hundreds of extra times during a typical trip. Out of sheer frustration, the flight attendants would trip the circuit breaker on the IFE system at the beginning of each long flight, shortly after departure. They would then blandly announce to the passengers that, sorry, the system was broken and there would be no movie on *this* flight.

The airline had spent millions of dollars constructing a system so obnoxious that its users deliberately turned it off to avoid interacting with it. The thousands of bored passengers were merely innocent victims. And this happened on long, overseas trips typically packed with much-sought-after frequent flyers. I cannot put a dollar figure on the expense this caused the airline, but I can say with conviction that it was catastrophically expensive.

The software inside the IFE systems worked with flawless precision but was a resounding failure because it misbehaved with its human keepers. How could a company fail to predict this sad result? How could it fail to see the connection? The goal of this book is to answer these questions and to show you how to avoid such high-tech debacles.

What Do You Get When You Cross a Computer with a Warship?

In September 1997, while conducting fleet maneuvers in the Atlantic, the USS *Yorktown*, one of the Navy's new Aegis guided-missile cruisers, stopped dead in the water. A Navy technician, while calibrating an on-board fuel valve, entered a zero into one of the shipboard management computers, a Pentium Pro running Windows NT. The program attempted to divide another number by that zero—a mathematically undefined operation—which resulted in a complete crash of the entire shipboard control system. Without the computers, the engine halted and the ship sat wallowing in the swells for two hours and 45 minutes until it could be towed into port. Good thing it wasn't in a war zone.

What do you get when you cross a computer with a warship? Admiral Nimitz is rolling in his grave! Despite this setback, the Navy is committed to computerizing all of its ships because of the manpower cost savings. To deflect criticism of this plan, it blamed the "incident" on human error. Because the software-creation process is out of control, the high-tech industry must bring its process to heel, or else it will continue to put the blame on ordinary users while ever-bigger machines sit dead in the water.

Techno-Rage

An article in the *Wall Street Journal* once described an anonymous video clip circulated widely by email that showed a "[m]ustachioed Everyman in a short-sleeved shirt hunched over a computer terminal, looking puzzled. Suddenly, he strikes the side of his monitor in frustration. As a curious co-worker peers over his cubicle, the man slams the keyboard into the monitor, knocking it to the floor. Rising from his chair, he goes after the fallen monitor with a final, ferocious kick."

The article went on to say that reaction to the clip had been "intense" and that it had apparently tapped into "a powerful undercurrent of techno-rage."

It's ironic that one needs to be moderately computer savvy to even send or view this video clip. The man in the video may well be an actor, but he touches a widespread, sympathetic chord in our business world. The frustration that difficult and unpleasant software-based products are bringing to our lives is rising rapidly.

Joke emails circulate on private email lists about "Computer Tourette's." This is a play on the disorder known as Tourette's syndrome, some of whose sufferers engage in uncontrollable bouts of swearing. The joke is that you can walk down the halls of most modern office buildings and hear otherwise-normal people sitting in front of their monitors, jaws clenched, swearing repeatedly in a rictus of tense fury. Who knows what triggered such an outburst: a misplaced file, an inaccessible image, or a frustrating interaction. Or maybe the program just blandly erased the user's only copy of a 500-page manuscript because he responded with a Yes to a confirmation dialog box, assuming that it had asked if he wanted to "save your changes" when it actually asked him if he wanted to "discard your work."

An Industry in Denial

We are a world awash in high-tech tools. Computers dominate the workplace and our homes, and vehicles are filling up with silicon-powered gadgets. All of these computerized devices are wildly sophisticated and powerful, but every one of them is dauntingly difficult and confusing to use.

The high-tech industry is in denial of a simple fact that every person with a cell phone or a word processor can clearly see: *Our computerized tools are too hard to use.* The technologists who create software and high-tech gadgets are satisfied with their efforts. The software engineers[1] who create them have tried as hard as they can to make them easy to use, and they have made some minor progress. They believe that their products are as easy to use as it is technically possible to make them. As engineers, their belief is in technology, and they have faith that

---

[1] *Throughout the computer industry, the term "software engineer" is used synonymously with the term "programmer"; throughout this book, I have done the same.*

only some new technology, such as voice recognition or artificial intelligence, will improve the user's experience.

Ironically, the thing that will likely make the *least* improvement in the ease of use of software-based products is new technology. There is little difference *technically* between a complicated, confusing program and a simple, fun, and powerful product. The problem is one of culture, training, and attitude of the people who make them, more than it is one of chips and programming languages. We are deficient in our development *process*, not in our development tools.

The high-tech industry has inadvertently put programmers and engineers in charge, so their hard-to-use engineering culture dominates. Despite appearances, business executives are simply not the ones in control of the high-tech industry. It is the engineers who are running the show. In our rush to accept the many benefits of the silicon chip, we have abdicated our responsibilities. *We have let the inmates run the asylum.*

When the inmates run the asylum, it is hard for them to see clearly the nature of the problems that bedevil them. When you look in the mirror, it is all too easy to single out your best features and overlook the warts. When the creators of software-based products examine their handiwork, they overlook how bad it is. Instead, they see its awesome power and flexibility. They see how rich the product is in features and functions. They ignore how excruciatingly difficult it is to use, how many mind-numbing hours it takes to learn, or how it diminishes and degrades the people who must use it in their everyday lives.

The Origins of This Book

I have been inventing and developing software-based products for 25 years. This problem of hard-to-use software has puzzled and confounded me for years. Finally, in 1992, I ceased all programming to devote 100% of my time to helping other development firms make their products easier to use. And a wonderful thing happened! I immediately discovered that after I freed myself from the demands of programming, I saw for the first time how powerful and compelling those demands were. Programming is such a difficult and absorbing task that it dominates all other considerations, including the concerns of the user. I could only see this after I had extricated myself from its grip.

Upon making this discovery, I began to see what influences drove software-based products to be so bad from the user's point of view. In 1995 I wrote a book[2] about what I had learned, and it has had a significant effect on the way some software is designed today.

---

[2] About Face: The Essentials of User Interface Design, *IDG Books, Foster City CA, 1995, ISBN 1-56884-322-4,* http://www.cooper.com. *In March 2003, my coauthor Robert Reimann and I released a revised second edition of the book. It was completely rewritten, including updated examples and seven brand new chapters. It is called* About Face 2.0: The Essentials of Interaction Design, *John Wiley & Sons, ISBN 0-76452-641-3.*

To be a good programmer, one must be sympathetic to the nature and needs of the computer. But the nature and needs of the computer are utterly alien from the nature and needs of the human being who will eventually use it. The creation of software is so intellectually demanding, so all-consuming, that programmers must completely immerse themselves in an equally alien thought process. In the programmer's mind, the demands of the programming process not only supersede any demands from the outside world of users, but the very languages of the two worlds are at odds with each other.

The process of programming subverts the process of making easy-to-use products for the simple reason that the goals of the programmer and the goals of the user are dramatically different. The programmer wants the construction process to be smooth and easy. The user wants the interaction with the program to be smooth and easy. These two objectives almost never result in the same program. In the computer industry today, the programmers are given the responsibility for creating interaction that makes the user happy, but in the unrelenting grip of this conflict of interest, they simply cannot do so.

In software, typically nothing is visible until it is done, meaning that any second-guessing by nonprogrammers is too late to be effective. Desktop-computer software is infamously hard to use because it is purely the product of programmers; nobody comes between them and the user. Objects such as phones and cameras have always had a hefty mechanical component that forces them into the open for review. But as we've established, when you cross a computer with just about any product, the behavior of the computer dominates completely.

The key to solving the problem is interaction design before programming. We need a new class of professional interaction designers who design the way software behaves. Today, programmers consciously design the code inside programs but only inadvertently design the interaction with humans. They design what a program does but not how it *behaves, communicates,* or *informs.* Conversely, interaction designers focus directly on the way users see and interact with software-based products. This craft of interaction design is new and unfamiliar to programmers, so—when they admit it at all—they let it in only after their programming is already completed. At that point, it is too late.

The people who manage the creation of software-based products are typically either hostage to programmers because they are insufficiently technical, or they are all too sympathetic to programmers because they are programmers themselves. The people who use software-based products are simply unaware that those products can be as pleasurable to use and as powerful as any other well-designed tool.

Programmers aren't evil. They work hard to make their software easy to use. Unfortunately, their frame of reference is themselves, so they only make it easy to use for other software engineers, not for normal human beings

The costs of badly designed software are incalculable. The cost of Jane's and Sunil's time, the cost of offended air travelers, and the cost of the lives of passengers on Flight 965 cannot easily be quantified. The greatest cost, though, is the opportunity we are squandering. While we let our products frustrate, cost, confuse, irritate, and kill us, we are not taking advantage of the real promise of software-based products: to be the most human, powerful, and pleasurable creations ever imagined. Because software truly is malleable far beyond any other medium, it has the potential to go well beyond the expectations of even the wildest dreamer. All it requires is the judicious partnering of interaction design with programming.

2

COGNITIVE FRICTION

It's one thing to see that a problem exists, but it's quite another to devise a solution. One key part of problem solving is the language we use. Over the years, I've developed many useful terms and mental models. They have proven vital to framing the problem presented by hard-to-use software-based products. In this chapter I will introduce those terms and ideas, showing how they can help bring the benefits of interaction design to our troubled process.

Behavior Unconnected to Physical Forces

Having just left the industrial age behind, we are standing at the threshold of the information age with an obsolete set of tools. In the industrial age, engineers were able to solve each new problem placed before them. Working in steel and concrete, they made bridges, cars, skyscrapers, and moon rockets that worked well and satisfied their human users. As we tiptoe into the information age, we are working increasingly in software, and we have once again brought our best engineers to the task. But unlike in the past, things haven't turned out so well. The computer boxes are fast and powerful, and the programs are generally reliable, but we have encountered a previously unseen dimension of frustrated, dissatisfied, unhappy, and unproductive users.

Today's engineers are no less capable than ever, so I must deduce from this that, for the first time, they have encountered a problem qualitatively different from any they confronted in the industrial age. Otherwise, their old tools would work as well as they ever did. For lack of a better term, I have labeled this new problem substance *cognitive friction*. It is the resistance encountered by a human intellect when it engages with a complex system of rules that change as the problem changes. Software interaction is very high in cognitive friction. Interaction with physical devices, however complex, tends to be low in cognitive friction because mechanical devices tend to stay in a narrow range of states comparable to their inputs.

Playing a violin is extremely difficult but low in cognitive friction because—although a violinist manipulates it in very complex and sophisticated ways—the violin never enters a "meta" state in which various inputs make it sound like a tuba or a bell. The violin's behavior is always predictable—though complex—and obeys physical laws, even while being quite difficult to control. In contrast, a microwave oven has a lot of cognitive friction, because the 10 number keys on the control panel can be put into one of two contexts, or modes. In one mode they control the intensity of the radiation, and in the other they control the duration. This dramatic change, along with the lack of sensory feedback about the oven's changed state, results in high cognitive friction.

The QWERTY keys on a typewriter, for example, don't have metafunctions. When you press the E key, the letter E appears on the page. When you press the key sequence ERASE ALL, the words ERASE ALL appear on the paper. On a computer—depending on the context—you may also get a metafunction. A higher-level operation occurs, and the computer *actually erases things.* The behavior of the machine no longer has a one-to-one correspondence to your manipulation.

Cognitive friction—like friction in the physical world—is not necessarily a bad thing in small quantities, but as it builds up, its negative effects grow exponentially. Of course, friction is a physical force and can be detected and measured, whereas cognitive friction is a forensic tool and cannot be taken literally. Don't forget, though, that such things as love, ambition, courage, fear, and truth—though real—cannot be detected and measured. They can't be addressed by engineering methods, either.

The skilled engineers who manufacture microwave ovens typically consult with human-factors experts to design the buttons so they are easy to see and press. But the human-factors experts are merely adapting the buttons to the user's eyes and fingers, not to their minds. Consequently, microwave ovens don't have much "friction" but have a lot of cognitive friction. It is easy to open and close the door and physically press the buttons but, compared to the simplicity of the task, setting the controls to achieve your goals is very difficult. Getting the microwave to perform the work you intend for it is quite difficult, though our general familiarity with it makes us forget how hard it really is. How many of us have cooked something for one second or one hour instead of for one minute? How many of us have cooked something at a strength of 5 for 10 minutes instead of a strength of 10 for 5 minutes?

On the computer screen, everything is filled with cognitive friction. Even an interface as simple as the World Wide Web presents the user with a more intense mental engagement than any physical machine. This happens because the meaning of each blue hyperlink is a doorway to some other place on the Web. All you can do is click on a hyperlink, but what the link points to can change independently of the pointer without any outward indication. Its sole function is pure metafunction. The very "hyper"ness is what gives it cognitive friction.

Design Is a Big Word

The theme of this book is that interactive products need to be designed by interaction designers instead of by software engineers. This assertion often generates instant antagonism from programmers who have been doing design all along. Furthermore, these programmers fear that by taking design away from them, I'm taking away the best and most creative aspect of their work, leaving them condemned to coding drudgery unleavened with fun. This is absolutely untrue. Their worry stems only from the imprecise nature of the term *design*.

The entire software-creation process includes design, all the way from selecting the programming language to choosing the color of the delivery truck. No aspect of this lengthy and involved process is more design-filled than the programming itself. Programmers make design decisions at every step of their process. The programmer must decide how each procedure will call each other procedure, how information and status will be shared, stored, and changed, and how the code's validity will be guaranteed. All of these decisions—and the millions more like them—are design decisions, and the success of each one depends on the programmer's ability to bring her experience and judgment to bear.

I draw a simple dividing line through this sea of design. I put the part of the design that will directly affect the ultimate end user of the product on one side. On the other side is all other design. In this book, when I speak of "interaction design," I am referring only to the former. I call the remaining design that doesn't affect the end user *program design.*

It is not possible to base the dividing line on purely technical criteria. It cannot be expressed in terms that are familiar to engineers because the differentiating factor is human, not technical, and engineering rules aren't applicable to people. For example, the interaction designer typically is agnostic about issues such as which programming language is to be used. However, occasionally the choice of language affects response time, which most assuredly is an interaction issue, and the designer will have something to say.

Almost all interaction design refers to the selection of behavior, function, and information and their presentation to users. End-product interaction design is the only part of the design that I want to take away from programmers and put into the hands of dedicated interaction designers.

The Relationship Between Programmers and Designers

In a technical world dominated by engineers, internal program design has held sway, and interaction design for the end user's benefit has been incorporated only on an after-the-fact, spare-time basis. One of the goals of this book is to reveal the benefits of inverting this priority and making interaction design the first consideration in the creation of software-based products.

Most Software Is Designed by Accident

Mud huts and subterranean burrows are designed—albeit without much conscious thought—by the demands of rock and thatch. Similarly, all software is designed by the arcane demands of programming languages and databases. Tradition is the strongest influence in the design of all of these media. The biggest difference is that the builder-designer of the hut will also be its primary occupant, whereas programmers typically don't use the software they design.

What really happens in most programming shops is that there is no one on staff who has a clue about designing for end users. However, these same clueless people are far from clueless about program design, and they have strong opinions about what *they* like, personally. So they do what they do, designing the interaction for themselves, subject to what is easiest and most enjoyable to code, and imagine that they are actually designing for users. While it seems to the programmer that lots of design is getting done, it is only lots of program design, and very little end-user design.

Because the lack of design is a form of design, whenever anyone makes decisions about program behavior, he is assuming the role of interaction designer. When a marketing executive insists that a favorite feature be included in the product, she is designing. When a programmer implements a pet behavior in the product, he is designing.

The difference between good design and this kind of inadvertent, mud-hut design isn't so much the tools used or the type of gizmos, but the motivation. The real interaction designer's decisions are based on what the user is trying to achieve. Ersatz designers' decisions are based on any number of other random rationales. Personal preferences, familiarity, fear of the unknown, directives from Microsoft, and miscues from colleagues all play a surprisingly large role. Most often, though, their decisions are based on what is easiest for them to create.

"Interaction" Versus "Interface" Design

I prefer the term *interaction design* to the term *interface design* because "interface" suggests that you have code over here, people over there, and an interface in between that passes messages between them. It implies that only the interface is answerable to the users' needs. The consequence of isolating design at the interface level is that it licenses programmers to reason like this: "I can code as I please because an 'interface' will be slapped on after I'm done." It postpones design until after programming, when it is too late.

Like putting an Armani suit on Attila the Hun, interface design only tells how to dress up an existing behavior. For example, in a data-reporting tool, interface design would eliminate unnecessary borders and other visual clutter from a table of figures, color code important points, provide rich visual feedback when the user clicks on data elements, and so on. This is better than nothing, but far from sufficient. Microsoft invests many millions of dollars on interface design, but its products remain universally unloved.

Behavioral design tells how the elements of the software should act and communicate. In our example, behavioral design tells us what tools you could apply to that table of figures, how you might include averages or totals. Interaction designers also work from the outside in, starting from the goals the user is trying to achieve, with an eye toward the broader goals of the business, the capabilities of the technology, and the component tasks.

You can go still deeper to what we call *conceptual design*, which considers what is valuable for the users in the first place. In our example, conceptual design might tell you that examining a table of figures is only an incidental task; the users' real goal is spotting trends, which means that you don't want to create a reporting tool at all, but a trend-spotting tool. To deliver both power and pleasure to users, interaction designers think first *conceptually*, then in terms of *behavior*, and last in terms of *interface*.

Why Software-Based Products Are Different

Cognitive friction creeps into all software-based products, regardless of their simplicity, and cognitive friction makes them much more difficult to use than equivalent mechanical-age products. As an example, here are the contents of my pants pocket: some coins, my Swiss Army knife, and my car keys. The knife is pure industrial age: You can see how it is built, how it works, and how to work it just by a cursory inspection—by manipulation. When you flip open the knife blade, you can see that it is sharp, and you can imagine the power it has for cutting.

The knife has a grand total of six blades, plus a toothpick and tweezers. The use of all of them is readily apparent. I can easily and intuitively discern how to manipulate the knife because of the way it fits my hand and fingers. The knife is a pleasure to use.

The keyless entry system accompanying my car keys is a different beast altogether. It only has two push buttons on it, so—from a manipulation point of view—it is much simpler than the knife. As soon as my hand grips the smooth, black-plastic case, my fingers naturally and intuitively discover the two push buttons, and their use is obvious: Press to activate. Ah, but there is silicon, not steel, behind those buttons, and they are far harder to work than they seem.

The large button locks the car and simultaneously arms the alarm. Pressing the button a second time disarms the alarm and unlocks the car. There is also a second, smaller button labeled Panic. When you press it, the car emits a quiet warble for a few seconds. If you hold it down longer, the quiet warble is replaced by the full 100-decibel blasting of the car alarm, whooping, tweeting, yowling, and declaring to everyone within a half-mile that some dolt—me—has just done something execrably stupid. What's worse, after the alarm has been triggered, the little plastic device becomes functionally inert, and further pressing of either button does nothing. The only way to stop that honking announcement of my palpable stupidity is to walk to my frighteningly loud car, enduring withering stares from passersby, unlock the driver's door with the key, then insert the key into the ignition and twist it. It really makes me feel like an idiot. If my car merely got robbed it would make me feel violated and sad, but it wouldn't make me feel stupid.

In my previous book, I stated that the number-one goal of all computer users is to not feel stupid. I further asserted that good interfaces should avoid presenting users with ejection-seat levers intermingled with the controls for common, everyday functions. Here is a classic example of a device that really makes users feel stupid by putting an ejector-seat lever right up front. Accidentally setting off the ejector-seat lever initiates a personally embarrassing episode tantamount to showing up at the office having forgotten your pants. My Swiss Army knife just doesn't have the capability of doing that.

Not only can I *not* imagine a reason why any person would want to use either of the functions on the second button, but I question why the makers of the control didn't take advantage of the golden opportunity to provide me with functions that *are* desirable and useful.[1]

As much as I appreciate that my car comes with an alarm, there are many times when I want to lock the car without arming the alarm. When I pop into the local Starbucks for some coffee, I don't need the level of protection that I need at, say, the airport. I would really like to have the ability to lock and unlock my car from the remote without involving the alarm system. This would be quite useful when I'm just driving to local shops or dropping my kids off at school.

Another quite useful and desirable feature would be an option to support an even more secure locking system. Occasionally, when I return to my previously locked car, I find that it has become unlocked in my absence. This happens when someone with a similar car made by the same manufacturer parks near my car. When that person presses the button to lock his car, it also gives the signal to unlock mine, disarming the alarm, and opening up my car to the depredations of any passing sociopath. This scenario is most disturbing in precisely the situation where it is most likely to occur: in large, urban parking lots, such as at airports, where my car is likely to spend several hours, or even days, exposed to the random distribution of keyless entry systems. It sure would be a useful application

---

[1] *I have repeatedly been told that women actually desire this function as a deterrent to criminal activity in dark parking lots, but every one of the tellers has been a technically trained male who would never use it himself. Much to my surprise, I recently read in the* Wall Street Journal *about a bona fide use for the Panic button. A family was camping in Yosemite National Park, and a wild bear began trashing their car in an attempt to get at the food locked within. The mother pressed the Panic button, and the alarm eventually discouraged the bear. Maybe that little button should be labeled "Bear Repellent."*

of the technology if I could lock and arm my car in such a way that I could unlock and disarm it only by personal application of the metal key in the door. Obviously, I know that the technology exists to do this because that is how the alarm itself is turned off after it is triggered. Unfortunately, the designers of the system made certain that regardless of how I lock the car, anyone's big button can unlock it.

The Swiss Army knife is complex and packed with features, some hidden quite cleverly, yet learning and using it is simple, predictable, and intuitive. Using the keyless entry system is difficult, problematic, and capable of instantly embarrassing me. It doesn't do what I want, and it doesn't give me the level of control over my car and its alarm that I consider normal and acceptable. In short, the interaction with the system sucks. It is plain old *bad*, and I hate it.

The Dancing Bear

On the other hand, if you made me choose between my knife and my keyless system, I'd toss away the knife in a New York minute. Immediately after first using my keyless entry system, I couldn't imagine ever *not* owning one. It is the single most convenient feature of my car, and I use it more often than any other one. I use it 10 times to every 1 time I use the knife. In spite of its weak and clumsy design, it is still a wonderful thing. It's like the fellow who leads a huge bear on a chain into the town square and, for a small donation, will make the bear dance. The townspeople gather to see the wondrous sight as the massive, lumbering beast shambles and shuffles from paw to paw. The bear is really a terrible dancer, and *the wonder isn't that the bear dances well but that the bear dances at all.*

The wonder isn't that the keyless entry system works well, but that the keyless entry system works at all. I am very willing to put up with interaction problems in order to gain the benefit of remote entry to my vehicle.

The prodigious gifts of silicon are so overwhelming that we find it easy to ignore the collateral costs. If you are stranded on a deserted island, you don't care much that your rescue ship is a leaky, rat-infested hulk. The difference between having a software solution for your problem and not having any solution is so great that we accept any hardship or difficulty that the solution might force on us.

The difficulty of devising a better interaction isn't what makes the problem so intractable. Instead, it is our almost universal willingness to accept bad interaction as an unavoidable cost. When we see that rusty rescue ship, we don't question its accommodations but just jump on and are glad for what we get.

Software experts are—of necessity—comfortable with high-cognitive-friction interaction. They pride themselves on their ability to work in spite of its adversity. Normal humans, who are the new users of these products, lack the expertise to judge whether this cognitive friction is avoidable. Instead, they rely on the cues offered by the nerds, who simply shrug and say that to use software-based products you have to be "computer literate." Software engineers blame the technology, telling users that difficult interaction simply comes with the territory, that it is unavoidable.

This is not true. Difficult interaction is very avoidable.

Cognitive friction doesn't come from technology, but from the people who control technology. They are masters because they know how to think in ways that are sympathetic to silicon, and they imagine that everyone thinks in the same way. They create technological artifacts whose interaction is expressed in the terms in which they are constructed. Instead of creating an automobile that is all leather and burl wood, they would create one that is all hot steel and grinding gears. As engineers, they think more about gears than about leather, so the interface to the human user is expressed in those "implementation" terms, which is why I call products designed this way as having an *implementation model.*

The Cost of Features

Most software vendors don't know how to make their programs easy to use, but they sure know how to add features, so that is what they do.

Physical objects, such as my Swiss Army knife, are subject to a natural brake on the proliferation of marginal features. Each new blade or accessory costs money for the manufacturer to build into the knife. The maker of the knife knows this, and each proposed new feature must pass a gauntlet of justification before it makes it into a shipping product. In engineering terms, this is called a *negative feedback loop,* in which intrinsic forces trend toward stability and equilibrium. For example, tire friction in your car creates a negative feedback loop in the steering system, so that when you release the wheel it tends to return to straight ahead.

In the business of software-based products, a different system prevails. Because functions and features are added in intangible software code and not in tangible steel, copper, or plastic, it appears to traditional manufacturing executives that additional features are nearly cost free. It seems to them that software is easy to add, change, and "improve."

Right now I'm listening to Jimmy Buffett on my computer's CD-ROM drive. The small program that plays the disc offers me a plethora of functions: I can move to the previous track or the next track, skip to random tracks, create a custom play list, play for a predetermined time, repeat play, view information about Buffett on the Web, put the album into my "collection," take notes on the various tracks, gather song names from a database on the Internet, examine information about the disc, create a list of favorite tracks, and more. All of these features are really nice, and I wouldn't necessarily delete them, but they all conspire to make the program extremely difficult to understand and use. What's more, when the phone rings and I need to quickly pause the disc, I can't find the pause function because it's buried among all of those other—free—functions. Those functions are not "free" to me. Some hapless engineer thought that he was doing me a favor by adding all of those free features, but I'd rather have a simple player with a quick and easy pause button.

Regarding my car's remote keyless entry system, I seriously doubt that any designer asked himself, "Which and how many functions are appropriate?" Instead, I'm certain that some junior engineer chose an off-the-shelf chip that coincidentally came with two channels. After using one of them to lock and unlock, he found himself with a free surplus channel. The engineer—possibly under the influence of an enthusiastic but ill-informed marketing manager— concocted the rationale that manually setting off the alarm would serve some purpose. He was proud of his ability to provide additional functionality for no apparent cost.

It's cheaper to put an entire microprocessor in your car key, microwave, or cell phone than it is to put in discrete chips and electronic components. Thus, a new technical economy drives the design of the product. Adding physical controls to devices is still governed by the negative feedback loop of manufacturing costs, but the process of adding functions and features in software is not. To software makers, it seems virtually free to add features, so any proposed feature is *assumed* to be a good investment until proven otherwise. Without a governor, the product rapidly fills up with unwanted features, which means complexity and confusion for the user. All of these features are touted as indispensable advantages and, of course, the main function that really is needed still remains. That bear is in there dancing away.

For desktop computers, the implications of the missing feedback loop are just as debilitating. The software maker imagines that it can add all of the features it wants, and they will be "free" as long as they are controlled through the standard mouse and keyboard. They can crowd the screen with hundreds of obscure icons, buttons, or menu items, all of which must ultimately be controlled by a key press or a mouse click. How is the user supposed to tell the difference between small, insignificant functions and those that have large, negative effects?

Virtually every commercially available software product has grown in complexity with each subsequent release. More features and functions are added as the product evolves, so more controls are added to the interface. The industry press calls it "bloatware." Products such as Lotus Notes, Adobe Photoshop, Intuit Quicken, and Microsoft Word are so encrusted with a bewildering array of features that users are confounded and use few of them effectively, if at all. Meanwhile, the myriad of marginal features crowd out the few really useful ones.

This problem is even more evident in enterprise software than in consumer products. Vendors such as Oracle, PeopleSoft, ADP, SAP, and Siebel all make complex, back-office software that's necessary for corporate operations. These products are very complex, obscure, and feature-laden. Each annual revision adds many new features but fails to make the existing features understandable or controllable except by users who receive months of rigorous training.

Apologists and Survivors

Dancing bearware is becoming omnipresent. The incredible power of computers means that few people can afford to ignore them. Even if you don't have a desktop computer, you probably own a cell phone and an ATM card, which are software-based products. It is unrealistic to simply say you won't use computers. They aren't just getting cheaper; they are getting ridiculously cheaper, to the point of ubiquity and disposability. Many familiar products that we imagine as mechanical (or electronic) are no longer made without computers. Cars, washing machines, televisions, vacuum cleaners, thermostats, and elevators are all good examples.

Although the usefulness of an industrial-age device was proportional to the difficulty of manipulating it, this relationship is missing in the information age, and the difficulty of operation increases more rapidly than the usefulness increases. An old-fashioned mechanical alarm clock has always been considered easy to operate. A contemporary, software-based alarm clock can be harder to work than a car.

High cognitive friction polarizes people into two groups. It either makes them feel frustrated and stupid for failing, or giddy with power at overcoming the extreme difficulty. These powerful emotions force people into being either an "apologist" or a "survivor." They either adopt cognitive friction as a lifestyle, or they go underground and accept it as a necessary evil. The polarization is growing acute.

⌘

I call the first group apologists, because its members take pains to justify their obeisance to the dancing bear. Like political-party sycophants wearing silly hats and carrying goofy signs, they tout the benefits while downplaying the disadvantages with unabashed partisanship. Virtually all programmers fall into this category, and their vested interest makes their motivation obvious, but it is surprising how many nontechnical users who are abused daily by bad interaction will excuse their oppressors by saying things like, "Oh, it's easy. I just have to remember to press these two keys, then give the system a valid name. If I forget what I called it, the system will let me look for it." They don't see how ludicrous it is for the system to "let them look for it." Why doesn't the computer do the looking, or the remembering? The apologists are the ones who defend the computer because it can accomplish a task that was heretofore impossibly difficult. They point to the bear and exclaim, "Look, it's dancing!"

Apologists remind me of the victims of the "Stockholm Syndrome." These are hostages who fall in love with their captors, declaring without irony or any vestige of rational perspective, "He's really a wonderful person. He even let us use the bathroom."

"Power user" is a code name for an apologist. Regardless of how hard an interaction is, or how uselessly obscure a feature is, the apologist will unerringly point to the power and functionality of the gadget, blithely ignoring the difficulty of actually using it.

One of my colleagues in the cellular-telephone business was complaining about how the engineers had made cell phones hard to use by packing in so many rarely used features. She said that cell phones were "wet dogs." When I inquired about her metaphor, she explained, "You have to really love a wet dog a lot to want to carry it around."

It is fascinating how computers seem to attract an inordinate number of highly intelligent, self-motivated people. These same people seem to also be attracted to dangerous and demanding sports such as heli-skiing, piloting, scuba diving, stock speculation, and technical rock climbing. Each activity demands rigorous training, and the slightest inattention can bring disaster. But if these avocations didn't have some huge appeal—some compelling attraction—wouldn't their adherents just watch TV instead? The common appeal is precisely what makes them so hard. It is the mental challenge of the very difficult, very unforgiving task. It is easy to picture the sweaty, exhausted, trekker chugging Gatorade, grinning, and saying, "Yeah, that last pitch was completely vertical and my quads were cramping as I worked the layback. Almost fell off a couple of times." He *likes* it tough! The tougher the better! That's why he does it!

Computers inspire people in the same way because they offer the same tough, ruthless challenges. If you aren't utterly on top of your game, computers will leave you whimpering in the dust. It is easy to picture the exhausted programmer chugging Coca-Cola, grinning, and saying, "Yeah, the fetch logic caused the crash, but only when the main heap grew beyond 64 meg; otherwise the cache wasn't activated. Almost couldn't find it!" He's having *fun*!

This is where apologists come from. They enjoy the tough challenge, the unforgiving nature. They like to work in an environment where their special abilities can make a difference, where they can stand out. The climber is apologizing for the steepness and difficulty of the cliff. The computer enthusiast apologizes for the obscurity and difficulty of the software interaction.

⌘

At the other pole are the survivors. They know that something is radically wrong, but they don't know what. They don't know much about computers or interaction, but they can see that there is a problem. They know what *hard* is, and they know what *easy* is, and they know full well that *computers are hard*.

However, just like everybody else, they cannot simply abandon the computer; they need it to do their jobs. They grit their teeth and put up with the abuse inflicted on them by the dancing bearware. They don't know there is a better way for the computer to behave, but they know that every time they use it, they feel a little smaller. Like a feudal peasant in the Middle Ages, they are powerless to change their status—or to even see the depth of their deprivation—but they are certain that they are oppressed.

The apologists say, "Look what the computer lets me do!" The survivors say, "I guess I'm just too stupid to understand these newfangled machines." The apologists say, "Look at this! A dancing bear!" The survivors say, "I need something that dances, so I guess a bear is the best I'm gonna get." The survivors are the vast majority of people who are not impressed by the newfound power, but who are mighty impressed by how stupid the interaction makes them feel.

Of course, virtually everyone in the computer industry, including everyone in allied industries that make products and services based on computers, falls firmly into the apologist camp. Their behavior reflects their point of view. They always defend their products on the basis of their power and capability. When attacked on human issues, they tend—like politicians—not to answer the proffered question, but instead to wax eloquently about the newly added features and capabilities of the product and the number of people using them. They ignore the poor quality of the dance to tout the mere fact of dancing.

The extremely rapid growth of the Internet and popular access to it via the World Wide Web has brought a whole invasion of new apologists and survivors to the computer world. The apologists point enthusiastically to all of the information and services that are now available online. Meanwhile, the survivors sit staring at their computer screens wondering how to find anything that might be of use to them. They wait endlessly for Web sites to download unnecessary pictures while still letting them get lost in complex hierarchies of unwanted information. The Web is probably the biggest dancing bear we've ever faced.

How We React to Cognitive Friction

Most people, even apologists, react to cognitive friction in the same way. They take the minimum they need from it and ignore the rest. Each user learns the smallest set of features that he needs to get his work done, and he abandons the rest. The apologists proudly point out that their wristwatches can synchronize with their desktop calendar systems, but they conveniently neglect to mention that it has been six months since they used that feature. They will get defensive about it if you press them on the point, but that is what makes them apologists.

My home-entertainment system has literally thousands of features. I'm not an apologist, but I certainly qualify as a gadget freak. I have learned how to use some of its gratuitous features, but they are too hard to use effectively. For example, my television has a feature called "picture-in-picture" (PIP). It superimposes a second, smaller screen showing another channel in the lower-right corner of the main screen. It is all done in software and can be completely controlled by buttons on the remote control. In theory, it is useful for such circumstances as keeping an eye on the football game in the PIP screen while I'm watching a movie on the main screen. When the salesperson demonstrated it to me in the electronics showroom, it seemed quite useful.

The problem is that it is just too difficult to control; there is too much cognitive friction involved in using it, and I cannot master it sufficiently well to make it worth the effort. It's just more enjoyable to watch one channel, as in the old days when one channel was all that the technology could deliver. Nobody else in my family has bothered to use the PIP facility even once, except by accident, and I occasionally come home to find someone watching TV with a PIP screen up. As soon as I walk in the room, he or she asks me to turn it off.

My TV has a 55" screen and a Dolby sound system, and it receives a digital signal from an orbiting satellite, but otherwise my family members and I *use* it in exactly the same way we used our snowy, tinny, 19" Motorola in 1975. All of those features go unused.

You can predict which features in any new technology will be used and which won't. The use of a feature is inversely proportional to the amount of interaction needed to control it. In other words, the bigger, brighter, sharper screen on my new TV demands no interaction on my part, so it is used 100% of the time my TV is on, and I'm quite happy with it. The satellite system is a very desirable dancing bear of a feature, so I put up with the complexity of source-signal switching to watch the satellite broadcast once a week or so. Nobody else in my family was able to figure out how to view the satellite until I created a plastic-laminated cheat sheet that sits on the coffee table with a checklist of switches, buttons, and settings that must be made to connect up. The PIP system not only uses a complex system of over a dozen buttons, but its interaction is very obscure and its behavior is unpleasant. After the first couple of tries, I abandoned it completely, as has everyone else.

This pattern of cognitive friction abandonment can be found in every office or household with every software-based product.

The Democratization of Consumer Power

Traditionally, the more complex a mechanical device was, the more highly trained its operators were. Big machinery was always isolated from the public and was operated by trained professionals in uniform. The information age changed everything, and we now expect amateurs to manage technology far more complex than our parents ever faced.

As more and more of our tools and systems get silicon brains, they are placed into the hands of untrained amateurs. Twenty-five years ago, trained human operators handled long-distance phone calls at our verbal request. Today, the most complex international calls are handled directly by any untrained amateur pushing buttons.

Just a couple of decades ago, even gas pumps were operated only by trained service-station attendants. Today, every individual is expected to be able to perform the gas-pumping transaction, as well as the associated financial transaction, using a credit or debit card. Twenty years ago, only trained tellers operated banks. Today, you operate your bank by using a gas pump or ATM.

The engineering process doesn't discern between the creation of a complex system that will be operated by a trained, paid professional and the creation of one that is to be operated by an indifferent amateur. The process of engineering doesn't have concepts to deal with that human stuff. It concentrates on the implementation issues: What is it made of? How will it be constructed? What controls will be needed to give input to all possible variables?

Blaming the User

Most software is used in a business context, so most victims of bad interaction are paid for their suffering. Their job forces them to use software, so they cannot choose *not* to use it—they can only tolerate it as well as they can. They are forced to submerge their frustration and to ignore the embarrassment they feel when the software makes them feel stupid.

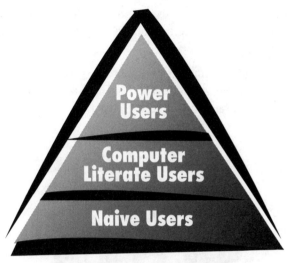

EUPHEMISM PYRAMID

For years, I've watched as dozens of software-industry executives have drawn on their whiteboards for me essentially the same diagram showing their view of the high-tech marketplace. It shows a pyramid—some draw it inverted—that is divided into three horizontal layers, each with an innocent-sounding phrase as a label. Each executive superimposes an amorphous blob on it showing the portion of the market they are aiming to conquer. But each label is a euphemism—really a veiled slur, like a code phrase you'd hear a bigot use to keep someone out of the country club. The three euphemisms are "naïve user," "computer-literate user," and "power user."

"Naïve user" is industry code for "stupid, incompetent user." And certainly these people are made to feel stupid, but they are not. It is the bad design of the interaction that is at fault. The apologists in the computer industry dismiss naïve users as insignificant, but that flies in the face of good sense. Why would a vendor write off the lion's share of the market? Because it removes the blame for failure from the executives and software engineers and places it squarely onto the shoulders of the innocent users.

The phrase "computer-literate user" really means the person has been hurt so many times that the scar tissue is thick enough that he no longer feels the pain. Computer literacy means that when your program loses your document, you have learned enough not to panic like Jane in Chapter 1, "Riddles for the Information Age," but to begin the slow, manual, utterly unnecessary search for it in the hierarchical file system without complaint. One characteristic of computer literacy is that it is like anesthesia: The patient drifts slowly and gently into unconsciousness. There is little point in constantly whining and complaining about a piece of software that is a fixed and permanent part of your job. Most people don't even realize how hard they are working to compensate for the shortcomings of a software-based tool.

Most apologists consider computer literacy to be a badge of accomplishment, like a Sharpshooter's Medal. Actually, it is more akin to a Purple Heart, an official recognition of having suffered a wound in battle.

Power users are simply apologists. They are techno-enthusiasts who have sufficiently overcome their better instincts to be useful consumers of high-cognitive-friction products. They take pride in the challenge, as they might in the challenge of scaling a rock wall in Yosemite.

Software Apartheid

There's an old joke in Hollywood that you can bump into a stranger in the grocery store and ask how his screenplay is doing. The stranger—without hesitation—will reply, "Great! I've just restructured the second act to tighten up the action!" The same joke is now true in Silicon Valley. You can buttonhole a stranger in line at Starbucks and ask how her Web site is doing. The stranger—without skipping a beat—will reply, "Great! I've just restructured the frames to tighten up the navigation!"

Here in Silicon Valley, we forget how skewed our population is, and we should frequently remind ourselves how abnormal we really are. The average person who uses a software-based product around here isn't really very average.

Programmers generally work in high-tech environments, surrounded by their technical peers in enclaves such as Silicon Valley; Route 128 outside Boston;

Research Triangle in North Carolina; Redmond, Washington; and Austin, Texas. Software engineers constantly encounter their peers when they shop, dine out, take their kids to school, and relax, and their contact with frustrated computer users is limited. What's more, the occasional unfocused gripes of the users are offset by the frequent enthusiasm of the knowledgeable elite. We forget how far removed we and our peers are from the inability of the rest of the country (not to mention the world) to use interactive tools without frustration.

We industry insiders toss around the term "computer literacy," assuming that in order to use computers, people must acquire some fundamental level of training. We see this as a simple demand that isn't hard and is only right and proper. We imagine that it isn't much to ask of users that they grasp the rudiments of how the machines work in order to enjoy their benefits. But it *is* too much to ask. Having a computer-literate customer base makes the development process much easier—of that there can be no doubt—but it hampers the growth and success of the industry and of society. Apologists counter with the argument that you must have training and a license to drive a car, but they overlook the fact that a mistake with a car frequently kills people, but a mistake with software generally doesn't. If cars weren't so deadly, people would train themselves to drive the same way they learn Excel.

The concept of computer literacy has another, more insidious, effect. It creates a demarcation line between the haves and have-nots in society. If you must master a computer in order to succeed in America's job market beyond a burger-flipper's career, then mastering the interactive system's difficulty prevents many people from moving into more productive, respected, and better-paying jobs.

Users should not have to acquire computer literacy to use computers for common, rudimentary tasks in everyday life. Users should not have to possess a digital sensitivity to work their VCR or microwave oven, or to get email. What's more, users should not have to acquire computer literacy to use computers for enterprise applications, when the user is already trained in the application domain. An accountant, for example, who is trained in the general principles of accounting, shouldn't have to be computer literate to use a computer in her accounting practice. Her domain knowledge should be enough to see her through.

As our economy shifts more and more onto an information basis, we are inadvertently creating a divided society. The upper class is composed of those who have mastered the nuances of differentiating between "RAM" and "hard disk." The lower class consists of those who treat the difference as inconsequential. The irony is that the difference *really is inconsequential* to anyone except a few hard-core engineers. Yet virtually all contemporary software forces its users to confront a file system, where your success is fully dependent on knowing the difference between RAM and disk.

Thus the term "computer literacy" becomes a euphemism for social and economic apartheid. Computer literacy is a key phrase that brutally bifurcates our society.

But what about people who are not inclined to pander to technocrats and who cannot or will not become computer literate? These people, many by choice, but most by circumstance, are falling behind in the information revolution. Many high-tech companies, for example, won't even consider for employment any applicant who does not have an email address or whose resume isn't online. I'm sure that there are many otherwise-qualified candidates out there who can't get hired because they are not yet wired. Despite the claims of the apologists, using email effectively is difficult and involves a significant level of computer literacy. Therefore, it artificially segregates the workforce. It is the moral equivalent of the banking technique of "redlining." In this illegal procedure, all houses in a given neighborhood are declared unacceptable as collateral for a housing loan. Although the red lines on the map are ostensibly drawn around economic contours, they tend to follow racial lines all too closely. Bankers protest that they are not racists, but the effect is the same.

When programmers speak of "computer literacy," they are drawing red lines around ethnic groups, too, yet few have pointed this out. It is too hard to see what is really happening because the issue is obscured by technical mythology. It is easy to see—regardless of how true—that a banker can make a loan on one house as easily as on another. However, it is not easy to see that a programmer can make interactive products easy enough for people from lower socioeconomic backgrounds to use.

As an industry, we are largely in denial about the problem of usable interactive products. There are too many apologists shouting about dancing bears. Their histrionics drown out our doubts about the efficacy of our software-based products. Before we begin to look for solutions, we must collectively come to our senses about the scope and severity of the problem. This is the goal of the next section.

Part II

It Costs You Big Time

3

Wasting Money

It's harder than you might think to squander millions of dollars, but a flawed software-development process is a tool well suited to the job. That's because software development lacks one key element: an understanding of what it means to be "done." Lacking this vital knowledge, we blindly bet on an arbitrary deadline. We waste millions to cross the finish line soonest, only to discover that the finish line was a mirage. In this chapter I'll try to untangle the expensive confusion of deadline management.

Deadline Management

There is a lot of obsessive behavior in Silicon Valley about time to market. It is frequently asserted that shipping a product *right now* is far better than shipping it later. This imperative is used as a justification for setting impossibly ambitious ship dates and for burning out employees, but this is a smoke screen that hides bigger, deeper fears—a red herring. Shipping a product that angers and frustrates users in three months is *not* better than shipping a product that pleases users in six months, as any businessperson knows full well.

Managers are haunted by two closely related fears. They worry about when their programmers will be done building, and they doubt whether the product will be good enough to ultimately succeed in the marketplace. Both of these fears stem from the typical manager's lack of a clear vision of what the finished product actually will consist of, aside from mother-and-apple-pie statements such as "runs on the target computer" and "doesn't crash." And lacking this vision, they cannot assess a product's progress towards completion.

The implication of these two fears is that as long as it "doesn't crash," there isn't much difference between a program that takes three months to code and one that takes six months to code, except for the prodigious cost of three months of unnecessary programming. After the programmers have begun work, money drains swiftly. Therefore, logic tells the development manager that the most important thing to do is to get the coding started as soon as possible and to end it as soon as possible.

The conscientious development manager quickly hires programmers and sets them coding immediately. She boldly establishes a completion date just a few months off, and the team careens madly toward the finish line. But without product design, our manager's two fears remain unquelled. She has not established whether the users will like the product, which indeed leaves its success a mystery. Nor has she established what a "complete" product looks like, which leaves its completion a mystery. Later in the book, I'll show how interaction design can ease these problems. Right now, I'll show how thoroughly the deadline subverts the development process, turning all the manager's insecurities into self-fulfilling prophecies.

What Does "Done" Look Like?

After we have a specific description of what the finished software will be, we can compare our creation with it and really *know* when the product is done.

There are two types of descriptions. We can create a very complete and detailed physical description of the actual product, or we can describe the reaction we'd like the end user to have. In building architecture, for example, blueprints fill the first requirement. When planning a movie or creating a new restaurant, however, we focus our description on the feelings we'd like our clients to experience. For software-based products, we must necessarily use a blend of the two.

Unfortunately, most software products never *have* a description. Instead, all they have is a shopping list of features. A shopping bag filled with flour, sugar, milk, and eggs is not the same thing as a cake. It's only a cake when all the steps of the recipe have been followed, and the result looks, smells, and tastes substantially like the known characteristics of a cake.

Having the proper ingredients but lacking any knowledge of cakes or how to bake, the ersatz cook will putter endlessly in the kitchen with only indeterminate results. If we demand that the cake be ready by 6 o'clock, the conscientious cook will certainly bring us a platter at the appointed hour. But will the concoction be a cake? All we know is that it is on time, but its success will be a mystery.

In most conventional construction jobs, we know we're done because we have a clear understanding of what a "done" job looks like. We know that the building is completed because it looks and works just like the blueprints say it should look and work. If the deadline for construction is June 1, the arrival of June doesn't necessarily mean that the building is done. The relative completeness of the building can only be measured by examining the actual building in comparison to the plans.

Without blueprints, software builders don't really have a firm grasp on what makes the product "done," so they pick a likely date for completion, and when that day arrives they declare it done. It is June 1; therefore, the product is completed. "Ship it!" they say, and the deadline becomes the sole definition of project completion.

The programmers and businesspeople are neither stupid nor foolish, so the product won't be in complete denial of reality. It will have a robust set of features, it will run well, and it won't crash. The product will work reasonably well when operated by people *who care deeply* that it works well. It might even have been subjected to usability testing, in which strangers are asked to operate it under the scrutiny of usability professionals[1]. But, although these precautions are only reasonable, they are insufficient to answer the fundamental question: Will it succeed?

Parkinson's Law

Managers know that software development follows Parkinson's Law: Work will expand to fill the time allotted to it. If you are in the software business, perhaps you are familiar with a corollary to Parkinson called the Ninety-Ninety Rule, attributed to Tom Cargill of Bell Labs: "The first 90% of the code accounts for the first 90% of the development time. The remaining 10% of the code accounts for the other 90% of the development time." This self-deprecating rule says that when

---

[1] *Usability professionals are not interaction designers. I discuss this difference in detail in Chapter 12, "Desperately Seeking Usability."*

the engineers have written 90% of the code, they *still* don't know where they are! Management knows full well that the programmers won't hit their stated ship dates, regardless of what dates it specifies. The developers work best under pressure, and management uses the delivery date as the pressure-delivery vehicle.

In the 1980s and 1990s, Royal Farros was the vice president of development for T/Maker, a small but influential software company. He says, "A lot of us set deadlines that we *knew* were impossible, enough so to qualify for one of those Parkinson's Law corollaries. 'The time it will take to finish a programming project is twice as long as the time you've allotted for it.' I had a *strong* belief that if you set a deadline for, say, six months, it would take a year. So, if you had to have something in two years, set the deadline for one year. Bonehead sandbagging, but it always worked."

When software entrepreneur Ridgely Evers was with Intuit, working on the creation of QuickBooks, he experienced the same problem. "The first release of QuickBooks was supposed to be a nine-month project. We were correct in estimating that the development period would be the same as a gestation period, but we picked the wrong species: It took almost two-and-a-half years, the gestation period for the elephant."

Software architect Scott McGregor points out that Gresham's Law—that bad currency drives out good—is also relevant here. If there are two currencies, people will hoard the good one and try to spend the bad one. Eventually, only the bad currency circulates. Similarly, bad schedule estimates drive out good ones. If everybody makes bogus but rosy predictions, the one manager giving realistic but longer estimates will appear to be a heel-dragger and will be pressured to revise his estimates downward.

Some development projects have deadlines that are unreasonable by virtue of their arbitrariness. Most rational managers still choose deadlines that, while reachable, are only reachable by virtue of extreme sacrifice. Sort of like the pilot saying, "We're gonna make Chicago on time, but only if we jettison all our baggage!" I've seen product managers sacrifice not only design, but testing, function, features, integration, documentation, and reality. *Most product managers that I have worked with would rather ship a failure on time than risk going late.*

The Product That Never Ships

This preference is often due to every software development manager's deepest fear: that after having become late, the product will never ship at all. Stories of products never shipping are not apocryphal. The project goes late, first by one year, then two years, then is euthanized in its third year by a vengeful upper management or board of directors. This explains the rabid adherence to deadlines, even at the expense of a viable product.

For example, in the late 1990s, at the much-publicized start-up company Worlds, Inc., many intelligent, capable people worked on the creation of a virtual, online world where people's avatars could wander about and engage other avatars in real-time conversation. The product was never fully defined or described, and after tens of millions of investment capital was spent, the directors mercifully pulled the plug.

In the early 1990s, another start-up company, Nomadic Computing, spent about $15 million creating a new product for mobile businesspeople. Unfortunately, no one at the company was quite sure what its product was. They knew their market, and most of the program's functions, but weren't clear on their users' goals. Like mad sculptors chipping away at a huge block of marble hoping to discover a statue inside, the developers wrote immense quantities of useless code that was all eventually thrown away, along with money, time, reputations, and careers. The saddest waste, though, was the lost opportunity for creating software that really was wanted.

Even Microsoft isn't immune from such wild goose chases. Its first attempt at creating a database product in the late 1980s consumed many person-years of effort before Bill Gates mercifully shut it down. Its premature death sent a shock wave through the development community. Its successor, Access, was a completely new effort, staffed and managed by all new people.

Shipping Late Doesn't Hurt

Ironically, shipping late generally isn't fatal to a product. A third-rate product that ships late often fails, but if your product delivers value to its users, arriving behind schedule won't necessarily have lasting bad effects. If a product is a hit, it's not a big deal that it ships a month—or even a year—late. Microsoft Access shipped several years late, yet it has enjoyed formidable success in the market. Conversely, if a product stinks, who cares that it shipped on time?

Certainly, some consumer products that depend on the Christmas season for the bulk of their sales have frighteningly important due dates. But most software-based products, even consumer products, aren't that sensitive to any particular date.

For example, in 1990 the PenPoint computer from GO was supposed to be the progenitor of a handheld-computer revolution. In 1992, when the PenPoint crashed and burned, the Apple Newton inherited the promise of the handheld revolution. When the Newton failed to excite people, General Magic's Magic Link computer became the new hope for handhelds. That was in 1994. When the Magic Link failed to sell, the handheld market appeared dead. Venture capitalists declared it a dry hole. Then, out of nowhere, in 1996, the PalmPilot arrived to universal acclaim. It seized the handheld no-man's-land *six years late*. Markets are always ready for good products that deliver value and satisfy users.

Of course, companies with a long history of making hardware-only products now make hybrid versions containing chips and software. They tend to underestimate the influence of software and subordinate it to the already-established completion cycles of hardware. This is wrong because as Chapter 1, "Riddles for the Information Age," showed, these companies are now in the software business, whether or not they know it.

Feature-List Bargaining

One consequence of deadline management is a phenomenon that I call "feature-list bargaining."

Years ago programmers got burned by the vague product-definition process consisting of cocktail-napkin sketches, because they were blamed for the unsuccessful software that so often resulted. In self-defense, programmers demanded that managers and marketers be more precise. Computer programs are procedural, and procedures map closely to features, so it was only natural that programmers would define "precision" as a list of features. These feature lists allowed programmers to shift the blame to management when the product failed to live up to expectations. They could say, "It wasn't my fault. I put in all the features management wanted."

Thus, most products begin life with a document variably called a "marketing specification," "technical specification," or "marketing requirements document." It is really just a list of desired features, like the list of ingredients in the recipe for cake. It is usually the result of several long brainstorming sessions in which managers, marketers, and developers imagine what features would be cool and jot them down. Spreadsheet programs are a favorite tool for creating these lists, and a typical one can be dozens of pages long. (Invariably, at least one of the line items will specify a "good user interface.") Feature suggestions can also come from focus groups, market research, and competitive analysis.

The managers then hand the feature list to the programmers and say, "The product must ship by June 1." The programmers—of course—agree, but they have some stipulations. There are far too many features to create in the time allotted, they claim, and many of them will have to be cut to meet the deadline. Thus begins the time-honored bargaining.

The programmers draw a dividing line midway through the list. Items above it will be implemented, they declare, while those below the "line of death" are postponed or eliminated. Management then has two choices: to allow more time or to cut features. Although the project will inevitably take more time, management is loath to play that trump so early in the round, so it negotiates over features. Considerable arguing and histrionics occur. Features are traded for time; time is traded for features. This primitive capitalist negotiation is so human and natural that both parties are instantly comfortable with it. Sophisticated parallel strategies develop. As T/Maker's Royal Farros points out, when one "critical-path feature was blamed for delaying a deadline, it would let a dozen other tardy features sneak onto the list without repercussion." Lost in the battle is the perspective needed for success.

Farros described T/Maker's flagship product, a word processor named WriteNow, as "a perfect product for the university marketplace. In 1987, we actually shipped more copies of WriteNow to the university market than Microsoft shipped Word. However, we couldn't hold our lead because we angered our very loyal, core fans in this market by not delivering the one word-processor feature needed in a university setting: *endnotes*. Because of trying to make the deadline, we could never slip this feature into the specification. We met our deadline but lost an entire market segment."

Programmers Are in Control

Despite appearances, programmers are completely in control of this bottom-up decision-making process. They are the ones who establish how long it will take to implement each item, so they can force things to the bottom of the list merely by estimating them long. The programmers will—in self-defense—assign longer duration to the more nebulously defined items, typically those concerned with substantive user-interface issues. This inevitably causes them to migrate to the bottom of the list. More familiar idioms and easy-to-code items, such as menus, wizards, and dialog boxes, bubble to the top of the list. All of the analysis and careful thinking done by high-powered and high-priced executives is made moot by the unilateral cherry picking of a programmer following his own muse or defending his turf.

Like someone only able to set the volume of a speaker that isn't within hearing distance, managers find themselves in the unenviable position of only having tools that control ineffective parameters of the development process. It is certainly true that management needs to control the process of creating and shipping successful software, but, unfortunately, our cult of deadline ignores the "successful" part to concentrate only on the "creating" part. We give the creators of the product the reins to the process, thus relegating management to the role of passenger and observer.

Features Are Not Necessarily Good

Appearances to the contrary, users aren't really compelled by features. Product successes and failures have shown repeatedly that users don't care that much about features. Users only care about achieving their goals. Sometimes features are needed to reach goals, but more often than not, they merely confuse users and get in the way of allowing them to get their work done. Ineffective features make users feel stupid. Borrowing from a previous example, the successful PalmPilot has far fewer features than did General Magic's failed Magic Link computer, Apple's failed Newton, or the failed PenPoint computer. The PalmPilot owes its success to its designers' single-minded focus on its target user and the objectives that user wanted to achieve.

About the only good thing I can say about features is that they are quantifiable. And that quality of being countable imbues them with an aura of value that they simply don't have. Features have negative qualities every bit as strong as their positive ones. The biggest design problem they cause is that every well-meant feature that *might possibly* be useful obfuscates the few features that *will probably* be useful. Of course, features cost money to implement. They add complexity to the product. They require an increase in the size and complexity of the documentation and online help system. Above all, cost-wise, they require additional trained telephone tech-support personnel to answer users' questions about them.

It might be counterintuitive in our feature-conscious world, but you simply cannot achieve your goals by using feature lists as a problem-solving tool. It's quite possible to satisfy every feature item on the list and still hatch a catastrophe. Interaction designer Scott McGregor uses a delightful test in his classes to prove this point. He describes a product with a list of its features, asking his class to write down what the product is as soon as they can guess. He begins with 1) internal combustion engine; 2) four wheels with rubber tires; 3) a transmission connecting the engine to the drive wheels; 4) engine and transmission mounted on metal chassis; 5) a steering wheel. By this time, every student will have written down his or her positive identification of the product as an automobile, whereupon Scott ceases using features to describe the product and instead mentions a couple of user goals: 6) cuts grass quickly and easily; 7) comfortable to sit on. From the five feature clues, not one student will have written down "riding lawnmower." You can see how much more descriptive goals are than features.

Iteration and the Myth of the Unpredictable Market

In an industry that is so filled with money and opportunities to earn it, it is often just easier to move right along to another venture and chalk up a previous failure to happenstance, rather than to any *real* reason.

I was a party to one of these failures in the early 1990s. I helped to start a venture-funded company whose stated goal was to make it absurdly simple to network PCs together.[2] The product worked well and was easy to use, but a tragic series of

---

[2] *Actually, we said that we wanted to make it "as easy to network Intel/Windows computers as it was to network Macintosh computers." At the time, it was ridiculously simple to network Macs together with AppleTalk. Then, as now, it was quite difficult to network Wintel PCs together.*

self-inflicted marketing blunders caused it to fail dismally. I recently attended a conference where I ran into one of the investors who sat on the doomed company's board of directors. We hadn't talked since the failure of the company, and—like veterans of a battlefield defeat meeting years later—we consoled each other as sadder but wiser men. To my unbridled surprise, however, this otherwise extremely successful and intelligent man claimed that in hindsight he had learned a fundamental lesson: Although the marketing, management, and technical efforts had been flawless, the buying public "just wasn't interested in easy-to-install local area networks." I was flabbergasted that he would make such an obviously ridiculous claim and countered that surely it wasn't lack of desire, but rather our failure to satisfy the desire properly. He restated his position, arguing forcefully that we had demonstrated that easy networking just wasn't something that people wanted.

Later that evening, as I related this story to my wife, I realized that his rationalization of the failure was certainly convenient for all the parties involved in the effort. By blaming the failure on the random fickleness of the market, my colleague had exonerated the investors, the managers, the marketers, and the developers of any blame. And, in fact, each of the members of that start-up has gone on to other successful endeavors in Silicon Valley. The venture capitalist has a robust portfolio of other successful companies.

During development, the company had all the features itemized on the feature list. It stayed within budget. It shipped on schedule. (Well, actually, we kept extending the schedule, but it shipped on *a* schedule.) All the quantitatively measurable aspects of the product-development effort were within acceptable parameters. The only conclusion this management-savvy investor could make was the existence of an unexpected discontinuity in the marketplace. How could *we* have failed when all the meters were in the green?

The fact that these measures are objective is reassuring to everyone. Objective and quantitative measure is highly respected by both programmers and businesspeople. The fact that these measures are usually ineffective in producing successful products tends to get lost in the shuffle. If the product succeeds, its progenitors will take the credit, attributing the victory to their savvy understanding of technology and marketing.

On the other hand, if the product fails, nobody will have the slightest motivation to exhume the carcass and analyze the failure. Almost any excuse will do, as long as the players—both management and technical—can move along to the next high-tech opportunity, of which there is an embarrassment of riches. Thus, there is no reason to weep over the occasional failure. The unfortunate side effect of not understanding failure is the silent admission that success is not predictable—that luck and happenstance rule the high-tech world. In turn, this gives rise to what the venture capitalists call the "spray and pray" method of funding: Put a little bit of money into a lot of investments and then hope that one of them gets lucky.

⌘

Rapid-development environments such as the World Wide Web—and Visual Basic before it—have also promoted this idea of simply iterating until something works. Because the Web is a new advertising medium, it has attracted a multitude of marketing experts who are particularly receptive to the myth of the unpredictable market and its imperative to iterate. Marketers are familiar with the harsh and arbitrary world of advertising and media. After all, much of advertising *really is* random guesswork. For example, in advertising, "new" is the single most effective marketing concept, yet when Coca-Cola introduced "New Coke" in the mid-1980s, it failed utterly. Nobody could have predicted this result. People's tastes and styles change randomly, and the effectiveness of marketing can appear to be random.

On the Web, the problem arises when a Web site matures from the online-catalog stage into the online-store stage. It changes from a one-way presentation of data to an interactive software application. The advertising and media people who had such great success with the first-generation site now try their same iteration methods on the interactive site and run into trouble, often without realizing it. Marketing results may be random, but interaction is not. The cognitive friction generated by the software's interactivity is what gives the impression of randomness to those untrained in interaction design.

The remarkably easy-to-change nature of the World Wide Web plays into this because an advertisement or marketing campaign can be aired for a tiny fraction of the cost (and time) of print or TV advertising. The savvy Web marketer can get almost instantaneous feedback on the effectiveness of an ad, so the speed of the iteration increases dramatically, and things are hacked together overnight. In practice, it boils down to "throw it against the wall and see what sticks." Many managers of Web start-ups use this embarrassingly simple doctrine of design by guesswork. They write any old program that can be built in the least time and then put it before their users. They then listen to the complaints and feedback, measure the patterns of the user's navigation clicks, change the weak parts, and then ship it again.

Generally, programmers aren't thrilled about the iterative method because it means extra work for them. Typically, it's managers new to technology who like the iterative process because it relieves them of having to perform rigorous planning, thinking, and product due diligence (in other words, interaction design). Of course, it's the users who pay the dearest price. They have to suffer through one halfhearted attempt after another before they get a program that isn't too painful.

Just because customer feedback improves your understanding of your product or service, you cannot then deduce that it is efficient, cheap, or even effective to toss random features at your customers and see which ones are liked and which are disliked. In a world of dancing bears, this can be a marginally viable strategy, but in any market in which there is the least hint of competition, it is suicidal. Even when you are all alone in a market, it is a very wasteful method.

Many otherwise sensitive and skilled managers are unashamedly proud of this method. One mature, experienced executive (a former marketing man) asked me, in self-effacing rhetoric, "How could anyone presume to know what the users want?" This is a staggering question. Every businessperson presumes. The value that most businesspeople bring to their market is precisely their "presumption" of what the customer wants. Yes, that presumption will miss the mark with *some* users, but not to presume at all means that *every* user won't like it. This foolish man believed that his customers didn't mind plowing through his guesses to do his design work for him. Today, in Silicon Valley, there might be lots of enthusiastic Web-surfing apologists who are willing to help this lazy executive figure out his business, but how many struggling survivors did he alienate with that haughty attitude? As he posted sketchy version after sketchy version of his site, reacting only to those people with the stamina to return to it, how many customers did he lose permanently? What did *they* want? It has been said that the way Stalin cleared a minefield was to march a regiment through it. Effective? Yes. Efficient, humanitarian, viable, desirable? No.

The biggest drawback, of course, is that you immediately scare away all survivors, and your only remaining users will be apologists. This seriously skews the nature and quality of your feedback, condemning you to a clientele of technoid apologists, which is a relatively small segment. This is one reason why so few personal-computer software-product makers have successfully crossed over into mass markets.

I am not saying that you cannot learn from trial and error, but those trials should be informed by something more than random chance and should begin from a well-thought-out solution, not an overnight hack. Otherwise, it's just giving lazy or ignorant businesspeople license to abuse consumers.

The Hidden Costs of Bad Software

When software is frustrating and difficult to use, people will avoid using it. That is unremarkable until you realize that many people's jobs are dependent on using software. The corporate cost of software avoided is impossible to quantify, but it is real. Generally, the costs are not monetary ones, anyway, but are exacted in far more expensive currencies, such as time, order, reputation, and customer loyalty.

People who use business software might despise it, but they are paid to tolerate it. This changes the way people think about software. Getting paid for using software makes users far more tolerant of its shortcomings because they have no choice, but it doesn't make it any less expensive. Instead—while the costs remain high—they become very difficult to see and account for.

Badly designed business software makes people dislike their jobs. Their productivity suffers, errors creep into their work, they try to cheat the software, and they don't stay in the job very long. Losing employees is very expensive, not just in money but in disruption to the business, and the time lost can never be made up. Most people who are paid to use a tool feel constrained not to complain about that tool, but it doesn't stop them from feeling frustrated and unhappy about it.

One of the most expensive items associated with hard-to-use software is technical support. Microsoft spends $800 million annually on technical support. And this is a company that spends many hundreds of millions of dollars on usability testing and research, too. Microsoft is apparently convinced that support of this magnitude is just an unavoidable cost of doing business. I am not. Imagine the advantage it would give your company if you didn't make the same assumption that Microsoft did. Imagine how much more effective your development efforts would be if you could avoid spending over five percent of your net revenue on technical support.

Ask any person who has ever worked at any desktop-software company in technical support, and he will tell you that the one thing he spends most of his time and effort on is the file system. Just like Jane in Chapter 1, users don't understand the recursive hierarchy of the file system—the Finder or Explorer—on Windows, the Mac, or Unix. Surprisingly, very few companies will spend the money to design and implement a more human-friendly alternative to the file system. Instead, they accept the far more expensive option of answering phone calls about it in perpetuity.

You can blame the "stupid user" all you want, but you still have to staff those phones with expensive tech-support people if you want to sell or distribute within your company software that hasn't been designed.

The Only Thing More Expensive Than Writing Software Is Writing Bad Software

Programmers cost a lot, and programmers sitting on their hands waiting for design to be completed gall managers in the extreme. It seems foolish to have programmers sit and wait, when they could be programming, thinks the manager. It is false economy, though, to put programmers to work before the design is completed. After the coding process begins, the momentum of programming becomes unstoppable, and the design process must now respond to the needs of programmers, instead of vice versa. Indeed, it is foolish to have programmers wait, and by the simple expedient of having interaction designers plan your next product or release concurrently with the construction of this product or release, your programmers will never have to idly wait.

It is more costly in the long run to have programmers write the wrong thing than to write nothing at all. This truth is so counterintuitive that most managers balk at the very idea. After code is written, it is very difficult to throw it out. Like writers in love with their prose, programmers tend to have emotional attachments to their algorithms. Altering programs in midstride upsets the development process and wounds the code, too. It's hard on the manager to discard code because she is the one who paid dearly for it, and she knows she will have to spend even more to replace it.

If design isn't done before programming starts, it will never have much effect. One manager told me, "We've already got people writing code and I'm not gonna stop." The attitude of these cowboys is, "By the time you are ready to hit the ground, I'll have stitched together a parachute." It's a bold sentiment, but I've never seen it work.

Lacking a solid design, programmers continually experiment with their programs to find the best solutions. Like a carpenter cutting boards by eye until he gets one that fits the gap in the wall, this method causes abundant waste.

The immeasurability and intangibility of software conspires to make it nearly impossible to estimate its size and assess its state of completion. Add in the programmer's joy in her craft, and you can see that software development always grows in scope and time and never shrinks. We will always be surprised during its construction, unless we can accurately establish milestones and reliably measure our progress against them.

Opportunity Cost

In the information age, the most expensive commodity is not the cost of building something, but the lost opportunity of what you are *not* building. Building a failure means that you didn't build a success. Taking three annual releases to get a good product means that you didn't create three good products in one release each.

Novell's core business is networking, but it attempted to fight Microsoft toe-to-toe in the office-applications arena. Although its failed efforts in the new market were expensive, the true cost was its loss of leadership in the networking market. The money is nothing compared to the singular potential of the moment. Netscape lost its leadership in the browser market in the same way when it decided to compete against Microsoft in the operating-system business.

Any developer of silicon-based products has to evaluate what the most important goals of its users are and steadfastly focus on achieving them. It is far too easy to be beguiled by the myriad of opportunities in high tech and to gamble away the main chance. Programmers—regardless of their intelligence, business acumen, loyalty, and good intentions—march to a slightly different drummer and can easily drag a business away from its proper area of focus.

The Cost of Prototyping

Prototyping is programming, and it has the momentum and cost of programming, but the result lacks the resiliency of real code. Software prototypes are scaffolds and have little relation to permanent, maintainable, expandable code—the equivalent of stone walls. Managers, in particular, are loath to discard code that works, even if it is just a prototype. They can't tell the difference between scaffolding and stone walls.

You can write a prototype much faster than a real program. This makes it attractive because it seems so inexpensive, but real programming gives you a reliable program, and prototyping gives you a shaky foundation. Prototypes are experiments made to be thrown out, but few of them ever are. Managers look at the running prototype and ask, "Why can't we just use this?" The answer is too technically complex and too fraught with uncertainty to have sufficient force to dissuade the manager who sees what looks like a way to avoid months of expensive effort.

The essence of good programming is deferred gratification. You put in all of the work up front, and then you reap the rewards later. There are very few tasks that aren't cheaper to do manually. Once written, however, programs can be run a million times with no extra cost. The most expensive program is one that runs once. The cheapest program is the one that runs ten billion times. However, any inappropriate behavior will also be magnified ten billion times. Once out of the realm of little programs, such as the ones you wrote in school, the economics of software take on a strange reversal in which the cheapest programs to own are the ones that are most expensive to write, and the most expensive programs to own are the cheapest to write.

Writing a big program is like making a pile of bricks. The pile is one brick wide and 1,000 bricks tall, with each brick laid right on top of the one preceding it. The tower can reach its full height only if the bricks are placed with great precision on top of one another. Any deviation will cause the bricks above to wobble, topple, and fall. If the 998th brick deviates by a quarter of an inch, the tower can still probably achieve 1,000 bricks, but if the deviation is in the fifth brick, the tower will never get above a couple dozen.

This is very characteristic of software, whose foundations are more sensitive to hacking than the upper levels of code. As any program is constructed, the programmer makes false starts and changes as she goes. Consequently, the program is filled with the scar tissue of changed code. Every program has vestigial functions and stubbed-out facilities. Every program has features and tools whose need was discovered sometime after construction began grafted onto it as afterthoughts. Each one of these scars is like a small deviation in the stack of bricks. Moving a button from one side of a dialog box to the other is like joggling the 998th brick, but changing the code that draws all button-like objects is like joggling the 5th brick. Object-oriented programming and the principles of encapsulation are defensive techniques whose sole purpose is to immunize the program from the effects of scar tissue. In essence, object orientation divides the 1,000-brick tower into 10 100-brick towers.

Good programmers spend enormous amounts of time and energy setting up to write a big program. It can take days just to set up the programming environment, before a line of product code is written. The proper libraries must be selected. The data must be defined. The storage and retrieval subsystems must be analyzed, defined, coded, and tested.

As the programmers proceed into the meat of the construction, they invariably discover mistakes in their planning and flaws in their assumptions. They are then faced with Hobson's choice of whether to spend the time and effort to back up and fix things from the start, or to patch over the problem wherever they are and accept the burden of the new scar tissue—the deviation. Backing up is always very expensive, but that scar tissue ultimately limits the size of the program—the height of the bricks.

Each time a program is modified for a new revision to fix bugs or to add features, scar tissue is added. This is why software must be thrown out and completely rewritten every couple of decades. After a while, the scar tissue becomes too thick to work well anymore.

Prototypes—by their very nature—are programs that are slapped together in a hurry so that the results can be assayed. What the programmer exchanges in order to build the prototype so speedily is the perfect squaring of the bricks. Instead of using the "right" data structures, information is thrown in helter-skelter. Instead of using the "right" algorithms, whatever code fragments happen to be lying around are drafted for service. Prototypes *begin* life as masses of scar tissue. They can never grow very large.

Some software developers have arrived at the unfortunate conclusion that modern rapid-prototyping tools—such as Visual Basic—are effective design tools. Rather than designing the product, they just whip out an extremely anemic version of it with a visual programming tool. This prototype typically becomes the foundation for the product. This trades away the robustness and life span of the product for an illusory benefit. You can get a better design with pencil and paper and a good methodology than you can with any amount of prototyping.

For those who are not designers, visualizing the form and behavior of software that doesn't yet exist is difficult, if not impossible. Prototypes have been drafted into the role of a visualization tool for these businesspeople. Because a prototype is a rough model created with whatever prebuilt facilities are most readily available, prototypes are by nature filled with expedient compromises. But software that actually works—regardless of how badly—exerts a powerful pull on those who must pay for its development. A running—limping—prototype has an uncanny momentum out of proportion to its real value.

It is all too compelling for the manager to say, "Don't throw out the prototype. Let's use it as the foundation for the *real* product." This decision can often lead to a situation in which the product never ships. The programmers are condemned to a role of perpetually resuscitating the program from life-threatening failures as it grows. Like the stack in which the first 25 bricks were placed haphazardly, no matter how precisely the bricks above them are placed, no matter how diligently the mason works, no matter how sticky and smooth the mortar, the force of gravity inevitably pulls it down somewhere around the 50th level of bricks.

The value of a prototype is in the education it gives you, not in the code itself. Developer sage Frederick Brooks says, "Plan to throw one away." You will anyway, so you might as well do it under controlled circumstances.

In 1988, I sold a program called Ruby to Bill Gates. Ruby was a visual programming language that, when combined with Bill's QuickBasic product, became Visual Basic. What Gates saw was just a prototype, but it demonstrated some significant advances both in design and technology. (When he first saw it, he asked, "How did you *do* that?") The Microsoft executive in charge of then-under-construction Windows 3.0, Russ Werner, was also assigned to Ruby. The subsequent deal we struck included having me write the actual program to completion. The first thing I did was to throw Ruby-the-prototype away and start over from scratch with nothing but the wisdom and experience. When Russ found out, he was astonished, angry, and indignant. He had never heard of such an outrageous thing, and was convinced that discarding the prototype would delay the product's release. It was a fait accompli, though, and despite Russ's fears we delivered the completed program on schedule. After Basic was grafted on, VB was one of Microsoft's more successful initial releases. In contrast, Windows 3.0 shipped more than a year late, and ever since it has been notoriously handicapped by its profuse quantities of vestigial prototype code.

In general, nontechnical managers erroneously value completed code—regardless of its robustness—much higher than design, or even the advice of those who wrote the code. A colleague, Clay Collier, who creates software for in-car navigation systems, told me this story about one system that he worked on for a large Japanese automotive electronics company. Clay developed—at his client's behest—a prototype of a consumer navigation system. As a good prototype should, it proved that the system would work, but beyond that the program barely functioned. One day the president of the Japanese electronics company came to the United States and wanted to see the program demonstrated. Clay's colleague—we'll call him Ralph—knew that he could not deny the Japanese president; he would have to put on a demo. So Ralph picked the president up at LAX in a car specially equipped with the prototype navigation system. Ralph knew that the prototype would give them directions to their offices in Los Angeles, but nothing else had been tested. To Ralph's chagrin, the president asked instead to go to a specific restaurant for lunch. Ralph was unfamiliar with the restaurant and wasn't at all confident that the prototype could get them there. He crossed his fingers and entered the restaurant's name, and to his surprise, the computer began to issue driving instructions: "Turn right on Lincoln," "Move into the left lane," and so on. Ralph dutifully followed as the president ruminated silently, but Ralph began to grow more uneasy as the instructions took them into increasingly unsavory parts of town. Ralph's anxiety peaked when he stopped the car on the computer's command and the passenger door was yanked open. To Ralph's eternal relief, the valet at the desired restaurant had opened it. A smile broke across the president's face.

However, the very success of this prototype demonstration backfired on Ralph. The president was so impressed by the system's functioning that he commanded that Ralph turn it into a product. Ralph protested that it was just a feasibility proof and not robust enough to use as the foundation for millions of consumer products. The president wouldn't hear of it. He had seen it work. Ralph did as he was told, and eight long years later his company finally shipped the first working version of the product. It was slow and buggy, and it fell short of newer, younger competitors. The *New York Times* called it "clearly inferior."

The expertise and knowledge that Ralph and his team gained by building the prototype *incorrectly* was far more valuable than the code itself. The president misunderstood that and, by putting greater value on the code, made the entire company suffer for it.

⌘

If you define the boundaries of a development project only in terms of deadlines and feature lists, the product might be delivered on time, but it won't be desired. If, instead, you define the project in terms of quality and user satisfaction, you will get a product that users want, and it won't take any longer. There's an old Silicon Valley joke that asks, "How do you make a small fortune in software?" The answer, of course, is, "Start with a large fortune!" The hidden costs of even well-managed software-development projects are large enough to give Donald Trump pause. Yacht racing and drug habits are cheaper in the long run than writing software without the proper controls.

4

THE DANCING BEAR

Even when survivors know that an interactive product makes them feel stupid, they cannot generally point this fact out without appearing to whine and complain, because they are surrounded by apologists. Nobody likes to complain, so survivors feel strong social pressure to join the apologists, make excuses, and blame themselves for their bad performance. But the instincts of the survivors are better than their conscious efforts to compensate. The software *does* make them feel stupid, and it doesn't have to. If you are one of these people, you might be asking yourself, "Just what does he mean by bad software? It gets the job done, doesn't it?" In the rest of this chapter, I'll describe what I mean by bad.

If It Were a Problem, Wouldn't It Have Been Solved by Now?

The sad thing about dancing bearware is that most people are quite satisfied with the lumbering beast. Only when they see some real dancing do they begin to suspect that there is a world beyond ursine shuffling. So few software-based products have exhibited any real dancing ability that most people are honestly unaware that things could be better—a lot better. Most people using spreadsheets and word processors on modern computers imagine that all the problems that a computer can solve *have* been solved, and solved adequately if not well. But this is far from the truth. An infinity of information-handling jobs remains unsolved and, in many cases, not addressed at all.

Consumer Electronics Victim

As consumers of software-based products, we are so used to accepting what we are given that we cannot see what could so easily be ours. Engineers make products that perform the tasks comprising the job but, lacking design, the collection of tasks still doesn't achieve the user's goals.

I have owned various videocassette recorders for over 20 years. All of them have had built-in facilities for delayed recording of shows, but none of these machines—even the $1,500, top-of-the-line model—gives me confidence that I will succeed. The interface the product presents to me is so hard to control, so hard to read, so unclear about terminology and settings, and so filled with hidden switches and modes that my success ratio has been a consistent 40%. More than half of the time, I find that I have recorded three hours of Brazilian soccer instead of the PBS special that I wanted. After years of struggling, I have merely conceded defeat and don't even try to record TV shows anymore. So has everyone in my family. So have all of my friends. We are survivors of dancing bearware.

In frustration, I go to the local Circuit City, my Visa card burning a hole in my pocket. "Here's a grand! Two grand," I shout, "for the salesperson who can bring me a VCR that I can use to record TV shows!" The shiny-suit set gather round and proffer their wares. From bargain-basement VCR to most expensive, there is no difference in interaction. Sure, there is a continuum of available features, but the actual way that I control the device is the same across the board. In other words, after 20 years of product maturation, I am no closer to being able to use the product than before. This is dancing bearware at its worst.

When I point this out to the salesman, he defends the device by saying that it is as good as it gets. He shows me where the brochure claims that it is "easy to use." Bill Gates once observed, with uncharacteristic cynicism, that the way you made software user friendly was by making a rubber stamp and stamping each box with the legend "USER FRIENDLY." Unintentionally, his method has become the computer industry's *real* method.

Pushbuttons don't map well to a continuum such as time, but a rotating knob does. If that VCR just had a simple rotating knob like my $11 Baby Ben alarm clock, I could set the time and banish the blinking "12:00" forever. If the device had a second knob to set the future record time, I could manage recording easily, too. As it is, by providing the flexibility to record *10* future shows, the device becomes unusable for recording *any one* show.

Products that are dancing bearware surround us. They have sufficient features to cover their cardboard boxes with callouts. They have enough options to fill the magazine reviewer's matrix of options with the word "Yes." But they don't make users happy or more effective. Most users can't make use of most of the options and features. Those who do are apologists who joyfully change their work habits to accommodate the idiosyncrasies of the software. They revel in the opportunity to tinker. They laboriously learn how to control new features that they will never actually use.

How Email Programs Fail

While vendors wage pitched battles in the software markets, users cower in their cubicles, fearful of wandering into no-man's-land. Email vendors, for example, add feature after feature to their checklists while still failing to address the fundamental needs of electronic communications.

New users of email are entranced by their novel ability to communicate directly, simply, and asynchronously with anyone else. But solving the tasks doesn't necessarily solve the user's goals, and that is why emailing remains in its primitive state. The problem lies in the misunderstanding of what email is really used for. Twenty years ago, getting *any* email was an important event. Because the medium made it clear that the message was important, the message itself wasn't anything special. In fact, it was just a simple, discrete file of plain ASCII characters with no special characteristics or relationships.

Today, we get a broad mixture of important and worthless emails. Any person who uses email discovers quickly what a powerful and useful medium it is, and her use of it rapidly escalates until she is running a significant part of her life and business on it. Many email users get dozens or hundreds of email messages every day. Most communications are sent either in response to some message, or in expectation of a reply. These sequences of messages, called threads, bounce back and forth between two or more people. On my computer, the ratio of threaded messages to singletons is about 50 to 1. And yet not a single email program available today treats email messages as part of a sequence.[1] They act as though threads either don't exist or are an insignificant attribute of only a few emails.

---

[1] *Some email programs let the user manually construct and manage a thread, but the cure is worse than the disease. Managing the feature is difficult, and threaded conversations are still treated as exceptional.*

It is easy to understand that viewing threads instead of messages lets the user clearly see the connections and flow between individual messages and how they form coherent conversations. When examined from a task or feature point of view, all you can see is that you need to either send or reply.

It is not a particularly difficult programming problem to handle email as a series of threaded conversations; it is just that it has never been done that way, and programmers are reluctant to innovate on the user's behalf and managers are fearful of forcing them down that unproven path.

Because the programmers view the software from the point of view of implementation, they see that messages are flowing back and forth and that users can put messages into folders, so the programmers don't see a problem. After they get the bear moving, they declare it a dance and cease any further instruction.

Email is only one example of software products that don't achieve the simple and obvious goals that they should. We are so impressed by the dancing bears that we fail to see the inadequacy of these products. Here are a few other examples.

How Scheduling Programs Fail

In a lawyer's office, advertising agency, accountant's office, or any other consulting business, there is a large and unfilled need for a program that manages the allocation of people to projects over time. This three-sided structure is common to all consulting companies, yet—amazingly—no program exists to provide this service.

From the programmer's point of view, project management is a scheduling issue, with the possible added twist of critical-path analysis, in which the start of one task is dependent on the completion of a preceding task. All project-management programs available today are based on this academically pure assumption.[2] The problem is that this vision of project management has very little to do with reality.

One fundamental assumption of project-management programs—that people need help understanding how to perform their projects—is wrong. Most people are pretty good at accomplishing their projects; after all, it's their job. What they really need help with is dovetailing multiple projects into the calendar. Resources—generally meaning people—work on multiple projects simultaneously. They start and finish projects in an unbroken, often overlapping, sequence, while other projects are temporarily waiting for their chance. It is not good enough to allocate people to projects one at a time. They have to be assigned to multiple projects at the same time.

To be useful, such resource-management programs must integrate the three dimensions of the problem: time, projects, and resources. Instead, we get programs that handle only two dimensions—time and resources—and their vendors insist

---

[2] *I'm as guilty as the next programmer. In 1984 I wrote Computer Associates' SuperProject, one of the first project-management programs. It ignored the interaction of multiple projects just as all of its successors have.*

that this is all we really need. Variously called "traffic," "project management," or "resource allocation," this critical application segment simply does not exist.

What's more, projects are constantly changing with respect to the plan. Any useful project-management program must be able to flow and adapt to changes as they spring up. A project-management system that doesn't incorporate robust and useful feedback mechanisms—so that the actual people doing the work can tell the system the truth about what is happening now—isn't very useful for real-world management.

How Calendar Software Fails

Virtually everyone uses a calendar for business planning. Many calendar programs are available for sale, yet every one of them ignores the most simple and obvious ways that people want to use calendars. Simply put, a calendar should reflect how people use time to manage their lives. In general, we can divide our time concerns into two types: deadlines and ongoing processes. A deadline is an instant in time when something is due, such as a project milestone. An example of an ongoing process is an overnight business trip. While I'm visiting Chicago for two days, for example, I'll have three meetings with various clients.

Every contemporary calendar program ignores deadlines and ongoing processes, but instead is based on the establishment of appointments. An appointment is a discrete meeting that begins at a certain time. Appointments are an important component of time management, but they are by no means the only one. Not only are other types of calendar entries ignored, but even appointments are misrepresented.

Tracking the start time of meetings is far more important than tracking the end times, yet calendar programs don't differentiate between the two. In the last 30 years, I've initiated and attended thousands of meetings. The starting time of these meetings is extremely important. For most of the meetings, however, the *end* time is not important, not needed, not specified, and not knowable in advance. Yet in every calendar program I've ever seen, appointments have an end time that must be specified in advance with the same precision, accuracy, and diligence with which the meeting's start time must be specified. The end time is used in precise calculations of availability that cannot possibly be accurate and are a significant distortion of reality. For example, if—using a typical calendar program—you invite me to a meeting at 3:00 p.m., the program will reject your invitation if I have a 35-minute meeting scheduled at 2:30 p.m. In the real world, I can easily duck out of my previous meeting five minutes early.

Also, none of these programs factor in the time it takes me to get to a meeting. If I need to be across town at 2:00 p.m., I have to head out the door at 1:30 p.m. Should I set the appointment in the program for 1:30 or for 2:00? A well-designed program should figure that out and help guide me to get going on time.

There are quite a few other forms of common time-related entries that are not accommodated. On any given day, I can have a dozen or more projects that are current, while at any given instant I will actually work on only one. The typical calendar program refuses to acknowledge this normal behavior and won't let me enter project-level items. I can't get around the dancing bear.

Mass Web Hysteria

The World Wide Web has opened the awesome resource of the Internet to just about anybody with a computer and a modem. The Web is a great tool, and it offers fantastic value. Surprisingly, the most important change the Web has made is to demonstrate just how easy it can be to use software. Many former apologists find the Web so simple to use that they are demanding that all software be that easy. In particular, they like the way browsers don't make them go through the annoying installation process.

Software executives, particularly corporate IT vendors, are eagerly leaping onto this bandwagon. They, too, are swooning in love with browser-based software because they can field their products without inflicting a nasty installation process on the users. Before the Web, all software products required a complex installation process; products that run in a browser do not. This seems to be—for most software executives—a technological leap surpassing the invention of the zipper.

But it is just a sham! There is no reason that any non-Web program—regardless of its technical details—can't have a completely invisible installation process. If your computer required software installation, it would require it with or without the browser. *The only reason why nonbrowser programs require installation is that this is the way programmers have always done things.* Putting a bunch of questions in the install program made their programming job easier. Early browsers didn't have facilities for asking those questions, so programmers merely shrugged their shoulders and stopped asking them. If further proof were needed, programmers hardly even noticed the setback, while for many users it made the Web the easiest platform they had ever used.

Installation aside, browsers are weak as kittens. Their interaction idioms are prehistoric. Their technical structure is a primitive joke. They are as flexible as an icicle. Any program running inside a browser must necessarily sacrifice enormous power and capability. It infuriates me that software managers are eager to carve the heart out of their applications by porting them to the Web to get the advantage of no installation, when they could have the same installation-free product merely by saying to their developers, "Get rid of the installation process, please!"

Users are demanding browser-based software because they don't know any better. Software developers, however, are going along with it for all of the wrong reasons. The Web is organized like the old Soviet Union, with central computers dictating the actions of powerless desktop machines. Programmers—particularly those in corporate IT departments—own the central computers, so, like the Soviet commissars, they stand to benefit by this move. Instead of getting the no-installation benefit for free, users are paying a huge cost in loss of long-term control over their information infrastructure.

What's Wrong with Software?

Much of my first book was devoted to answering this question in detail. However, I'd like to take a few pages to provide you with a glimpse of some interaction-design principles that are effective in designing better software-based products.

Software Forgets

Every time you use a program, you learn a bit more about it, but the program doesn't remember a thing. Troy Daniels is our media producer. He practically lives in Adobe Photoshop. Yet, every time he opens Photoshop, it has forgotten everything and anything he has ever done with it. It doesn't remember where he keeps his image files, nor does it remember the typical work that he does with them. Controls and functions that he uses constantly are given the same emphasis in the interface as controls that he has never used and likely never will.

Software Is Lazy

Most application programs just don't work very hard for users. This is not to say that they don't work hard, but they often waste enormous effort trying to please users by treating them the way programmers wish to be treated. It's like giving your wife an electric drill for her birthday. Just because *you* like electric drills doesn't mean that *she* does. If we could only get the programmers to put their efforts behind something that the user really desires, we could make the user much happier without working the programmer any harder.

Software Is Parsimonious with Information

Just like the ATM that doesn't tell me how much money is in my account, most interactive products are very stingy with information. They also tend to camouflage the process—what is *happening*—as well as the information relevant to that process. The typical user of an interactive system cannot tell the state of the system until it blurts out a message indicating total failure. For instance, my new clock-radio I described in Chapter 1, "Riddles for the Information Age," fools me by inadvertently concealing its state. The system seems to be working just fine, but it isn't, and there is simply no way of knowing.

If you ever find yourself with a pad of paper taking marginal notes as you work in some program, you know that you are a victim of an information-stingy program. It would be so easy for any program to put lots more helpful information on the screen, but few programmers think about it. For example, when my email program receives an incoming message, it displays a tiny envelope icon. The same little envelope is visible whether I have one new message or a thousand. It doesn't give me any clue about the depth of my digital inbox. That parsimony doesn't let me see the big picture.

Software Is Inflexible

When people can see the big picture, they often tailor their actions to it, but software rarely is so flexible. When a person sees that the stack of forms in his inbox has grown to a depth of six inches, he knows that he must take some drastic action to keep from getting swamped. The way almost all software programs are written, they can only see the single form on the very top of the stack—never beyond it. If a computer program's inbox is stacked six inches or six feet deep—metaphorically speaking—the computer still behaves as though it has only a single form awaiting its ministrations. The converse is true, too. When there is only one form in the human's inbox, he might take advantage of the lull to help his colleague with a taller pile. The computer would never do that.

When a manual, human process is computerized, the programmers (or analysts) study the current behavior of users performing the manual job, and they distill the tasks or functions out of it. These tasks are then programmed into the computer. Typically, all of the nontask aspects of the job are simply lost.

In a manual, human system, the person in charge can pull her brother-in-law's form off the bottom of the stack and expedite its handling. Alternatively, the annoying caller who behaves rudely gets his form moved way to the bottom of the stack. This system flexibility is a key to maintaining social order. In computerized systems, an inhuman rationality is imposed that wears away at the fabric of civilization.

Human users prefer systems that let them fudge things a little. They want to be able to bump the pinball machine just a little bit—not enough to tilt the game, but enough to have some positive influence on the outcome. This fudgability is what makes our manual systems work so much better—albeit more slowly—than our computerized ones.

Software Blames Users

When a program does have a problem, it invariably dumps it in the user's lap, and it typically blames the user for the problem, too. If a human being has an accident, he will usually work to make up for it. For example, if I'm at a friend's house for dinner, and I spill someone's glass of wine, I'll use my napkin to stop the wine from spreading, and then I'll pour the person a new glass. Because I show concern and helpfulness, no offense is taken, and the accident is clearly seen for what it is.

Recently I used a vendor's program to access the vendor's own support site. For some unknown reason, the program failed to make a connection. It issued an error message telling me, erroneously, offensively, and entirely unhelpfully, that I was not connected to the Internet. It was as if the program spilled my wine, refused to clean it up, and then blamed me for it.

When an interactive product has a small problem, it often drops everything and collapses into a useless, inert heap. When it collapses, it tends to cause a lot of collateral damage. For example, an installation program will ask the user several questions before it begins loading the new program onto the hard disk. In the old days, if it ran out of disk space, it would just crash. Modern install programs are hardly better. If they run out of room, they might issue an error message, but then would stop running, forgetting all the settings you have meticulously keyed in. If you clear out some space on your hard disk and run the install again, the first thing it does is ask you all those questions again, instead of remembering what you keyed in.

Software Won't Take Responsibility

Confirmation dialog boxes are one of the most ubiquitous examples of bad design—the ones that ask us if we're *sure* that we want to take some action. In the early days of desktop computing, programs would take irreversible actions the instant the user entered a command. Typing in "erase all" would do just that, immediately, irreversibly. As soon as the first user inadvertently erased his entire disk, he no doubt complained to the programmer, and the programmer added what he considered to be an adequate level of protection. After the user gives the "erase all" command, but before the computer executes it, the program displays a dialog box asking the user to confirm the erase instruction.

It is all so logical, yet it is all so wrong.

A confirmation dialog box is a convenient solution for the programmer because it absolves him from the responsibility of being the agent of an inadvertent erasure. But that is a misunderstanding of the real issues. The erasure is the user's responsibility, and she has already given the command. Now is not time for the program to waver. It should go ahead and perform the requested task. The responsibility that is actually being dodged is the program's responsibility to be prepared to *undo* its actions, even though the user requested them.

Humans generally don't make decisions in the same way that computers do, and it is quite normal and typical for a person to change his mind or to want to undo a decision he made earlier. In the real world outside of computers, most actions can be deferred, changed, or reversed. There is no reason that this can't also be true for software-based products, except that the programmers who create them don't think that way.

The ATM in Chapter 1 abdicates responsibility with confirmations, just as desktop software does. When I insert my card, the ATM demands that I acknowledge that I have inserted my card. When I request a withdrawal, it demands that I acknowledge that I wish to withdraw money. When I enter an amount, it demands that I acknowledge that I have entered an amount. Why doesn't the machine just trust me? Why doesn't it just proceed with the transaction?

It can give me the opportunity to extricate myself from the transaction at any time in a much easier way. If the ATM merely offered a big red CANCEL button that I could press at any time, it could assume that I am intelligent and capable, and that I know what I want and what I am doing, instead of assuming that I am stupid, incompetent, and confused about what I want.

I'm sure that some of the people who use the ATM *are* stupid and incompetent, but nobody—not even a stupid and incompetent person—likes to be treated as if he is stupid and incompetent. Besides, it never generates customer loyalty and good feelings to treat your clients that way.

Fixing the problem isn't difficult. The program should put the word "Withdraw" at the top of the screen and *leave it there throughout the transaction*. Then it should put the $1.50 charge up on the screen, and *leave it there, too*. Then it should add the word "Checking," along with my account number, balance, and withdrawal limit, and *leave them visible*. Then, when I come to the amount question, I am a fully informed consumer, instead of a confused victim of an interrogation. I can make the crucial decision: the amount, from a position of knowing what is legal, available, ready, and appropriate.

A system that is forthcoming with useful information such as I have described is very typical of how human systems work because humans need to see the big picture. Computers, on the other hand, need to see only a small bit of information to take the next step in the process, and that is exactly how this interaction is modeled: It assumes that the person standing there in the cold, punching buttons while her friends impatiently stamp their feet, is another computer, not a warm-blooded human being with feelings.

⌘

Many newcomers to the world of computing imagine that software behaves the way it does for some good reason. On the contrary, its behavior is often the result of some whim or accident that is thoughtlessly propagated for years. By bringing timely interaction design to the creation of software-based products, we can change its behavior to something more pleasant and productive for humans.

5

Customer Disloyalty

The real benefit of offering a well-designed product or service is the fierce loyalty it generates in your clientele. In this chapter, I'll show how that loyalty can buoy your company through the more difficult passages of business evolution and arm you against your competitors. I'll also show how vulnerable you are without it.

Desirability

Larry Keeley of the Doblin Group has created an intriguing conceptual model of three primary qualities in high-technology business. Keeley calls the first quality *capability*, and it is what technologists bring to the party. They ask, "What are we capable of? What is possible?" Engineers must know what can and can't be built. A product can't be a success unless it can be built and made to work.

Keeley calls the second quality *viability*, and it is the contribution of business-people. They ask, "What is viable? What can we sell?" Business executives must know what can and can't be created and sold at a profit. A product can't be a success unless it can support a growing company.

Because all successful high-technology businesses need a balance of both of these qualities, the tension between their constituents is strong. Businesspeople are totally dependent on technologists for their ability to create things that work. And technologists are totally dependent on businesspeople to provide them with the tools for their efforts. This makes for an uneasy symbiosis.

Programmers like to add features and functions to their products. They find a creative challenge in making the program's inner workings run at a high level of efficiency. It is an expression of capability, and some technologists can be happy without ever shipping a viable product. If their employing company fails, they merely switch jobs. Their individual success is independent of the success of the business.

On the other hand, businesspeople like to own market share and sell lots of product. They find a challenge in motivating people to buy their product. It is an expression of viability, and some businesspeople can be happy without ever shipping a technically sophisticated product. Most businesspeople would be quite satisfied to sell pet rocks, as long as they sold lots of them.

Although the two sides depend on each other, their divergent goals create a structural weakness in their relationship. It is as unstable as a two-legged stool, and this is where Keeley's third quality comes in, as a balancing third leg for the stool.

Keeley calls the third quality *desirability*, and it is what designers supply. They must ask, "What is desired? What do people want?" Designers determine product behavior that will make people happy and satisfied. A product can't be a long-term success unless it delivers power and pleasure to the people who must actually use it.

Design takes a product that can be built and performs well, and that can be distributed and sold profitably, and makes it a success by making it into something that *people really want*. This third leg brings stability and converts an interesting technological achievement into a long-term success.

Although it's possible to draw out something desirable in an existing product, Keeley believes—and I agree—that it is more sensible to *first* decide what customers will find desirable, and then challenge the engineers and businesspeople to build and sell it. This approach can yield significant advantages to the savvy player. It pulls you out in front of the competition. While they are back in the pack, reacting to each other's competitive moves, wrestling with "possible?" and "viable?" questions, you are out in clear air focusing on your customer's as-yet-unmet needs. Let your competitors fight among one another while you leap directly to providing your customers what they desire most.

For example, in the early 1990s, Borland International was a serious player in the Windows software market, and I had the opportunity to learn about its business while I did some consulting there. The company was a remarkable marriage of highly skilled businesspeople and razor-sharp software engineers. Seemingly every day I was introduced to another impressive skunk-works project. A top-notch businessperson and an equally bright software engineer headed each such project.

Each project had similar qualities: cool technology, clearly demonstrated market need, obvious commercial potential, and bright people. At first, the effect of seeing so many talented people at work on such cool stuff was impressive. But after a while, the true nature of these projects became apparent: Very few of these awesome projects ever actually shipped. None had envisioned their customers. Little revenue was generated and lots of money was squandered, and after five years of this tug-of-war between capability and viability, Borland unsurprisingly fell on hard times and was forced to lay off the majority of its people.

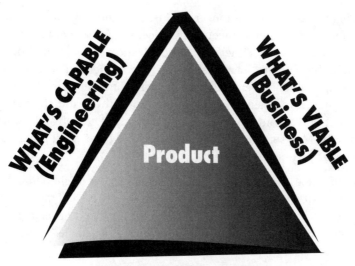

WHAT'S CAPABLE (Engineering)

WHAT'S VIABLE (Business)

Product

WHAT'S DESIRABLE (Design)

Borland, like most contemporary high-tech companies, had no significant design talent on its staff, and there was little understanding of the role of design in either its business or its technical culture. Consequently, it was very difficult for Borland to convert any of its capable, viable projects into desirable products.

Desirability is easy to confuse with need, but they are dramatically different. I *desire* a six-week vacation in Bermuda, but I don't *need* it. If I have gallstones, I *need* gall bladder surgery, but it is not something that I *desire*. As a real-estate agent, Sally *needs* to sell four houses this year. But Sally *desires* to make four families happy and comfortable. She *needs* to use the multiple-listing-service (MLS) software to sell property, but she *desires* that the MLS program not make her feel stupid.

In the short term, a person can be powerfully influenced by needs, but over the long term, what a person desires can have a greater and more-profound effect. People's desires always have a way of emerging after their needs are satisfied. When a person needs something, she will do what is needed to get it, but when she desires something, *she is loyal to it*. She knows that it is a discretionary purchase, and she will buy what makes her happy and will not necessarily judge rationally. When a consumer desires a product or a brand, his loyalty is one of the strongest forces in business.

Keeley's tripod model shows us how to generate customer loyalty. A software company can be *viable* by meeting real-estate agent Sally's needs. But it shows us that it can grow stronger, last longer, and lead an industry by satisfying Sally's *desires*. If the product merely meets Sally's needs, it forces her to become either an apologist or a survivor. Either way, although she needs to learn how to use it, she won't be happy with it, and she won't recommend it to her colleagues. However, if the product meets Sally's *desires*, it becomes her friend and helpmate in her everyday work. Sally becomes a fan, an enthusiast. Sally tells her colleagues and friends about the product. She is happy at her job and takes pride in her work. If the MLS software gives Sally power and pleasure, it generates strong customer loyalty within her.

A product that doesn't have desirability designed into it might address a robust market need, but any success it enjoys will be the success of the dancing bear. The single greatest weakness of dancing bearware is that it never generates customer loyalty. Without the long-term brand loyalty of satisfied customers, your entire company is highly vulnerable to competition.

A Comparison

Three well-known high-tech companies illustrate the dynamics of Keeley's tripod model with their varied strengths and weaknesses: Novell, Microsoft, and Apple.

A lack of customer loyalty is what typically brings a company to its knees over the long term, despite the strength of any market need it fulfills. Novell is an excellent example of this. In the early 1990s, the only practical way to network your office's desktop computers together was with Novell NetWare. NetWare—the product—passed the capability test, and Novell—the company—passed the viability test. The need for local area networks (LANs) was enormous, and no other vendor had been able to satisfy it. Some companies, such as Banyan and Corvus, had also solved the technical problem; they, too, met the capability test, but they failed the viability test—their business structures failed. None of these companies made a desirable product, so although Novell prospered, only those customers driven by a powerful immediate need installed a NetWare LAN, and it remained an unloved dancing bear.

Novell grew fat and happy, but NetWare was egregiously designed, and installing, changing, and maintaining it required an expensive, trained specialist. What's more, the network behaved rudely and inappropriately, frustrating users. Novell failed to realize this, probably because millions bought NetWare, but its customer base was motivated by need, not by desire.

In the early 1990s, Microsoft, 3Com Corporation, and even Apple began to ship LAN products that were as capable as NetWare but that didn't force customers to depend so heavily on third-party experts for installation and—especially—maintenance. Novell watched in mute horror while its leadership position evaporated. As soon as there was competition, Novell's customers' lack of loyalty told. Novell's business today consists largely of maintaining those customers who were already technologically committed to the company. New customers went elsewhere.

Novell was a company that was viable and extremely capable. It had powerful technology and adequate business, but suffered from a complete lack of design.

⌘

Microsoft's story is easy to tell. Its products are technically competent but rarely innovative. Microsoft prefers to follow in the R & D footsteps of others.[1] But Bill Gates is arguably the most talented businessman of his generation, if not of the twentieth century. He has a remarkable ability to extract success from nearly every venture he makes, despite the obstacles.

Microsoft does little or no design, and its products are famous for making people feel stupid. They are also famous for giving people good value with a robust feature set.

Many businesses and professionals are committed to using Microsoft products, but most of them are driven to that point by economic imperatives and the lack of alternatives. Few other companies can provide a full solution, as Microsoft can. However, don't confuse economic necessity with customer loyalty. Few users are loyal to Microsoft.

Microsoft is a company that is somewhat capable but astonishingly viable. Microsoft has adequate technology and superb business, which makes up for its lack of design in the short term.

⌘

Customer loyalty can be an asset of fabulous value to a shrewd company, and Apple is justly famous for its inclusion of design at all levels of the company. Every aspect of Apple's corporate identity, products, and marketing is infused with a remarkable sense of design. The awards and honors that have been heaped on Apple are far too numerous to count, but one look at its software, hardware, packaging, documentation, or just the parties the company throws at MacWorld, and you can see that design is close to its heart.

Devotion to design and attention to the details of interaction have created for Apple a customer loyalty that borders on—and frequently transgresses into—fanaticism. Macintosh users are the most loyal product owners in the entire world of software-based products. No other product or manufacturer inspires personal loyalty to the degree that Apple does. Consumers drive around with

---

[1] *An old industry joke says that Microsoft's R & D department is in Cupertino, referring to the Silicon Valley location of Apple's Advanced Technology Group.*

Apple bumper stickers and Apple license-plate frames on their cars, wear Apple T-shirts, and sport Apple attitudes everywhere. They extol the virtues of Macs to anyone who will listen. Even though in most situations a Wintel computer will satisfy the person's every need better, more cheaply, and faster than a Mac, the Macintosh always seems to be the one chosen. At a recent design conference, the only speaker who used a Wintel box instead of a Mac apologized profusely to the audience for her disloyalty, as though she had sold out the one true computer of anyone with the slightest sense of design.

Apple's technological prowess is good but not great. From a capability point of view, Apple is no better than Microsoft in innovation.

It took Apple a dozen years to lose the market leadership that Novell lost in one. Few of Apple's problems were attacks from outside. Instead, it suffered from a staggering variety of self-imposed problems. For example, in the mid-1980s, Steve Jobs, the company's founder and visionary, was ousted and replaced by a non-computer-using soft-drink executive who made an unending series of bad business decisions. Products were overpriced and badly marketed. Third-party software vendors were viciously snubbed, and the Mac was kept a closed system—a strategy widely blamed for the dethroning of other market-leading platforms, such as VMS, MVS, and OS/2.

All of these blunders would easily kill any normal company, but Apple's use of design to make the Macintosh desirable earned it unheard-of customer loyalty. The Mac fulfilled the user's needs only as well as Windows ever did, and in many cases less well, but the fulfilling of needs isn't the vital ingredient in market success.

After continued management thrashing, after spectacular financial losses, after creating lackluster products, after squandering billions of dollars on wasted R & D, after losing two-thirds of its market share, the company still has the most fanatically loyal customer base of any computer company. This bestows many formidable business advantages on Apple. Many of these advantages are difficult to quantify, and none of them is tallied on the company's financial statements, but they are as real and as valuable to stockholders as a dividend check.

Apple's design-inspired customer loyalty drives Mac fans to shut their eyes to the many advantages available from other manufacturers. This reluctance to leap to other vendors gives Apple time to react to the competition's innovations. Customer loyalty gives Apple the support to weather surprises brought about by advances in technology. Novell's slide began the moment a competitor—Microsoft—offered a viable networking product. Novell's huge market share utterly failed to insulate it against the market forces. On the other hand, Apple—which never owned more than 15% of the computer market—has steadfastly resisted the onslaught of numerous powerful and cheap competing computers.

Apple is a company whose products are desirable. Its commitment to design has allowed it to overcome lackluster technology and survive calamitously self-destructive behavior.

Had Novell added design to its mix, it could have overcome its weak business moves. If Microsoft ever awakens to the value of interaction design, the competition might as well hang up its gloves and go home. Apple was as self-destructive as a grunge-rock star, but if it can continue to clean up its act, it might become viable again.

Business students at Harvard and Stanford are not usually taught the value of design in their case studies. Although design is essential to the success even of industrial-age products, its application is easier. Also, those industrial-age products are older, and their problems and solutions are well known. In the information age—in the age of rapid innovation and extreme cognitive friction—design is a primary necessity.

Time to Market

After a vendor has claimed a market by being the first to offer needed functionality, there is little advantage to hurrying to market with something equivalent. You have already lost the time-to-market race, so no amount of raw speed can ever gain that position for you. However, it is quite possible to take leadership from the market pioneer with better design. Design makes your product desirable, and that will make your customers actively seek out your product instead of the competitor's, regardless of who got there first.

The company that first claimed the market had to make certain sacrifices to get there. Chances are that design was an early casualty. This makes that company quite vulnerable to design, even if it is not vulnerable to speed.

Being the first to add extra features, however, is not the same thing. Features do not benefit users the way that good behavior and primary problem-solving abilities do, and adding features won't have the same beneficial effect that better behavior will. In a marketplace of equally poorly designed products, added features will not influence a broad segment of the market.[2]

Many markets consist of multiple vendors selling similar products, none of which are designed, but all of which compete on features. Every time one vendor introduces a new feature, all of the other vendors add that feature in their next version. These markets are characteristically balkanized into many tiny segments. There is no dominant product or manufacturer. For example, the market for personal information managers (PIMs) is fought over by more than a dozen vendors. The same is true for cellular telephones.

---

[2] *As Geoffrey Moore points out in his excellent book,* Crossing the Chasm, *the additional features have appeal only to the early adopters, not to the larger marketplace.*

The battle between capability and viability can go on unabated for years with users getting no relief. The only force that can convert a fragmented, feature-dominated market into a more stable, design-dominated market is the imposition of some outside force. The outside force can be the Brobdingnagian business acumen of Bill Gates, or it can be the studied application of design.

But all of Bill Gates's hard work is still not making his products lovable. What's more, the average level of desirability of almost all high-tech products remains about on a par with Microsoft's, despite all of the intelligence, sincerity, and hard work invested in them by their makers. In the next section, I'll show that simple but almost universal flaws in our process for creating software-based products are causing this proliferation of unpleasant, undesirable, dancing-bearware products.

Part III

6

The Inmates Are Running the Asylum

Despite the widely varied nature of the products described in Chapter 1, "Riddles for the Information Age," they all share a common frustration-inducing unpleasantness. In this chapter, I'll show that this recurrent pattern is due to the inadvertent hijacking of the industry by technical experts. Despite all of the marketing rhetoric, the form of our products is really determined by the people least equipped to determine it.

Driving from the Backseat

An article[1] about the spectacular failure of high-tech startup company General Magic is revealing. The author innocently touches on the root cause of the product's lack of success when she says that Marc Porat, the president, "launched his engineering team to design the device of their dreams." There is no irony in her statement. It seems perfectly natural for the engineering team to do the designing, yet that is precisely the cause of the problem. Later in the article, she quotes one of the engineers as saying, "We never knew what we were building. We didn't write specifications until 8 to 12 weeks before we finished." Again, neither the engineer nor the author notes the irony. The article seems to suggest that things would have worked out better for General Magic if only the engineers had drafted those specifications a month earlier.

No matter how early in the development process specifications are drafted, they cannot substitute for interaction design. And no matter how hard they try, programmers cannot consistently arrive at a successful design. Not only are their methods, training, and aptitude wrong for the job, but they are caught in a strong

---

[1] *Michelle Quinn, "Vanishing Act,"* San Jose Mercury News West Magazine, *March 15, 1998.*

conflict of interest between serving the user's needs and making their programming job easier. Yet, in company after company, software engineers are allowed to control the development process, often from start to finish. Sometimes their control is overt, but more typically it is indirect.

I witnessed this subtle control at a very successful, midsized Silicon Valley company. At the meeting was the president, a very savvy, veteran businessman who founded the company, along with the senior programmer responsible for building the product. The president showed us the product and demonstrated its power, which we could clearly see, but we could also see that its power was hard to use and its interface was overly complex. Our design team and I instantly recognized that the programmers had "designed" the product while they constructed it in the way a beaver "designs" his dam while he builds it.

The president complained that a competitor with a weaker product was stealing away market share. He was at a loss to explain why because he knew that his product was more powerful. Although the president had called us in to help him fight off the competition, he had given his senior programmer the authority to take whatever action he deemed appropriate. It was clear to us that the product badly needed some behavioral changes, and we presented our case to them both. To us, it was a simple and straightforward redesign project that would take a few months of effort and would make their product enormously more useful, practical, powerful, and pleasurable—more competitive. However, the senior programmer astonished us by asking that we *not actually make any changes to the product's interaction.* He considered it just fine the way it was. He felt that the product's market difficulties stemmed only from the company's sales force not being sufficiently well trained in the product's use. He wanted us to prepare some in-house promotional materials so their salespeople could be more effective. He was in complete denial about his product's shortcomings, despite the incontrovertible evidence that an "inferior" product was beating it.

Programmers devote so much of their time and energy to learning about software that it was inconceivable to him that his users would not want to take the time to understand his work. He was willing to accept that the problem lay with his own company, but not with his role within it. He blamed the sales force for not helping the customers learn about the product. He was willing to do the work to solve the problem by accepting the task of developing the new training aids, yet he was utterly oblivious to any hint of his own culpability in the product's fall from grace.

The high-handedness of this engineer was breathtaking. Not only was he blinded by his own pride in his demonstrated ability to build a powerful product, but he was blinding his boss—the president—to his obvious inability to design it in such a way as to make their users happy.

The company's product was the first of its kind, pioneering a new method of tracking manufacturing systems. The company was a fast-growing darling of Wall Street with a spectacularly successful initial public offering of stock two years before. The company had been praised in the business press and lavished with awards from civic and business groups. It seemed that it was doing everything right, and its market capitalization certainly attested to its success.

But success like that is watched just as closely by competitors as it is by its investors, partners, and other supporters. The company's competitors clearly saw the strength of the market, and just as clearly saw the weakness of this company's product. They could see how powerful and feature-packed it was, but they could also see that it was a dancing bear. It delivered new functionality, but it didn't make its users happy. It danced, but it didn't dance well. It didn't take a rocket scientist to spot the vulnerability of this company, so the competition copied many of the features of the product but made its product easier to use. Its management reports could be understood and manipulated by managers, while the older company's reports were obscure and static. The upstart competitor had stolen *60%* of market share away from the older company with a product that was less powerful!

The president's own engineering background hampered him. It had helped him to create his powerful product, but it now stood in his way, making it difficult for him to see what an obstacle his senior programmer was. Deeply ingrained in the software-nerd ethic, he saw his senior programmer's attitude as perfectly normal, while our team was flabbergasted. The president was not in charge. His senior programmer was driving the entire business from the back seat.

Hatching a Catastrophe

My colleague Scott McGregor sent me the following story when I asked him if he knew of any cases where development projects got out of control because of a lack of design. His story is a tragic one, made ever more so by the fact that it is so typical of our industry.

Scott is a very talented man, as his well-written story attests. He is also a skilled designer with a fine pedigree—academic and practical—in both software engineering and design. He joined a small, venture-funded start-up company in Silicon Valley. The original founders of the company also had well-established credentials, including several successful years at Apple. Scott invited me over one afternoon to meet the founders and to pitch my company. The CEO and the vice president of engineering showed our team what they were working on, and we were impressed. The product idea was excellent. It exploited an aspect of productivity software in a very clever way. The product was based on an appropriately small amount of good technology that served a very real marketplace need.

They had everything they needed to succeed—except for design. Here is Scott's story in his own well-crafted words:

> Our CEO said we would beat others because we were so fast and spry, and he went on to recommend with pride that we were following a "ready, fire, aim" strategy to reach success before other companies were even done aiming. Of course when we fired, it was obvious that we had shot ourselves in the foot!
>
> Although we met our schedule of delivering our 1.2 release on December 31, we did it by saying that Release 1.2 is whatever is done at 5:00 p.m. on December 31. There was no fixed spec that engineers were building from. Substantial new changes showed up for the first time without any prior warning on December 29.
>
> Earlier, I had suggested that we needed to follow a design method. I said that we should begin by identifying who all the key users and other stakeholders were and write up profiles on them, and then develop statements of their goals and the tasks they would go through to accomplish those goals. Then, from those tasks, I suggested we could come up with proposed visual representations of key objects and interaction behaviors. Once we had done this, we could start building it.
>
> Unfortunately, our management felt all that was a luxury we couldn't afford. We didn't have the time for that. Instead, we visited many customer prospects, and the CEO would relate our grand vision. People loved it, but they wanted to know specifics. But each prospect had a different axe to grind in the specifics. One wanted a product for their sales people, another for independent resellers, a third for customers. One had many documents they wanted to manage, another was interested in Web pages, etc. With each customer contact the definition for 1.2 grew, becoming the union of all imagined product features.
>
> Even more unfortunately, prospects would talk about some new thing they wanted, but didn't talk about features they already had in their existing software or their browsers and which they took for granted. Since these weren't talked about they were never added to the product spec, and they were never built.
>
> Our newly hired vice presidents of sales and marketing could not get the product to install on their systems for weeks. When they did get it to work, it corrupted or lost all their data several times a day. Performance continued to degrade. In a demonstration with no more than 100 data views, performance was acceptable but slow, and that is all the developers ever tested. But real-world use called for over a thousand views, and performance was downright snail-paced.

There were three major screens in the product, but to simply edit a document required jumping between each of the three screens several times. Many single tasks required the user to make a dozen mouse clicks with windows coming and going, and lots of switching between the mouse and the keyboard.

In the end the product was impossible to learn, was unusable from a cognitive and performance standpoint, had poor reliability and destroyed data regularly. Although it was full of lots of "differentiating" features, it was missing necessary basic features that were standard in all other competing products.

As might be expected, by the end of February, the board took action, and the CEO and VP of engineering were forced to step down.

This is of course just a single anecdote. It might appear to be an isolated incident, except for the fact that this has happened repeatedly at companies where I have worked over the last 20-plus years.

One thing I've noticed is that you get what you measure and reward. Prior to January, the only measures that our board had were dates and the features promised. They never set out measures for minimum quality (e.g., mean time between data corruption, crashes, etc.) so quality was sacrificed. There were never any measures for performance (e.g., number of seconds between the key press and something happening) so these got arbitrarily long. There were never any measures about how long it would take to learn something, or how often a user could work without an error, so learnability and usability were sacrificed. But the things that were measured—the schedule and the list of features—were achieved, and because there wasn't a full description of the features, many of them were achieved in name only.

Scott is highlighting a fundamental truth: You can "expect what you inspect." If you repeatedly point to the calendar, your project will be on time, and if you ignore user satisfaction, your users will be trod upon. Scott continues his narrative:

Investors repeatedly say, "We don't have enough money to spend on building a product we can't sell, so we have to know our customers before we start." Yet engineering managers seem to constantly believe that "We don't have enough time and money to spend designing—we could design forever and run out of money before we had a product to build." So in the end, they keep building new products rather than improving the design—until the money runs out.

Looked at with some detachment, the past few months seems sort of like an old screwball comedy movie, or a soap opera without the romance. And I can appreciate it all as such. Of course, if I only looked at it that way, I wouldn't have bothered to go into it in such detail. However, I am passionate about this. I feel there is a moral imperative to stop wasting people's lives in useless activities.

In *About Face* you wrote how important it is to stop wasting users' time. I wholeheartedly agree. But that is just the tip of the iceberg. That only happens when products actually get to market and are purchased. But there are many more projects that are canceled before they get to market or which fail to be purchased. Every engineer I've ever met cared deeply that the products she worked on might never be used. But when the resulting product was canceled or failed due to lack of design it meant that their effort was wasted. And the world doesn't have so much of these skills that it can afford to waste them. That's the moral imperative that I see, not just "stop wasting users' time," but stop wasting everyone's, including programmers, time and lives.

It was very painful to watch in a Cassandra-like role—foretelling the impending doom, but unheeded, and watching opportunities to avoid the doom pass. I've come to the conclusion that operant conditioning is so powerful that it allows a person properly conditioned to be impervious to reasoning based upon facts and figures.

I want to emphasize that Scott's experience is not atypical. Here is a story from another industry colleague, John Rivlin. John runs a small but very successful software design and development firm in Palo Alto, California. He sent me this story:

We always do detailed product designs prior to beginning any software project. This particular case is no exception. We started the project by creating a 15-page spec outlining the user interaction of the software we were proposing to write. It included the overall assumptions of the project so that we could move beyond the initial one-sentence description. This is important because we work on a fixed cost estimate where *we* assume the risk.

The client's development manager running the project concurred with the notion of writing a specification, and we agreed on a fixed cost to do so. The specification was then completed and submitted to the development manager's boss, the chief technology officer. The response we got was "Why have you spent so much time writing a spec? You have used up a major piece of the budget. We don't write specs here. We just go off and get the job done." Upon further examination, it also became clear that his assumptions about functionality were significantly different than those of his development manager. This discrepancy was only made visible by the "wasted" specification, but not even this persuaded him that designing software is a good thing. This is the CTO of a publicly traded technology company with annual revenues exceeding $100,000,000. The inmates are truly running the asylum.

Although the fear that many development managers hold for design is irrational, it is often based on very real personal experience. Previously, in the quest for better products, managers have asked programmers to design interaction, and the results have been painfully unproductive. Anyone untrained in interaction-design methods tends toward self-referential design, in which one imagines himself as the user, and programmers naturally fall into this trap. Any group of people designing self-referentially will have a devilish time getting to closure on issues because they have no firm, common ground about users, and the process drags on interminably.

Computers Versus Humans

Software is more like a bridge than an edifice. Although it runs on high-technology microprocessors, it must be operated and used by mere mortals. Amid all the attention and excitement about new technology, we overlook the incredible differences between computers and the humans who have to use them.

For example, because computers have memories, we imagine that they must be something like our human memories, but that is simply not true. Computer memories work in a manner alien to human memories. My memory lets me easily recognize the faces of my friends, whereas my own computer never even recognizes me. My computer's memory stores a million phone numbers with perfect accuracy, but I have to stop and think to recall my own.

For software to be robust and strong, it must be written in perfect harmony with the demands of silicon. For programmers to be professional, they must also work in this same harmony.

For users to be happy and effective with software, it must be written in harmony with the demands of human nature. The problem, of course, is that those human demands are so radically different from the demands of silicon.

Clearly, one side of software—the inside—must be written with technical expertise and sensitivity to the needs of computers. But equally clear, the other side of software—the outside—must be written with social expertise and sensitivity to the needs of people. It is my contention that programmers can do the former, but it takes interaction designers to do the latter.

COMPUTERS	Humans
INCREDIBLY FAST	Incredibly Slow
ERROR-FREE	Error-Prone
DETERMINISTIC	Irrational
APATHETIC	Emotional
LITERAL	Inferential
SEQUENTIAL	Random
PREDICTABLE	Unpredictable
AMORAL	Ethical
STUPID	Intelligent

Computer industry guru Jerry Weinberg says, "Once you eliminate your number one problem, you promote number two."[2] For decades, the computer industry's number-one problem has been efficiency. Computers were—relatively speaking—small, expensive, slow, and weak. We lionized the hacker-gods who could make programs that operated as efficiently as possible so as to maximize the productivity of the expensive mainframe computer. Essentially, it was far cheaper to train people to deal with obscure—but efficient—software than it was to buy more computers. The driving inevitability of plummeting computer costs has utterly obliterated that problem. Today, it is far more expensive to pay for the human costs of adapting to "efficient" software than it is to make the software conform to the expectations of the humans.

The solution is obvious: Make the software serve the users. But standing in the way is the culture we've so carefully built over the last 50 years that puts the hacker-gods in the driver's seat. The community of software engineers is generally willing to accept interaction design into the process. They say, "Sure, wait until we're done, and then do all the design you want." Unfortunately, design has to come before construction, so the programmer's openness to design is largely ineffectual. It's like a cement-truck operator telling the carpenters they can build all the forms they want as soon as he is done pouring the concrete.

Teaching Dogs to Be Cats

As a fallback position, software engineers are always willing to learn how to design. I'm constantly asked to "teach me to design." I applaud their open-mindedness, but I despair for its effectiveness. Any software engineer good

---

[2] *Gerald Weinberg,* The Secrets of Consulting: A Guide to Giving & Getting Advice Successfully, *Dorset House, 1985, ISBN 0-932633-01-3.*

enough to call herself a professional is well steeped in that literal/deterministic/sequential way that silicon behaves—far too steeped to have much simultaneous effectiveness in the irrational/unpredictable/emotional world of humans. I'm not saying that a programmer cannot become a designer; I'm just saying that it is nearly impossible to do either task well while attempting both simultaneously.

Every software engineer thinks that he is different, that he is the one who can do both. This is simply not true, as the failure of General Magic showed. Bill Atkinson and Andy Hertzfeld headed General Magic's development effort. These two men were the lead software engineers on the Apple Macintosh and are arguably the two most talented, creative, and inventive programmers ever. Their simultaneous design and programming on the Macintosh was a success in 1984 (although Jef Raskin, who did no programming, contributed much of the design). However, things changed quite a bit in the ensuing 14 years, and their methods were no longer viable. In early 1993, I interviewed Andy Hertzfeld at General Magic's engineering headquarters—Andy's living room in Palo Alto—and he described his design/programming philosophy to me. I listened in amazement, knowing that the odds would be severely stacked against him. Who but history could second-guess an engineering talent as towering as Andy's?

There is no doubt that the product General Magic had in mind was, and still is, extremely desirable. There is no doubt that its technology was superb. There is no doubt that Marc Porat's ability to establish strategic partnerships and make business deals was second to none. There is no doubt that the company was well sired and well funded. So what caused its demise? I offer interaction design, or a lack of it, as the smoking gun. Despite its stellar pedigree and awesome talent, General Magic's product was *engineered* and not *designed*.

The current thinking in the industry ignores this obvious deduction, as Michelle Quinn's article shows. The balance of the article seems to lay the product's failure on Porat's hubris and ego, but there's not a CEO in Silicon Valley who doesn't have hubris and ego in abundant quantities. They surely cannot be the reason for the company's failure.

Our high-tech culture is so inbred that we have little perspective on our own failures and foibles. You cannot be a successful reporter of high technology unless you are a computer-savvy nerd—an apologist—yourself, so the reporters blame our failures on personal demons, bad luck, and acts of God.

⌘

Software programming is not a true profession, like law, architecture, or medicine, so titles in our industry are very unreliable. Several of my friends who are top-notch computer programmers call themselves "software designers," a title that is not truly correct. If you ask Andy Hertzfeld, he will willingly accept the sobriquet "designer."

Many programmers believe themselves to be talented designers. In fact, this is often true, but there is a tremendous difference between designing for *function* and designing for *humans*.

Even if programmers haven't acquitted themselves well of the design task, they have at least kept many projects from unraveling completely. When a usurper approaches, they are careful not to let control get into the hands of irresponsible people. Most programmers are extremely responsible, and they often view outside consultants, marketers, and managers as flighty and incompetent.

Programmers have sensitive bull detectors, and all it takes to inure them to outside interference is a couple of episodes in which marketers or managers demand changes "to make the interface better" that turn out to be ineffective. Whether these changes are good or bad, they force the programmer into extra work. Each change also degrades the quality of the code because each change leaves behind inevitable splices and scars in the code. When someone declares that the program will be easier to use if all of the OK buttons are placed in the upper-right corner of each dialog box, the programmer's experience and wisdom tells him that it is just a waste of time—*his time*. And he is correct in his fear.

After a few of these wild-goose chases, they begin to treat all outside design direction merely as advice. It's as though the builders have had to rip out too many ill-conceived walls, so now they look at the blueprints with a jaundiced eye and resolve that they won't take them too literally.

⌘

Software engineers draw diagrams on the whiteboard showing the back-end data-handling code and the front-end user-interface code as two separate boxes. But there is really no difference in the code. It's not like one wall is made of granite blocks, mortared in place by a journeyman mason, while the adjoining wall is made of wooden lumber nailed in place by carpenters and covered with Sheetrock screwed in place by union drywallers. The assignments, pointers, and function calls are all pretty much the same, whether the software is responding to a user's mouse movement or reorganizing a database deep inside the program's guts. The same programmer often writes the system internals *and* the user-interaction code. She uses the same language, libraries, tools, and techniques to code it. Who is to say where the dividing line is between software for computers and software for users?

Programmers are used to apportioning the programming tasks on functional lines, and it is not at all clear to them why taking one slice out of the whole program, crossing many functional boundaries, and turning it over to an outsider is a good thing. It is hard for engineers to see that the C code used to interact with a database is hugely different from the C code used to interact with a human.

⌘

My colleague Jim Gay told me the following story. It illustrates how easy it is for smart engineers to pick the problems that amuse and interest them, rather than choosing to solve the problems that really need solving.

> TransPhone was a start-up company in the e-commerce arena. Our basic idea was to build a simple-to-operate consumer screen phone to enable Internet commerce. Critical to the success of our model was a simple, easy-to-use interface with which noncomputer people would be comfortable. TransPhone turned to an interaction-design firm for help in defining this interface.

> Our attitude was that we had the user interface almost done, but it could use a little tweaking. However, in the very first meeting, the designers repeatedly stated that they had no idea what it was that we were actually trying to do, or who we were trying to do it for. We believed that they were trying to oversimplify a problem that was, in reality, quite complicated. The meeting ended with the designers assigning us the task of more concisely defining our objectives. We, on the other hand, were beginning to feel that the designers did not have a clue what it was we were trying to do.

> We proceeded to build an improved prototype to show to prospective partners, but the TransPhone device just didn't click with our prospects. We continued to assume that it was just our demo that was not compelling enough. TransPhone ceased operations a few weeks after the second prototype was completed.

> Recalling that original meeting with the interaction designers, it is now clear that they homed in on the critical problem facing us in the first few minutes of our initial meeting: What was our objective, and who were we doing it for? This question was never adequately answered. Had we addressed it at the beginning, perhaps one of two things would have happened: Either we would have come up with an answer (and with it a chance for success), or we would have been unable to come up with the answer (in which case we could have minimized our investor's losses).

> The lesson in this experience is that product design is a critical part of the business cycle. Our failure to address fundamental design issues in

favor of pressing forward with engineering and sales ultimately doomed our company. In hindsight, when we couldn't find prospects that truly understood what we were trying to do, we should have revisited the basic assumptions of our business. I believe that this would have most likely led to a different, and simpler, product. Instead, we added more bells and whistles that probably made our value proposition more obscure than it already was.

Just like the General Magic guys, Jim found out the hard way that cool technology and a red-hot market can't overcome the dead weight of ill-conceived code. It's not enough to bridge the gap between technology and need. Somebody needs to make humans want to cross that bridge.

Most of our technological history is an industrial one, and both the problems and the solutions that define it are on a human scale. There is friction between humans and mechanical devices, but there is also a balance between them. In the information age, as computers invade our lives, and more and more products contain a chip of silicon, we find that what lies between us humans and our devices is cognitive friction, which is something new and something that we are ill prepared to deal with. Our engineering skills are highly refined, but when we apply them to a cognitive-friction problem, they fail to solve it. Over the years, our software engineers have gotten better and more skilled, yet their track record in making software powerful and pleasurable remains about the same as it has always been.

I believe that our failure to solve the problem with engineering methods is proof that engineering methods cannot solve the problem. I'll go further and state that engineering methods are one of the root causes of the problem. Asking engineers to fix the problem is like asking the fox to solve the henhouse security problem.

7

Homo Logicus

With my tongue firmly planted in my cheek, I call programmers *Homo logicus*: a species slightly—but distinctly—different from *Homo sapiens*. From my own observations, I have isolated four fundamental ways in which software engineers think and behave differently from normal humans, and I will discuss them in detail in this chapter. Programmers trade simplicity for control. They exchange success for understanding. They focus on what is possible to the exclusion of what is probable. And they act like jocks.

Homo logicus

The Jetway Test

I use a humorous litmus test that I call the *Jetway Test* to highlight the difference. To perform this test, all you have to do is visualize yourself walking down the corridor of a Jetway as you board an airliner. As you step onto the aircraft, you have a choice of going left into the cockpit or right into the cabin.

To the left, the cockpit is a kaleidoscope of complex controls and gauges, with every surface covered with instruments, knobs, and levers. To the right, in stark contrast, lies the cabin, where everything is gently rounded, smooth, and a calm-inducing shade of beige.

To turn left into the cockpit means that you must learn and master all the complicated technical stuff. You must know what every one of those instruments means. In exchange for understanding all that complexity is the certain knowledge that *you are in control* and that you are responsible for landing the aircraft at the right place.

To turn right into the cabin means that you relinquish all authority over the flight. In exchange for abdication of control, you get to relax, knowing that you will arrive at the proper destination without dealing with anything more complex than turning the reading light on and off.

The Jetway Test neatly divides the human race into two categories: Those who turn left strongly desire to *be in control* and to *understand* how the technology works, and those who turn right strongly desire to *simplify* their thinking and to have confidence in the *success* of the flight. Programmers—*Homo logicus*—always want to turn left. Users—*Homo sapiens*—always want to turn right.

The Psychology of Computer Programmers

Because our goal is to create software-based products that are both powerful and pleasurable for human users, understanding the psychology of the user might seem a natural prerequisite. This is, of course, true, but it obscures another more important, but far less obvious, point. Determining the solution and getting that solution implemented are two very different actions. I'd rather have a partial design actually built than have a better design sit in useless, dusty majesty on the shelf. To get our designed products actually created and into the hands of users, a far more important prerequisite is to understand the psychology of the builders—the programmers.

Nothing will change unless we can influence the software developers. Even if the programmers agree that the user should be better treated—and they usually do—that doesn't necessarily mean that they will do what is necessary to actually accomplish this goal. You are not going to get them to change just by asking them. In order to effect a real solution, we need insight into their thinking so that we can figure out how to *motivate* them to create interaction that is good for users. For the interaction designer, understanding psychology is very important, but it must include the psychology of the software engineer as well as the psychology of the user.

The implication of this is clear: Programmers are somehow different from ordinary people. Their stereotypical behavioral differences have been the subject of jokes for years: the social awkwardness, the pocket protectors, the bookish manner. Those are just the easily noticeable—and easily ridiculed—surface differences. The really substantive differences are not only far subtler, but they have a more profound effect on the cognitive friction–rich interactive products that programmers build.

Many observers of the computer industry have taken pains to point out these differences. Robert Cringely calls programmers "stinking gods among men," referring simultaneously to their superior attitudes and their hygiene habits.

Po Bronson is another shrewd observer and talented writer. He has cast his sharp eye and sharper wit onto the high-tech world. In a parody of Steven Covey, he has developed what he calls the Seven Habits of Highly Engineered People. They are remarkably revealing in their hyperbole:

1. They will be generous in their selfishness.
2. Blindness improves their vision.
3. They'll not only bite the hand that feeds them, but they'll bite their own hand.
4. They will try very hard to maintain the image that they care very little about their image.

5. They'll keep fixing what's not broken until it's broken.
6. "I didn't answer incorrectly, you just asked the wrong question."
7. They consider absence of criticism a compliment.

Programmers Trade Simplicity for Control

Homo logicus desire to have control over things that interest them, and the things that interest them are complex, deterministic systems. People are complex, but they don't behave in a logical and predictable way, like machinery. The best machinery is digital, because it can be the most complex, sophisticated, and can be easily changed by the programmer.

Controlling humans is less appealing from the programmer's point of view. In the novel *The First $20 Million Is Always the Hardest*,[1] author Po Bronson has his programmers play practical jokes on humans to demonstrate that they can control them, but the programmers take more satisfaction in making the computers jump to their bidding.

The price of control is always more effort and increased complexity. Most people are willing to make a moderate effort, but what differentiates programmers from most people is their willingness and ability to master extreme complexity. It is a satisfying part of the programmer's job to know and manage systems composed of many interacting forces. Flying airplanes is the archetypal programmer's avocation.[2] The cockpit control panel of an airplane is packed with gauges, knobs, and levers, but programmers thrive on these daunting complexities. *Homo logicus* finds it fun and engaging, despite (because of!) the months of rigorous study required. *Homo sapiens* would rather ride along as passengers.

For *Homo logicus*, control is the goal and complexity is the price they will pay for it. For normal humans, simplicity is the goal, and relinquishing control is the price they will pay. In software-based products, control translates into features. For example, in Windows 95, the Find File function gives me lots of control over the procedure. I can specify which area of my disk to search, the type of file to search for, whether to search by filename or by file contents, and several other parameters. From a programmer's point of view, this is very cool. For some extra up-front effort and understanding, he gets to make the search faster and more efficient. Conversely, the user's point of view is less rosy because he *has to* specify the area of the search, the type of file to search for, and whether to search by name or contents.

---

[1] *Po Bronson,* The First $20 Million Is Always the Hardest, *Avon Books, New York, New York, 1997, ISBN: 0-380-73155-X.*

[2] *All right, I confess: I'm a private pilot. Quintessential programmer-nerd Gary Kildall took me flying for the first time in his Piper Archer in 1979, and in that short flight I became hooked. The computer programmer in me loves all of that pointless complexity.*

Homo logicus
wants control—
accepts complexity
as trade-off

Homo sapiens
wants simplicity—
accepts less control
as trade-off

Homo sapiens would gladly sacrifice the odd extra minute of compute time if they didn't have to know how the search function works. To them, each search parameter is just another opportunity to enter something incorrectly. The probability of making a mistake that causes the search function to fail is higher, not lower, with the added flexibility. They would gladly sacrifice all that unnecessary complexity, control, and understanding in order to make their job simpler.

Programmers Exchange Success for Understanding

Homo logicus are driven by an irresistible desire to understand how things work. By contrast, *Homo sapiens* have a strong desire for success. Programmers also want to succeed, but they will frequently accept failure as the price to pay for understanding.

An old joke about engineers gives some insight into this need to understand:

> Three people are scheduled for execution: a priest, an attorney, and an engineer. First, the priest steps up to the gallows. The executioner pulls the lever to drop the hatch, but nothing happens. The priest claims divine intervention and demands his release, so he is set free. Next, the attorney takes a stand at the gallows. The executioner pulls the lever, but again nothing happens. The attorney claims another attempt would be double jeopardy and demands release, so he is set free. Finally, the engineer steps up to the gallows and begins a careful examination of the scaffold. Before the executioner can pull the lever, he looks up and declares, "Aha, here's your problem."

Understanding the problem with the scaffold was more compelling than staying alive.

When I lecture to groups of computer programmers, I ask for a show of hands of how many in the audience, when they were a child, took a clock apart to see how it worked. Typically, two-thirds of the audience will raise their hands. I then ask how many of them ever got that clock back together again, and all but a few hands will drop. I then ask how many considered this experiment to be a failure, and most of the audience will laugh as they realize that they got full satisfaction out of breaking their clocks. *Homo logicus* want to understand how that clock works—that is their goal—and they are quite willing to sacrifice a working clock to achieve that goal. *Homo sapiens*, on the other hand, like to have clocks that work. Their goal is to be able to know what time it is, and in exchange, they will forego knowing what makes the clock tick.

Homo logicus
wants to understand—
accepts failure
as trade-off

Homo sapiens
wants success—
accepts less understanding
as trade-off

Interaction designer Jonathan Korman points out:

> Most people cannot understand the degree to which computers fascinate programmers. The difficulties of learning about computers only strengthen the programmer's sense of satisfaction. Their interest runs so deep that it never occurs to them that others might not feel the same way, so they interpret others' frustration as stemming from inability rather than from disinterest.

Programmers' drive to understand makes them instinctively create interaction that closely follows the internal functioning of the product. Instead of making the program mirror the end user's goals, it reflects the working of the mechanism within. Programmers are naturally comfortable with it because when they understand how the software works, they understand how to use it. We call this common interaction style *implementation model.* For example, computer documents are permanently stored on disk drives, but programs can only modify documents while they are temporarily stored in RAM. Programmers are very comfortable with this technical distinction, so the interface to their programs reflects the two storage types. Exposing the two types to the user is as unnecessary as putting a switch on the dashboard of your car to force you to select between radial and bias-ply tires.

Normal humans are quite content not to know how something works, even though they use it and depend on it in their everyday lives. They see implementation-model interfaces as imposing an unnecessary burden of understanding on them. Programmers find such attitudes inscrutable.

Programmers Focus on What Is Possible to the Exclusion of What Is Probable

Programmers share the mathematician's abstract view of complex systems, so it is not surprising that they look at things differently from most people. Here's what I mean: Imagine that you flipped a coin 1,000,000 times, and 999,999 times the coin landed heads up. To a mathematician, the assertion that "the coin always lands heads up" is false. That single tails-up result disproves the assertion. In mathematical terms, a proposition is true only if it is *always* true, and this way of thinking is very familiar and reasonable to *Homo logicus* because, not surprisingly, it's the way computers behave.

On the other hand, most normal people will declare the proposition true because of the preponderance of heads to tails. They also will claim that not only is the proposition true, but it is overwhelmingly, convincingly, indisputably true. The odds are a million to one! In the context of human behavior, million-to-one odds are definitive. They are odds beyond consideration. There's a better chance that I will get hit by lightning, accidentally fall off a bridge, or win the lottery than that the coin will land tails up.

The probability that the proposition is true is enormous, and *Homo sapiens* live in a world of probabilities. However, there is always that possibility that the proposition is false, and programmers live in the world of possibilities. If it might happen, it is something that *must* be considered. In the world of software—the world of precisely articulated propositions—enormously remote possibilities are issues that cannot be ignored.

Homo logicus
concerned
with possible cases—
accepts
advance preparation
as trade-off

Homo sapiens
concerned
with probable cases—
accepts
occasional setbacks
as trade-off

Programmers call these one-in-a-million possibilities *edge cases*.[3] Although these oddball situations are unlikely to occur, the program will crash whenever they do if preparations are not made. Although the likelihood of edge cases is small, the cost for lack of preparedness is immense. Therefore, these remote possibilities are very real to the programmer. The fact that an edge case will crop up only once every 79 years of daily use is no consolation to the programmer. *What if that one time is tomorrow?*

Arguably, the single most important difference between amateur programmers and experienced professionals is the journeyman's obsessive emphasis on preparing for edge cases. This fanatic preparation for the possible has the inevitable consequence of obscuring the probable. This results in products whose interaction is encrusted with little-used or never-used controls that obscure the frequently used ones. Users' most common complaint is that software is hard to use because it has too many options all jumbled into the interface without any discrimination.

The profusion of unneeded and unwanted features brought about by the programmer's possibility thinking is an excellent example of what Po Bronson means by programmers being "generous in their selfishness." They give us lots of what *they* want.

⌘

A common joke among programmers is that there are only three numbers: 0, 1, and infinity. In the world of computer processing, this makes a lot of sense. In the

---

[3] *They are also variously called* corner cases, special cases, *and* boundary conditions.

binary world inside a computer, a process either happens or it doesn't—1 or 0. If any process can happen more than once, that means it can happen an infinite number of times.

Setup and shut-down code is written so that it can be executed only once. If the program tries to execute it a second time, the computer will probably crash, or at least provoke some major errors. Other parts of programs are designed for more than one execution. Almost any part of any program that *can* be executed a second time without crashing can also be executed as many times as desired. For the code—for the programmer's *Homo logicus* point of view—there is little difference between two executions and two million or two billion executions.

Humans are different. They understand 0 and 1, but they also have a firm grasp on 2, 7, and 31. Most humans have a harder time visualizing a million things than they do visualizing 300 things. A typical human does things in quantities that are in a programmer's no-man's-land. Enthusiastic amateur skiers, for example, might go skiing a dozen weekends each season. Over a span of 40 years of active skiing, that is fewer than 500 times in a lifetime! Modern digital computers can process 500 things in the blink of an eye. An enthusiastic user of any program will still only use it a few thousand times, yet programmers still think in terms of an infinite number of occurrences.

Good programmers purposefully turn a blind eye to practical numbers such as 500 because doing so ensures that their programs will be better able to handle a possible 501st occurrence. This is what Po Bronson means when he says, "Blindness improves their vision."

Programmers Act Like Jocks

Probably the most surprising thing about good programmers is that they act like jocks. I use the term very consciously because it is freighted with overtones of immaturity, egotism, and competitiveness, as well as physical strength and coordination.

The term *jock* reminds me of high-school physical-education classes. Some teenaged boys are gifted with bigger, stronger musculature and well-coordinated bodies. These boys excel in organized athletics, but they also find that they can dominate the smaller, weaker kids in unofficial contests of strength and agility. These jocks not only dominate on the diamond or gridiron, but they dominate the weaker boys in the locker room and on the school playground, outside of sanctioned competition.

A 6-foot-tall, 17-year-old boy has the strength of a man but lacks the man's maturity. This man-boy is unsympathetic to those who are weaker than he is. He is in the throes of adolescence and is as yet untempered by the strictures of adult society.

His attitude is brutish and simple: Keep up or die. His actions say: "If you can't do what I do, then you are a worthless loser." Any kid on the playground who can't compete physically is rejected and is not considered acceptable. Because the jock has the physical strength to dominate, he does.

An interesting thing happens to this jock dynamic, however. Once out of school and into the real world, the ability to physically dominate another person quickly loses its power and usefulness. In high school, if the jock felt threatened by a chubby kid with glasses, a couple of well-placed fists and the haughty laughter of the varsity team served to put the kid in his place. In the world of business, fists and taunts can no longer be used. It is not acceptable behavior to administer wedgies or snap towels in the conference room, nor is it effective. Although the jock might still have the physical power to dominate another, weaker, person, doing so can only backfire if the weaker person is his peer, supervisor, or manager.

The jocks, who were so immature in high school, find themselves learning a very humbling lesson. When they emerge into the wider world, they find their wings are clipped by society, and they learn to coexist successfully with people of lesser physical ability. Jocks are well represented in business, and they tend to do well in it, overall. They make the transition successfully, if not willingly or happily. They retain their natural sense of competition, but they have now earned a level of maturity and selflessness that makes them good citizens.

Programmers are just like jocks. When programmers were in high school, many of them lacked the physical coordination of the jocks, but they were gifted with quicker, stronger minds and well-coordinated mental abilities. They excelled in some organized activities, such as forensics, lit club, and the chess team.

In the throes of adolescence, their gifts aren't worth as much as muscle. They are easily dominated on the school playground by stronger boys. A skinny 17-year-old boy who has a man's mastery of calculus, physics, and computer science might still be a physically weak boy ignored on the gridiron and rejected in the dating game. We call this kid a nerd.

This nerd-boy is unsympathetic to those who are weaker than he is. Privately—for he doesn't have the physical strength to do so publicly—he laughs and makes fun of bigger boys who lack his wit and brainpower. His attitude is brutish and simple: Keep up or die. Any kid on the playground who isn't competitive is rejected and is not considered acceptable. He gives no thought to these weaker people's feelings or their other talents. His value system is expressed in a simple pecking order based on inner development of his mental acuity. Within the confines of his nonjock peers, his attitude is: If I can beat you in a mental contest, then I am your master and I am better than you.

Like jocks gifted with athletic talent, good programmers are also gifted with a natural talent, and they are just as competitive as any young athlete is. It can be harder to see this competitive drive because programming is essentially an invisible, solo sport. But don't let their quiet demeanor fool you; programmers are zealous competitors, and really good programmers are as cutthroat as any Olympic hopeful.

An interesting thing happens to this nerd dynamic, however. Once out of school and into the real world of adulthood, the ability to mentally dominate another person is not lost in the transition to a mature, civil, adult society. The nerd is protected by social strictures and can no longer be beaten up on the playing field. Physical bullying ceases to be acceptable behavior as adolescents mature into adulthood, but mental bullying becomes a stronger and stronger weapon in adulthood.

This mental-jock dynamic—the ability to mentally dominate another person—gains tremendous power in the adult world of the information age. In civil society, it has become perfectly acceptable behavior to administer mental wedgies with inscrutable software, or to snap emotional towels at long-suffering humans just trying to get some cash from their ATMs.

The jocks, who were so powerful in high school, find themselves utterly at the mercy of their former victims. The humbling process of becoming an adult makes most jocks become decent humans, and many of them have confessed to me no small embarrassment over their adolescent behavior.

The 6-foot-4-inch-tall former All-State point guard finds his physical prowess is useless in the boardroom, whereas the 5-foot-7-inch-tall former astronomy-club treasurer finds his mental prowess allows him to weave and jab and punch with unmatched agility. The endlessly adolescent nerd-boy lawyer can dominate in court with his keen tongue and keener mind. The nerd-boy doctor now has the power of life or death over his former-jock patients. And—surprise—the pasty-faced nerd-boy computer programmer turns out to have the most astonishing amount of power ever before wielded because he now controls everyone's access to vital information.

There is no maturation process to temper their exercise of that power. They dominate others with their mental ability because they can, and they see nothing wrong with humiliating users with dauntingly complex products. They sneer, joke, and laugh about the "lusers" who simply are not smart enough to use computers. Their work habits, too, of isolation, pressure, and long, odd hours offer little civilizing influence.

Not until my late 20s did I realize what a bully I was. The only difference was that I used my programming skills as my fists, and my mastery of complex systems as my height and reach. And I swinishly hooted at those who could not keep up with the complexities of using computers.

8

An Obsolete Culture

Programming is a somewhat alien activity, but it is emotionally very powerful. This power is what makes the job of programming into something more akin to a calling, its jargon more like a distinct language, and the brotherhood of software engineers into a cohesive culture. In this chapter, I will show how the culture of programming influences the nature of software-based products.

The Culture of Programming

I read an interesting story in a Sunday supplement about an American couple who retired to Mexico. They purchased a lot on the outskirts of a large city and hired an American architect to design their dream home. They then hired a Mexican building contractor and turned the blueprints over to him. As construction proceeded, they were flabbergasted to find that the building wasn't turning out the way the architect had specified.

The blueprints showed the front wall of the house containing four windows whose manufacturer and part number were precisely specified. The owners discovered that the actual wall contained three windows from another maker with quite different appearance and size. When they queried the Mexican builder, he shrugged and said, "They're windows. The plan says windows go in this wall. What is the problem?"

The owners and architect were from one culture, sharing one set of values, and the builder came from another culture and valued aspects of the problem differently. No doubt he was able to procure the windows for much less money and effort, and—in his world—these considerations took precedence. The American owners and architect believed that the blueprints implied full and exact compliance. The Mexican builder believed that the blueprints were a suggestion, not a requirement. He believed that his imperatives of thrift and acquisition ease naturally outranked any exactitude in the specifications. He was sincerely trying to fulfill the architect's vision but was applying his own cultural filters—his own values—to the problem.

Reusing Code

Just as the Mexican builder put construction cost ahead of design considerations, engineers, left to their own devices, will value programming efficiencies more than user needs. The strongest evidence of this is the reuse of code that has been written for some previous project or that can be purchased for some nominal sum from outside vendors. Prewritten code not only saves time, but it has already been proven to be usable by other programmers and to be bug free in operation. One of software's unique properties is that any procedure can be invoked with a single command, but there is no limit to the magnitude of the invoked procedure. In other words, as long as the procedure is already written, all it takes is a single command to employ it. Therefore, any prewritten module of code is a significant boon to programmers. They can plug it into their program as a black box whose inner workings need never be plumbed. The programmer is spared not only lots of coding, but lots of thinking and testing, too. To most programmers, code reuse is more important than almost any other technical consideration. Famous open-source guru Eric Raymond says, "Good programmers know what to write. Great ones know what to reuse."

The primary side effect of code reuse is that large portions of most programs exist not because some interaction designer wanted them to exist, but because some other programmer already did the work on someone else's budget. Much of the software that we interact with exists for the sole reason that it existed before.

For example, our desktop software has so many menus and text-based dialog boxes because all windowing systems—Microsoft Windows, Mac OS, OS/2, Linux—provide prewritten code modules for these functions. Conversely, none of those systems provides much prewritten code for dragging and dropping, which is why you see so few direct-manipulation idioms in software interaction. A dialog box can be constructed in about 6 or 8 lines of easy, declarative code. A drag-and-drop idiom must be constructed with about 100 lines of very intricate procedural code. The choice—for the programmer—is obvious. The benefit for the end user is generally overlooked in this economy.

I see the Mexican-builder story played out in software development all of the time, mostly because of the programmer's compulsion to reuse code. Ed Forman, the head of development at Elemental Software, creates a detailed and accurate sketch of exactly what he wants the screen to look like before assigning it to his programmers. And yet, Ed says, the program that comes back to him is always just a pale shadow of what he drew.

It works like this: Ed's sketch shows dark-gray buttons on a light-gray background. The programmer will begin construction by copying the source code from some other—already working—part of the program. This is a good way to save programming time and effort, apparently benefiting everyone—except that the existing code has an extra dark-gray border around the buttons. The dark-gray border also comes with a text legend. Instead of removing the text and the border to comply with Ed's sketch, the programmer will just leave it there, thus saving lots of code. The code requires some text for the legend, so he just puts something appropriate—from his technical point of view—there.

When Ed finally sees the program, complete with the unwanted border and confusing text legend, he shakes his head in amazement. When he points out the differences to the programmer, the programmer doesn't see a problem. Just like the Mexican builder, programmers believe that their own imperatives of construction simplicity and ease of acquisition—of prewritten source code in their case—take precedence over any *suggestions* made by others.

Ed is amused as well as frustrated by this, but he is at a loss to explain the phenomenon. His programmers are uniformly intelligent, capable, and deeply concerned about the quality of their products and the success of their company, but they simply cannot resist the siren's song. Sure, they will try to build Ed's vision, but not at the expense of their own implementation priorities.

⌘

A fascinating aspect of the imperative to reuse code is the willingness with which programmers will adopt code with a questionable pedigree. Some inexperienced programmer will hack out the first interaction idea that pops into his head, but once it is written, that piece of code becomes the basis for all subsequent efforts because it is so aggressively reused.

In Windows, for example, the really experienced programmers built the internal processing of the operating system, but the first sample applications that showed third-party developers how to communicate with the user were written by a succession of summer interns and junior coders at Microsoft. The Windows internal code has been upgraded and rewritten over six major releases, and it has steadily improved. However, an embarrassingly large number of popular applications have in their hearts long passages of program code written by 21-year-old undergraduates spending a summer in Redmond. The same is true for the Web. Amateur experimenters hacked out the first Web sites, but those who followed cloned those first sites, and their sites were cloned in turn.

As you can see, there is a clear conflict of interest between what the user needs and what the programmer needs. We anticipate conflict of interest in countless activities and professions, and we have built-in safeguards to curb its influence. Judges and lawyers have skills in common, but we never let lawyers adjudicate their own cases. We never let basketball players referee their own basketball games. The conflicting interests are clearly visible, yet we consistently let programmers make design decisions based on personal implementation considerations.

It is a widely held view, in both the software-product industry and in corporate IT departments, that programmers are the people best equipped to design software because they are the local experts with the most thorough knowledge of the pertinent issues. Although it seems innocent and natural to let programmers determine the form and behavior of the software they will build, the trap of conflicting interests is unavoidable. The trap is insidious not because of the differences between the programmer and the user, but because of the similarities. The user wants to achieve his goals, and the programmer wants to achieve hers. The problem comes from the subtle differences between those goals.

⌘

Programmers become so familiar with code reuse that they often copy existing techniques even when they aren't actually copying code. This comes naturally, coupled with programmers' tendency towards conservatism. For example, most programs have lots of confirmation screens, virtually all of which are unnecessary. Many of them exist because they existed in reused code, but many of them exist because programmers are simply habituated to putting them in.

For example, I ran into Jeff Bezos, the founder of Amazon.com, at a conference and told him how much I like the "1-Click" interface on his Web site. This interface allows you to purchase a product with—big surprise—one click. The interface is really well designed, because it pushes all of the annoying details out of the interface and lets the user merely click one button without reentering shipping and billing information.

Jeff was pleased to hear that I liked 1-Click, and he told me that when he and his designers had cooked up the idea, they presented it to the programmers, who duly nodded and agreed that they could do such a thing. The programmers went off and coded for a while, then brought the finished work to Jeff for him to try. He found a book he wanted and pressed the 1-Click button, whereupon the program asked him a confirming question! The programmers had converted his one-click interface into a two-click interface. To the programmers, this was simply an additional click—what's the big deal? To Jeff—and to every user—it is a 100% inflation rate! Jeff had to wheedle and cajole before the programmers really made the 1-Click interface have only one click. Jeff won't tell me how much 1-Click has increased sales, but I can tell you that it has doubled my personal book-buying rate.

I have seen this behavior countless times, even from the most conscientious and capable programmers. They take our precisely rendered screen shots and treat them as vague suggestions for the interface. They take our list of functions and features and cherry-pick those items from it that they personally agree with or that are particularly easy for them to build.

The Common Culture

The nature of war and the demands of military training are common in every country. This gives rise to the strong cultural similarity shared by soldiers everywhere, regardless of which ideology they might choose to defend. The same is true in programming shops.

The collective psychology of *Homo logicus* engenders a common culture of software development. The accepted way that software-based products are built is astonishingly similar, from camera company to auto company to bank to navy, which is why products as diverse as cameras, Porsches, ATMs, and Aegis cruisers all behave in a similar, recognizable, computer-like way.

One aspect of this culture is a reverence for technical skill. This reverence has the effect of elevating the importance of programming skill into areas in which it is no longer relevant, such as interaction design. Thirty years ago, when computers lived in glass houses and were used only by trained programmers, the self-referential design work of programmers was adequate and appropriate. As computers edged out into the consumer market, programmers still did the design, by historical default. Development managers ask, "Why should I pay interaction designers for what I get free from my programmers today?" This is a good question, except that the underlying assumption is incorrect. He is not getting interaction design, free or otherwise, from his programmers. Rather, the interface he gets is one designed to please only the authors: people with atypical training, personality, and aptitude.

This highlights another key point regarding the culture of software development. Although it is founded on the particular nature of programmers, it is propagated by their managers, many of whom—it must be said—are former programmers. Jeff Bezos says that the most vociferous defense of the two-click interface came from the product manager!

The reverence for technical skill has another effect. Most people assume that programming is more technical than design. I won't dispute that, but I strongly disagree with the conclusion typically drawn from it that programming should therefore come before design in the development process. This has the effect of making the user conform to the technology. If the interaction design came before the programming, the technology would conform to the user's goals instead. I have heard high-tech executives say, "We'll bring designers in after the programmers build the functionality." This has the effect of making moot most of the interaction designer's opportunities to contribute.

Programming Culture at Microsoft

It is hard to overestimate the depth and power of the software-development culture. Fred Moody's 1995 book about Microsoft, *I Sing the Body Electronic*,[1] gives an indication of how deeply entrenched the nerd culture is through an examination of this most archetypal software-development shop. The journeyman author and computer-industry-beat reporter spent a year inside Microsoft, observing the creation of a new multimedia product that came to be called *Explorapedia*. Moody was given unfettered access to Microsoft, and his book paints a revealing portrait of life and culture inside the industry-leading company. As you can tell from its products, Microsoft reveres programming, but has little or no awareness of interaction design. The book provides a fascinating study of what happens in a programming culture.

In his introduction, Moody sets the stage:

> The Microsoft approach to corporate organization is to form small teams around specific products and leave them alone to organize and work as they wish. It is a risky approach, for these crews are left unsupervised to a degree unthinkable in standard American corporations.

Microsoft is famous for hiring extremely bright, highly aggressive, young people right out of school. Moody says, "I felt like I was watching a gang of adolescents who had sneaked into some corporate headquarters after hours, taken over its boardrooms, and were playing at being businesspeople." Microsoft is also

---

[1] *Fred Moody, I Sing the Body Electronic, 1995, Viking, New York, New York, ISBN 0-670-84875-1.*

famous for pushing these youngsters very hard to get the most and best out of them. Moody says, "The atmosphere on the campus is one of unrelenting anxiety and constant improvisation."

The book is a remarkable chronicle of how arbitrary, demoralizing, and unprofessional Microsoft's development methods often are. Moody himself was—quite admittedly—baffled by what he saw, although he was convinced that he had seen something important. What he saw right away is that programmers run the show. Even when they don't do so explicitly, they do so implicitly by the force of their will. Moody never once questions his and everyone else's assumption that programmers *should* be in the driver's seat, yet he constantly remarks on the friction, dissension, unpleasantness, and sense of failure that it brings about:

> This is not to say that I understand what exactly is going on at Microsoft. For the sad fact of the matter is that I left the company's campus more confused than I was when I entered. And looking back over these pages now leaves me even more perplexed, as I still cannot manage to tell whether they contain a story of success, of failure, of success disguised as failure, or of failure disguised as success.

What he was witnessing, of course, was the creation of a dancing bear: a drearily hard-to-use product whose sole virtue is delivering features unavailable anywhere else.

The development of *Explorapedia* was a classic example of how screwed up our typical development process has become. There is no doubt in my mind that the product was a failure. What confused Moody was that the product shipped on time and made money. In the final pages of his book, which Moody calls a "Postmortem," he says:

> It never occurred to me when I first approached Microsoft that I might end up chronicling a failed project. Yet from almost the beginning until near the end of my stay there, I believed that I was indeed observing an object lesson in how not to develop a product. Since everyone connected with [*Explorapedia*] was so miserable, so angry, and talked so incessantly about frustration and disappointment, I could only assume that chance had hooked me up with a catastrophe. But in fact the [*Explorapedia*] project was an unqualified success.

In the next sentence, Moody all but calls it a dancing bear: "While each particular feature in Explorapedia is a pale version of the feature first envisioned…the encyclopedia nevertheless entered the marketplace as the sole product of its kind." It's easy to win when you have no competition and you are backed with Microsoft's awesome brand, vendor leverage, and prodigious bank account.

By far the most damning thing is the weakness of the product. Near the end of the book, he quotes Sara Fox, one of the designers, as she looked at

> ...the Dorling Kindersley book upon which [*Explorapedia*] was based, and had been shocked to see that the book allowed browsers more freedom to explore at random than did the computer. Yet the computer was supposed to be this grand force of liberation from the strictures of the printed book. In the book, she pointed out, the text flowed freely around pictures, and readers could browse through it at their leisure, taking in volumes of content at a glance. In [*Explorapedia*], they would be funneled through the pop-ups in numerical order, allowed only a few sentences of content at a time. It was a hideous paradox: the computer actually would be more restrictive than the book. "Dorling Kindersley did the opposite of what we're doing, and we turned into gatekeepers."

At Microsoft, the most important projects are conceived, managed, and coded by programmers. The multimedia CD-ROM project that Moody observed was something of an exception in that "designers" were involved at every step of the way. But they in no way exhibited the skill set that I consider mandatory for the role of interaction designer. They seemed to be ignorant of all of the things important for an interaction designer: a strong understanding of what programmers actually do, an understanding of interaction-design principles and methods, and a taxonomy and tools for understanding their users. Moody makes clear that the only skills the Microsoft designers brought were a quick wit, boundless energy, and a sense of aesthetics.

Thus, it was inevitable that he would observe a very dysfunctional model. "It was a designer's assignment to try to pile on features, a developer's role to resist for the sake of meeting a deadline, and a program manager's job to mediate and render verdicts." Any adversarial relationship such as this is bound to take a heavy toll. The people, product, or company will suffer.

The Microsoft employees who worked on the project remain as unenlightened as Moody. Kevin Gammill, the lead programmer, says:

> "Carolyn keeps calling it the Project From Hell, and Craig's always talking about how he's never been through anything like this. But Craig's also always talking about how we made this mistake and this mistake and this mistake on *Encarta* and now here we are making it again. And Sara always says, 'A product cycle is so...*cyclic.*' Every project here is like this! We keep saying that we learn from our mistakes...but we keep going through the same [expletive] over and over again."

Reading the intimate portraits of Gammill is as fascinating as watching a train wreck. A reader not familiar with the software industry might be tempted to write

off the descriptions as hyperbole or accuse Moody of picking an unrepresentative example of the breed. But Gammill is an archetype whose behavior is very
typical. I've met hundreds of men—and a few women—just like him.

> Even under relatively normal conditions, it was hard for his teammates
> to talk to Gammill. An enormous cultural chasm stretched between
> developers and designers at Microsoft. Often it was impossible for a
> developer to make a designer understand even the simplest elements of
> a programming problem. Just as often, designers would work for weeks
> on some aspect of a product only to be rudely told, when they finally
> showed it to a developer, that it was impossible to implement.

> Although conditions had improved in recent years, the two camps liter-
> ally spoke different languages and came to the world of computing from
> opposite intellectual, cultural, psychological, and aesthetic poles.
> Designers came to Microsoft from the arts; developers from the world of
> math and science. Developers looked down on designers because their
> thinking seemed fuzzy and unstructured, their tastes arbitrary.
> Designers felt that developers were unimaginative, conservative, and
> given to rejecting their designs out of hand without trying to find a way
> to make them work. Because programming was inexplicable to design-
> ers, they had no way of assessing a developer's insistence that their
> designs were unprogrammable. "Designers," Tom Corddry liked to say,
> "are invariably female, are talkative, live in lofts, have vegetarian diets,
> and wear found objects in their ears. Developers are invariably male, eat
> fast food, and don't talk except to say, 'Not true.'" He might have added
> that designers and developers deal with conflict in markedly different
> ways. When developers, who are given to bursts of mischievous play,
> begin peppering a designer's door with firings from a Nerf-ball gun, their
> victim calls the supervisor to complain. A developer would fire back.

I want to make perfectly clear that what Microsoft and Moody call a "designer" is
what I call a *visual designer*. Visual designers have a well-developed aesthetic
sense, think visually, can draw or paint, and are a part of every one of my company's design projects. However, they add their magic to our designs only after
the heavy lifting of conceptual and behavioral design work has been completed
by trained interaction designers.

By the way, Corddry's snappish "Not true" is a good example of Po Bronson's "I
didn't answer incorrectly, you just asked the wrong question."

Moody was very aware of the unique cultural quirks of programmers and devoted many colorful paragraphs to describing their abrasive, arrogant, demanding
attitude, yet he never really fathomed their values. In his description of an

encounter between burger-eating programmer Gammill and a female, "vegetarian," visual designer named Carolyn Bjerke, Moody makes a fundamental misinterpretation:

> While Gammill's replies to Bjerke's questions tended toward playful banter, his demeanor and posture were undeniably hostile. He sat with his back ramrod-straight, tapping one foot frenetically on the floor while he drummed the table with his fingers. He gave the impression that he would rather be anywhere else in the world. You could gauge his reaction to Bjerke's question by the increase in the rate of his finger- and foot-taps; they accelerated in direct proportion to the difficulty of the feature in question.

Moody attributes Gammill's irritation to the "difficulty" of the undertaking. Nothing could be further from the truth. Programmers *love* difficult tasks. The more difficult the problem is, the more satisfaction there is in solving it. Difficulty is often the prime motivator for good programmers. Gammill's irritation is based on the prospect of having to write uninspiring code, and on his loss of control to a person he does not respect: Bjerke, the nontechnical person whose design decisions seem arbitrary to Gammill. Of course, Gammill would never state this—he is probably unaware of it himself—but would use the red herring of "difficulty" to lay off the blame.

If someone is to lead a development team, he or she must own the respect of the programmers. The work that programmers do is frighteningly complex and demanding, and they defend their turf ferociously. Anyone who attempts to guide programmers will fail unless he knows and respects the programmer's job inside and out. At Microsoft—as in most shops—there are programmers and there are "lesser" people, and those lesser people cannot possibly hope to influence the product-development cycle.

But Microsoft is undeniably successful, and this has one unfortunate side effect. Many companies are motivated to copy Microsoft's culture as a means of copying its success. It is a common mistake to copy the trappings of success, rather than the root cause of it. It's like seeing General George Patton's pearl-handled revolvers and drawing the erroneous conclusion that to be a good strategist one must wear ornate sidearms.

Moody unintentionally makes another interesting point about our software-development culture. Many executives with lots of experience in creating and marketing software products have never applied interaction design. Lacking design, some of their previous products were successes and some were failures, but the process they used to create them was the same. From this they deduced that the success or failure of a software product is due only to chance; software success is simply a crapshoot. In Moody's story, all the signs pointed to failure, yet the product was a success. For General Magic, discussed in Chapter 6, "The Inmates Are Running the Asylum," all the signs pointed to success, yet the product was a failure. Looking in the wrong places, they fail to discern a pattern, so they simply assume that results are random. The problem is reminiscent of physicians in the nineteenth century, before it was discovered that the anopheles mosquito carried malaria, who were unsure of the disease's source. It was thought to float on the evening air, striking randomly, and one's only defense against the often-deadly fever was luck. After the cause-and-effect relationship was discovered, the disease was quickly brought to heel.

Cultural Isolation

In most development shops, the most-experienced programmers take responsibility for the most-demanding parts of the program. In return for this effort, they are given some modicum of immunity from having to field annoying technical-support calls. When users of the program call from the field, they are routed to technical-support personnel or to more junior programmers. On the rare occasion that a user gets through to the senior coder, it is because that user has already demonstrated her expertise to the junior programmer or the tech-support person. The result of this filtering process is that the more senior programmers are, the less contact they have with typical, run-of-the-mill users. By extension, they mistakenly assume that "their" users are representative.

For example, at Sagent Technology—a vendor of datamart-management software in the enterprise-computing market—Vlad Gorelik is the database guru, and his programming expertise is legendary. The only customers he speaks with directly are those who can palaver about "query segmentation," "task partitioning," and "data cubing" at Vlad's exalted level. It is not surprising, then, that Vlad imagines the typical user of Sagent's *Information Studio* product to be a seasoned database expert.

Conversely, Alice Blair, the *Information Studio* product manager, spends the lion's share of her time speaking with prospective buyers of the product. She counsels these people on what the product does and explains its basic functions. Consequently, Alice's view of her customer base is skewed toward first-time users and those with only very basic computer skills. It is no surprise that she imagines that most customers need hand-holding.

Kendall Cosby works in tech support at Sagent. He speaks with neither experts nor first timers. Mostly, he works with intermediate end users. Because the product is used as a decision-support tool, he is in constant contact with financial and marketing analysts who know little about computers and databases, yet whose jobs depend on their ability to probe into their datamarts to understand sales trends. Because Kendall's customer isn't very computer savvy, he wants the product to hide or eliminate complex functionality. Of the three, Kendall's customer view is the most accurate, yet because of their roles, Vlad and Alice have greater influence on the product's design.

There's an old story about several blind men encountering an elephant for the first time. One grasps its leg and proclaims that the elephant is "very like a tree." Another touches its side and states that it is "very like a wall." Another grasps its trunk and declares it to be "very like a snake." Like the blind men and the elephant, Alice, Kendall, and Vlad have very different opinions of what their clients are like because they are each confronting a different subset of their users. What's more, they all have clear, empirical evidence to back their deductions. In order to get an accurate portrayal, someone divorced from the day-to-day imperatives of both development and sales is needed.

Skin in the Game

One strong cultural determinant of software engineering is that it is done alone. Programmers sit alone. Only one programmer can type in code at one time. Code is largely invisible inside a computer, and it is almost never read. Reading someone else's code is less like reading a book than it is like reading someone's lecture notes, written in a private, inscrutable shorthand. Programming is so complex that it takes single-minded focus and lots of uninterrupted time. Programmers have a strong sense of this insularity and of what it implies. Nobody can have significant control over what a programmer does inside his own program. Programmers know that the quality of their code is largely a matter of their own conscientiousness. The boss can demand quality, but the boss isn't going to invest the time and effort required to verify that such quality exists. It can take more time to decipher a programmer's code than it took to write it. Programmers know this, and they know that their personal decisions and actions have more leverage on the final product and the user's satisfaction than any other consideration. Ultimately, they will personally hold the bag for the product's success. They know that they have a lot of skin in the game.

The lonely work of the programmer gives him a strong sense of his power. Some programmers are uncomfortable with the sense of power, but they are even more uncomfortable delegating authority to others with less skin in the game. When marketers, managers, or designers give advice to them, programmers regard the suggestions with a healthy dose of skepticism. If they take the advice and it turns out to be bad, they know the advisor will be long gone and that the blame will fall squarely on the programmer.

Letting programmers do their own design results in bad design, but it also has a collateral effect: The programmers lose respect for the design process.

Programmers have been successfully bluffing their way through the design process for so long that they are conditioned to disregard its value. When a trained interaction designer is finally hired, the programmer naturally treats the designer's work dismissively.

This leads to a general lack of respect for the interaction designer, the design process, and sadly, the design itself. This disrespect reinforces the cultural valuation of the design as opinion and vague advice, rather than as a clear, specific, and unequivocal statement. Because the programmer rightly assumes that his fancy carries equal weight to mere opinion, he feels free to cherry-pick elements of the design from the specification. Instead of seeing the written design specification as a blueprint, he sees it as the op-ed page of the newspaper. Some items are interesting but untrue; others are true but irrelevant. Unfortunately, the programmer is making these decisions on the basis of implementation considerations or on a self-referential basis, so they are frequently wrong.

On the other hand, every programmer has horror stories to tell of good products that failed because of dunderheaded design imperatives from managers who were equally confused about what users might be looking for. I remember one senior executive who hated to type, demanding that all of his company's programs be controllable only by the mouse. I also remember another senior executive who was clumsy with a mouse, declaring that all of his company's programs must be controllable only with the keyboard. These destructive, self-referential designs caused despair to ripple through both companies.

⌘

Certainly some programmers are consciously malicious and destructive, but— judging from the many programmers I have met—they as are rare as hen's teeth. Their training and discipline are so tough that it is inevitable, as they reach the peak of their abilities, that they see nonprogrammers as less competent. Software engineers respect others in their own areas, but when a nonprogrammer ventures into the world of programming, as Moody describes, programmers become condescending or even elitist.

The programmer has every right to sneer at the amateur who pokes his nose into the highly technical world of software development. Likewise, if the programmer knocked on the controller's door and began recalculating business ratios, the controller would be justified in sneering at the presumption and arrogance of the interloping programmer.

The difficulty arises because designing interaction and implementing interaction are so thoroughly mixed in the typical development process. Although a manager might request a change in the program's behavior, she wouldn't presume to ask the programmer to use different construction methods. But because the behavior and its implementation are so tightly bound, it is impossible to assail one without appearing to assail the other. This is part of the difficulty Moody observed at Microsoft.

Most people involved in the creation of software-based products want theirs to be easy to use. Consequently, they are constantly encroaching on the programmers. The developers never have a surplus of time, so this poaching can make them testy. Many retreat into solitude and communicate only reluctantly with other, nonprogramming team members. Tamra Heathershaw-Hart related this story to me about getting information from programmers when she worked as a technical writer:

> I discovered that bribery worked a lot better than begging. I used chocolate most of the time. The bribery method worked so well that I once had an engineering manager apologize on his knees in public for forgetting to tell me about a product change. (Yes, he got his treat anyway.) At one company I had a chocolate-craving engineer tell me all his co-workers' changes, just so he could get *their* chocolate. Before the bribery method I spent a lot of overtime hours trying to figure out what stuff in the product had changed. Afterwards, I managed to cut my overtime by more than half.

This anecdote is amusing because—if we have any experience at all in the software-development business—we recognize its truth. If you heard a story about a company's controller having to bribe an accounts-receivable clerk with chocolate to get information on today's deposits, you'd be astonished, indignant, and incredulous.

⌘

Many executives are accustomed to having their subordinates respond immediately to any directive—or even mild suggestion—that they might offer. They imagine that programmers—being technical—are not very high up the totem pole of authority and will obediently follow direction from their higher-ups. From the programmer's point of view, the executive doesn't have any skin in the game, so obedience is problematic. The independent-minded software engineer won't change his code just because someone tells him to, regardless of the magnitude of that person's title.

If you want to change some existing code, you have to first change the programmer's mind. He will have a vested interest both in the existing code and in avoiding the seemingly unnecessary effort of changing it. You cannot merely demand, let alone ask, but you must present a rational, defensible reason for making the change. It must be presented in terms the engineer can understand, and it has to be presented by someone with skin in the game.

Paul Glen's book *Leading Geeks*[2] is a remarkably accurate and revealing analysis of how programmers think and behave. If you wish to learn more about programmers and programming culture, I strongly recommend Glen's book.

Scarcity Thinking

One of the strongest influences on software design is what I call *scarcity thinking*. This comes from two forces working in concert. The newness of the computer software industry is well known, but our very youth conspires to make us a very nonintrospective industry. We are too busy assimilating new technologies to reflect on the misconceptions surrounding the older ones. Consequently, the software industry resounds with myths and misunderstandings that go quite unquestioned.

Astonishingly, the simple and obvious fact that computers are vastly more powerful, cheaper, and faster than they were just a few years ago hasn't really penetrated the practice of software construction. Consequently, most software products don't work very hard to serve the user. Instead, they are protective of the central processing unit (CPU) in the mistaken impression that it is overworked. The result is that software-based products tend to overwork the human user. Design guru Bill Moggridge calls this attitude "be kind to chips and cruel to users."

In the last decade, the incredible advances in computer construction have put awesome power on the average desktop for bargain prices. Any student or homemaker can have power that General Motors' corporate data-processing center would have lusted after in 1974. Yet most software is still built today with tools, technologies, methods, and mind-sets that come directly from that world of scarcity thinking. Developers are conditioned to ask themselves, "Can we fit it in? Will it respond fast enough? What nonessentials can we discard to make it more efficient?" It forces out of consideration more-relevant questions, such as, "Will the user understand it? Can we present this information in a way that makes sense? Is the sequence of instructions appropriate for what the user wants? What information does the user need most?"

With few exceptions, most CPUs are spending the overwhelming majority of their time idling—doing nothing. Yes, some processes are compute-bound, but they are much fewer and rarer than we are led to believe by hardware vendors who want to sell us the latest and greatest and most-powerful electronic wonders. It would not be in their best interest to let consumers know that their CPUs work hard only in very brief spurts and sit idling for 75%–80% percent of the time.

---

[2] *Paul Glen* Leading Geeks: How to Manage and Lead the People Who Deliver Technology, *2003, John Wiley & Sons, New York, New York, ISBN: 0-7879-6148-5.*

Just two or three decades ago, computers were so weak and precious that any good idea was likely to be restrained by the feebleness of the host computer. The main thrust of computer science back then was to develop technologies that relieved the strain on the scarce computing resource. Such widely used technologies as the relational database, ASCII code, file systems, and the BASIC language were designed primarily to ease the load on the computer. Software written during that time gave priority to performance at the expense of other considerations, such as ease of use. But don't forget that prewritten code is like a force of nature, and much of that old code, written for weak computers, is running on modern, abundantly powerful systems.

The Process Is Dehumanizing, Not the Technology

Since Charlie Chaplin in *Modern Times*, the popular thinking has been that technology dehumanizes us. I disagree with this notion. Before technology, tyrants, barbarians, and warriors dehumanized their victims with fists and stones. It doesn't require sophisticated tools to dehumanize your fellow human—a glance or a kick does it as well. It is not technology that is dehumanizing. It is the technologists, or rather the processes that technologists use, that create dehumanizing products.

Of course, the more powerful the technology, the more damage a bad process can inflict. Conversely, designed properly, that same technology can be a great gift to humanity. High technology can go either way. It's the people who administer it who dictate the effect.

Interactive systems do not have to be dehumanizing, but for this to occur, we have to revamp our development methodology so that the humans who ultimately use them are the primary focus. The single most important process change we can make is to design our interactive products completely before any programming begins. The second most important change is to turn the responsibility for design over to trained interaction designers. In the next few chapters, I will show what can be accomplished by taking these steps.

Part IV

INTERACTION DESIGN IS GOOD BUSINESS

9

DESIGNING FOR PLEASURE

As Albert Einstein said, "You can't solve a problem with the same thinking that created it." I've just devoted many pages to identifying that old thinking and showing how it doesn't work. Now it's time to talk about a new method that *will* work. I've been developing this method, called Goal-Directed design, since 1992, and the designers in my consulting firm use it for all of our projects. It consists of some novel ways of looking at problems, some powerful guiding axioms, and some remarkably effective mental tools. In the next few chapters, I'll present an overview of three of the most powerful of these tools, along with some case studies of how they are applied and the kind of results you can expect.

Personas

The most powerful tools are always simple in concept, but they often must be applied with some sophistication. That is certainly true of interaction design tools. Our most effective tool is profoundly simple: *Develop a precise description of our user and what he wishes to accomplish.* The sophistication comes from how we determine and use that precise description.

The most obvious approach—to find the actual user and ask *him*—doesn't work for a number of reasons, but the main one is that merely being the victim of a particular problem doesn't automatically bestow on one the power to see its solution. The actual user is still a valuable resource, and we devote considerable attention to him or her, but we never let the user directly affect the solution.

The actual method that works sounds trivial, but it is tremendously powerful and effective in every case: We make up pretend users and design for *them*. We call these pretend users *personas*,[1] and they are the necessary foundation of good interaction design.

Personas are not real people, but they represent them throughout the design process. They are *hypothetical archetypes* of actual users. Although they are imaginary, they are defined with significant rigor and precision. Actually, we don't so much "make up" our personas as *discover* them as a byproduct of the investigation process. We do, however, make up their names and personal details.

Personas are defined by their goals. Goals, of course, are defined by their personas. This may sound tautological, but it is not. Personas reveal themselves through our research and analysis in much the same way that the sequence of tectonic events reveal themselves to geologists through the study of sedimentary layers: The presence of a fossil defines a stratum, and a stratum defines the presence of a fossil. I'll talk a lot about goals in the next chapter, but we discover them in the same way we discover personas. We determine the relevant personas and their goals in a process of successive refinement during our initial investigation of the problem domain.

Typically, we start with a reasonable approximation and quickly converge on a believable population of personas. Although this iterative process is similar to the iterative process used by software engineers during the implementation process, it is significantly different in one major respect. Iterating the design and its premises is quick and easy because we are working in paper and words. Iterating the implementation is slow and difficult because it requires code.

Design for Just One Person

If you want to create a product that satisfies a broad audience of users, logic will tell you to make it as broad in its functionality as possible to accommodate the most people. *Logic is wrong.* You will have far greater success by designing for a single person.

Imagine that you are designing an automobile to please a wide spectrum of people. You could easily identify at least three subgroups: the soccer mom, the carpenter, and the junior executive. Mom wants a safe, stable vehicle with lots of space and big doors for hauling the kids, dogs, groceries, and other stuff. Joe, the carpenter, wants a rugged vehicle with all-wheel drive and abundant room for ladders, lumber, bags of cement, and tools. Seth, the young executive, wants a

---

[1] *For all of you Latin scholars and typographers out there, you will be happy to know that the battle between "personas" and "personæ" rages hotly and daily at Cooper Interaction Design. Designers on the "personas" side argue that pronunciation is less ambiguous, gratuitous ligatures can be eliminated, and the word appears conventional and unthreatening to our clients. Designers on the "personæ" side argue that the pronunciation is easy once you hear it, the opportunity for a gratuitous ligature is like manna from heaven, and that our clients are bright enough to deal with arcane and obsolete phraseology. It sounds to me a lot like programmers arguing about algorithms, so, in this book, I'll stick to "personas."*

sporty car with a powerful engine, stiff suspension, convertible top, and only enough room for two.

The logical solution is shown in the illustration. It's a combination vehicle with a little bit of what each driver wants: a convertible van with room for kids and lumber. What a goofy, impossible car! Even if it could be built, no one would want it. The correct solution is to build a minivan for Mom, a pickup truck for Joe, and a sports car for Seth.

Making three different products in software is a lot easier than making them in steel. Whereas there really must be three vehicles, one software product can usually be configured to behave like three different ones (with the caveat that the job of configuring it must not be dumped in the user's lap).

Every time you extend the functionality to include another constituency, you put another speed bump of features and controls across every other user's road. You will find that the facilities that please some users will interfere with the enjoyment and satisfaction of others. Trying to please too many different points of view can kill an otherwise good product. However, when you narrow the design target to a single persona, nothing stands between that persona and complete happiness.

Robert Lutz, the chairman of Chrysler, says that 80% of people in focus groups hated the new Dodge Ram pickup. He went ahead with production and made it into a best-seller because the other 20% *loved* it. Having people love your product, even if it is only a minority, is how you succeed.

The broader a target you aim for, the more certainty you have of missing the bull's-eye. If you want to achieve a product-satisfaction level of 50%, you cannot do it by making a large population 50% happy with your product. You can only accomplish it by singling out 50% of the people and striving to make them 100% happy. It goes further than that. You can create an even bigger success by targeting 10% of your market and working to make them 100% *ecstatic*. It might seem counterintuitive, but designing for a *single user* is the most effective way to satisfy a broad population.

The Roll-Aboard Suitcase and Sticky Notes

The roll-aboard suitcase is a good example of how powerful designing for one person can be. This small suitcase with the built-in wheels and retractable handle revolutionized the entire luggage industry, yet it wasn't designed for the general public. It was originally designed just for airline flight crews, a very narrowly defined target user. However, the product's design purity pleased this group enormously. The rest of the traveling public soon saw that it solved their luggage problem, too. Carrying it through crowded airports was as easy as maneuvering it down airliner aisles or stowing it aboard planes.

After the roll-aboard succeeded in its target segment, it was launched into other markets. Now you can buy double-sized roll-aboards, designer roll-aboards, armored-equipment roll-aboards, and kids' roll-aboards. Today, purchasing luggage without built-in wheels and a retractable handle is difficult.

As another example, an adhesive engineer at 3M named Art Fry used his own very specific requirements as a basis for creating what is arguably the most widely used and widely appreciated office tool. When he sang in the church choir, paper bookmarks always fell out of his hymnal, making him lose his place. Unwilling to damage the church's property with sticky tape, he looked for a better solution. He remembered an adhesive that he had worked on a few years earlier that was discarded because it didn't stick well enough. He used that failed adhesive to coat some small squares of yellow paper for bookmarks. This is how the 3M Post-it Note was born.

Happy users make remarkably effective and valuable assets. By narrowing your focus, you can generate fanatical customer loyalty in your target market. As discussed in Chapter 5, "Customer Disloyalty," customer loyalty can sustain you in difficult times. Not only will loyal users climb mountains and wade rivers to purchase and use your product, but they are the most powerful marketing tool known. Loyal users will personally recommend you to their friends. After you get buzz going about your product, you can build on it and extend your product into other segments of the market.

The Elastic User

Although satisfying the user is our goal, the term "user" causes trouble. Its imprecision makes it as unusable as a chainsaw is for removing someone's appendix. We need a more precise design tool.

Whenever I hear the phrase "the user," it sounds to me like "the elastic user." The elastic user must bend and stretch and adapt to the needs of the moment. However, our goal is to design *software* that will bend and stretch and adapt to the user's needs. Programmers have written countless programs for this mythical elastic consumer, but he simply doesn't exist. When the programmer finds it convenient to dump the user into the Windows file system to find the information she needs, he defines the elastic user as an accommodating, computer-literate power user. Other times, when the programmer finds it convenient to step the user through a difficult process with a mindless wizard, he defines the elastic user as an obliging, naïve, first-time user. Designing for the elastic user gives the developer license to code as he pleases while paying lip service to "the user." *Real* users are not elastic.

Programmers have an expressive taxonomy for describing the construction of software. Good programmers don't toss around gross generalizations about different computers and systems. A programmer would never say, "This will run well on a computer." Which computer? Which model? What operating system? What peripherals? Similarly, designers must never be so vague as to say their program "is designed for the user," or that "it will be user friendly." If you hear someone speaking like that, it is likely a way to justify the imposition of his own self-interest instead.

In our design process, we never refer to "the user." Instead, we refer to a very specific individual: a persona.

Be Specific

The more specific we make our personas, the more effective they are as design tools. That's because personas lose elasticity as they become specific. For example, we don't just say that Emilee uses business software. We say that Emilee uses WordPerfect version 5.1 to write letters to Gramma. We don't just let Emilee drive to work. We give her a dark-blue 1991 Toyota Camry, with a gray plastic kid's seat strapped into the back and an ugly scrape on the rear bumper. We don't just let Emilee go to work. We give her a job as a new-accounts clerk in a beige cubicle at Global Airways in Memphis, Tennessee. This distinctive specificity is very powerful as a design and communications tool. Consequently, all of our personas are articulated with singular detail and precision.

As we isolate Emilee with specific, idiosyncratic detail, a remarkable thing happens: She becomes a real person in the minds of the designers and programmers. We can refer to her by name, and she assumes a tangible solidity that puts all of our design assumptions in perspective. As she loses her elasticity, we can identify her skills, her motivations, and what she wants to achieve. Armed with this knowledge, we can then examine her in light of the software's subject area to see whether she is really an archetypal user. After a designer has some experience, he can usually synthesize a valid persona on the first try.

Giving the persona a name is one of the most important parts of successfully defining one. *A persona without a name is simply not useful.* Without a name, a persona will never be a concrete individual in anyone's mind.

All things being equal, I will use people of different races, genders, nationalities, and colors as personas. However, I try not to play against type because this can confuse everyone. Stereotypical personas are more effective if the stereotyping lends more credence to the persona. My goal here is not to be politically correct but to get everyone to believe that my personas are real. If my persona is a nurse, I will use a woman rather than a man, not because there are no male nurses, but because the overwhelming majority of nurses are female. If the user is a computer technician, our persona will be Nick, a pimply faced 23-year-old former member of the high-school audio-visual club, rather than Hellene, a statuesque, 5-foot-11-inch beauty who went to Beverly Hills High. I am shooting for believability, not diversity.

To make each persona more real to everyone involved in the product creation, I like to put faces to the names and give each persona an image. I usually purchase, for a small fee, faces from stock photo libraries on the Web. Occasionally, I've used sketched caricatures. You can cut them out of magazines if you want.

A fully realized, thoroughly defined user persona is a powerful tool. Until the user is precisely defined, the programmer can always imagine himself as the user or allow the user to become elastic. A completely defined user persona is key to the suppression of any tendency for the developer to usurp or distort the user persona's role. Long before a single line of code is written, a well-defined user persona becomes a remarkably effective tool for interaction design.

Hypothetical

It is important not to confuse a precise user taxonomy with a real person. Real people are of great interest as raw data, but they are frequently useless—and often detrimental—to the design process. A fine wine helps a successful dinner; raw Cabernet Sauvignon grapes—tiny, tough-skinned, and seed-filled—would ruin it. Many scientists, with a reverence for the empirical, confuse real users with imaginary—but more valuable—design personas.

The other major problem with real users is that, being real, they have funny quirks and behavioral anomalies that interfere with the design process. These idiosyncrasies are not extensible across a population. Just because one user has a distaste for direct manipulation doesn't mean that all—or even a plurality of—users do. The same works in reverse, too. Our real user might be fully capable of getting over some cognitive bump in the interaction road, whereas the majority of other users cannot. The temptation to attribute such capabilities to all users because one very real human exhibits them is strong but must be avoided.

In particular, we see this from company presidents. For example, one president we have worked with hates typing and wants to do all of his work without a keyboard. He has issued a directive that all of his company's software will be controlled only from the mouse. It is reasonable to want to use just the mouse to control the software, but it is not reasonable to shut out all those users who are more comfortable with the keyboard. The president is not a very representative persona.

Precision, Not Accuracy

As a design tool, it is more important that a persona be precise than accurate. That is, it is more important to define the persona in great and specific detail than that the persona be the precisely correct one. This truth is surprising because it is the antithesis of the *goal* of interaction design, in which accuracy is always more important than precision. The end result is to have a program that does the right thing, and we are willing to accept some friction in the system to obtain it.

In mechanical devices, moving linkages must be without slack. That is, a piston must move with minimal tolerances in its cylinder. If there were play in the linkage, the piston would quickly slap itself into self-destruction. It matters less that the piston is too short or too long for the cylinder than that it fits without loose-ness. The same is true of personas. It matters more that the persona is expressed with sufficient precision that it cannot wiggle under the pressure of development than it does that it be the right one.

For example, if we were designing the roll-aboard suitcase, for our persona we could use Gerd, a senior captain flying 747s from Vancouver to Frankfurt for Lufthansa.

On the other hand, we can't extend our persona to include *any* commercial flyer. Sonia, for example, attends classes at Embry-Riddle Aeronautical University in Daytona Beach and will be a professional pilot when she graduates. She flies every day, but only in small, single-engine propeller planes, and never stays overnight away from home. From a luggage point of view, Sonia is an edge-case pilot. As soon as you blur the definition of Gerd to include Sonia, you make him approximate instead of exact. You get into endless, unproductive discussions about whether Sonia is or is not an airline pilot and what special features her baggage needs.

On the other hand, we could certainly design a roll-aboard by using Francine, a newly minted flight attendant on Reno Air, as a persona. She flies the length of California three times a day, serving drinks and handing out peanuts. Gerd and Francine are dramatically different personas, but their suitcase goals and needs are equivalent.

Programmers live and die by edge cases, and they will bring that awareness to the persona-selection process. They will argue that Sonia has a valid claim on persona-hood because she occupies a pilot seat. But whereas programming is defined by cases at the edge of the paradigm, design is defined at the center. If there is any doubt at all about a persona being very close to the center, that persona should be shunted out of consideration.

In the interest of being precise in the definition of personas, averages have to be ruled out. An average user is never actually average. The average person in my community has 2.3 children, but not a single person in my community actually has 2.3 children. A more useful representative would be Samuel, who has 2 children, or Wells, who has 3. Samuel is useful because he is a person. Yes, he is hypothetical, but he is specific. Our parent of 2.3 children cannot possibly be specific, because if he were, he wouldn't have that impossible average.

Average personas drain away the advantages of the specificity of precise personas. The great power of personas is their precision and specificity. To deal in aggregates saps that power.

Personas are the single most powerful design tool that we use. They are the foundation for all subsequent Goal-Directed design. Personas allow us to see the scope and nature of the design problem. They make it clear exactly what the user's goals are, so we can see what the product must do—and can get away with *not* doing. The precisely defined persona tells us exactly what the user's level of computer skill will be, so we don't get lost in wondering whether to design for amateurs or experts.

The personas we invent are unique for each project. Occasionally, we can borrow from previous projects, but because precision is the vital key, it is rare to find two personas exactly alike.

A Realistic Look at Skill Levels

One of the really valuable contributions of personas is that they give discussions of skill levels a refreshing breath of realism. The scope of variation of users' skill levels is huge, and personas make that fact easy to see. The widely held, more-traditional model of user skill levels was shown as the euphemism pyramid in Chapter 2, "Cognitive Friction." At the top of the pyramid are "power users," assumed to be perfectly knowledgeable about computers, but lacking the training to program. The central trapezoid is "computer-literate users," who are imagined to have a fundamental understanding of how computers work, but who don't avail themselves of all its coolest features. "Naïve users" fill the bottom of the pyramid, and they are estimated to be as dumb as a brick and completely clue free.

Here are some examples of personas that shatter the pyramid's false assumptions:

Rupak works as a network installer in Los Angeles. He works with computers all day every day and is very adept at getting them to function, but he doesn't really understand how they work. He survives through his reservoir of superstition and lore, his capacity for rote learning, and his endless patience.

Shannon is an accountant at a health spa in Tempe, Arizona. She is clueless about the Web, email, networks, the file system, and most everything else about computers, but she is an astonishing whiz with the Microsoft Excel spreadsheet program. She can whip out a new spreadsheet—complete with charts and graphs—that shows sales trends in no time at all.

Dexter is the vice president of business development at Steinhammer Video Productions in Hollywood. Dexter has a pager, two cell phones, a pocket computer, and a wireless modem stashed in the pockets of his double-breasted suit as he walks between sound stages. He is a master of technology, and he can solve any problem. His colleagues are always calling him over to help find lost files for them, but he is really too busy for those time-wasting exercises. Clint is holding on line three!

Roberto is a telemarketing representative for J. P. Stone, the mail-order merchant of rugged outdoor clothing. He sits in a carrel in a suburb of Madison, Wisconsin, wearing a telephone headset and using a PC to process phoned-in orders. Roberto doesn't know a thing about high technology or computers, but he is a steady, conscientious worker and has a wonderful ability to follow complex procedures without difficulty. After a few days of training, he has become one of J. P. Stone's most productive and efficient reps. He says, "I *like* the computer!"

Interestingly, neither Rupak, Shannon, Dexter, nor Roberto comes close to fitting into any of the slices of the pyramid. Even aside from its oppressive stereotyping power, the pyramid is remarkably unrepresentative of the population. Oversimplified models of markets don't help with design problems.

Personas End Feature Debates

Surprisingly, another extremely important contribution of personas is their value as a communications tool. The cast of characters becomes a design taxonomy with great power to explain our design decisions. Even more, they become a spotlight, showing the programmers, marketers, and managers that our design decisions are obviously correct.

It is vitally important that everyone on the design team not only become familiar with the cast of characters, but that each persona become like a real person—like a fellow member of the development team. Programmers—with their mathematical nature—have a natural reluctance to think about specific user cases, preferring instead to think about general cases. This spills over into their thinking about users, and they are always imagining users in the aggregate, the average, or the generic. They much prefer to speak of "the user" than of Judy, Crandall, Luis, Estelle, Rajiv, and Fran.

Before personas are put to use, a typical conversation between a programmer and a manager engaged in interaction design would go something like this:

Programmer: "What if the user wants to print this out?"

Manager: "I don't think we really need to add printing in version one."

Programmer: "But someone might want to print it."

Manager: "Well, yes, but can't we delay putting printing in?"

The manager cannot win this discussion because she has not advanced an argument with the force of reason. Regardless of its truth, it is stated merely as her amorphous desire to do things differently, and the programmer's logic of what "might" happen is irresistible.

After the cast of characters is developed, we have our taxonomy for expressing precisely who needs what in the program. But programmers are hard to move, and a typical discussion with a client programmer early in the relationship goes like this:

Programmer: "What if the user wants to print this out?"

Interaction designer: "Rosemary isn't interested in printing things out."

Programmer: "But someone might want to print it."

Interaction designer: "But we are designing for Rosemary, not for 'someone.'"

At this point, we are at a standoff. The programmer is still using the term "user" and is still stuck in the world of possibility thinking. However, our invocation of the persona Rosemary is not an amorphous, unformed desire. Instead, it is a specific person with a demonstrated skill set and objectives. We finally have an argument that is compelling.

However, because programmers have possession of the code, they can—and will—still do what they want, regardless of the strength of our arguments. The key to success is getting the programming staff to buy into the existence and reality of the cast of characters. Every one of our designers resolutely insists on expressing all design issues in terms of named personas. We *never* fall back into the "user" construct. We never let the programmer—or anyone else—get away with assertions about "the user." After a while, this consistency pays off, and the programmers begin to adopt personas and refer to them by name. Although this seems like a subtle change, when the programmers begin to speak of personas by name of their own volition, it is really a dramatic, watershed event that changes the nature of the collaboration between designers and developers.

This watershed occurs in every one of our successful design projects. When it happens, the entire process shifts into high gear. The conversations now sound more like this:

Enlightened programmer: "Would Rosemary want to print this out?"

Happy interaction designer: "No. Although Jacob will want some printed reports on a quarterly basis."

Enlightened programmer: "Well, if they are so rarely needed, we should save ourselves time and effort by not writing a fancy, proprietary report-writing feature, but instead license a commercially available tool."

Happy manager: "And that shaves two weeks off of the shipping schedule!"

I have seen dramatic changes come over our client companies after the watershed. Before, they were stuck in endless feature wrangling, and issues once thought resolved would reappear for further discussion every couple of weeks. Afterwards, design issues are raised, answered, and put away once and for all.

Some of our client companies have printed T-shirts with a picture of an important persona on it for each of the developers. We have had other clients print posters with personas to put on the walls of the programming shop. These efforts help to unite the programmers in a mutual understanding of their ultimate customer.

Both Designers and Programmers Need Personas

On the other hand, we have worked with companies where the programmers are simply too embarrassed to actually call users by their names, and they would not buy in to the idea of precise personas. They would continually backslide into "user-speak," and their products suffered enormously.

I know a programmer who simply doesn't understand how personas work. Under the pressure of arguments from my colleagues and myself, he has admitted that personas are important. However, he misses the central point of specificity, so he tends to use the term "persona" as a synonym for "user." He says, "We have to fulfill the needs of the personas." Although he uses the term, he rejects the specificity, which is the active ingredient, so he loses any value.

Another client gave us just a few days to make some recommendations. We created a persona named Edgar, who was not defined with much detail. We then entered some protracted discussions with the client on issues that extended beyond the original project scope. We quickly found that Edgar began to multiply. Different teams within the client adopted different Edgars, each with different qualities.

Marketing professionals will be instantly familiar with the process of persona development because it is very similar to what they do in the market-definition phase. The main difference between marketing personas and design personas is that the former are based on demographics and distribution channels, whereas the latter are based purely on users. The two are not the same and don't serve the same purpose. The marketing personas shed light on the sales process, whereas the design personas shed light on the development process.

As we begin to develop ideas for design solutions, we can constantly hold them up against our personas to see how well we have done. We become character actors, inhabiting the minds of our personas. This is easy to do because they are so narrowly defined. When you try on a persona and examine a product or a task, you can tell right away whether or not the design has succeeded in making that persona happy.

It's a User Persona, Not a Buyer Persona

A frequent mistake is to design for someone who is close to the product but is not the actual user. Many products are designed for the writer who will review the product in consumer publications. In the information-technology business, the IT manager who purchases the product will rarely be the one to actually use it. Designing for the purchaser is a frequent mistake in the computer business.

While you cannot ignore the IT manager's needs, the IT manager will ultimately be happier if the product makes the *real* end user happy. After all, if the end user is happy and productive, it is a success for the IT manager. We have seen a recurring pattern in which clients ignore this advice and pander to these gatekeepers of technology. After these IT managers deploy the software to the real end users, they are besieged with complaints and discover that the users are disinclined to use the product that so beguiled the IT manager. They then turn on the software vendor, demanding that the interaction be made more satisfactory for the end user.

The Cast of Characters

We give every project its own cast of characters, which consists of anywhere from 3 to 12 unique personas. We don't design for all of them, but they are all useful for articulating the user population. Some are defined only to make it clear that we are *not* designing for them. In one project, for example, our project concerned a technical help-desk management system. We defined three people, two of them in-house help-desk technicians. Leo Pierce was a marketing assistant in the company's product division. He used a computer in his daily work and was occasionally a consumer of help-desk services. Alison Harding was a company technician whose job entailed going from office to office with her aluminum tool case, fixing technical problems for the likes of Leo. Ted van Buren was a help-desk representative who spent his day answering phone calls from people like Leo and dispatching Alison to Leo's office to fix his computer.

Our client, Remedy Inc, was revising its flagship product, Action Request System (ARS), and wanted to make it "easier to use." By developing these three personas (and a few others), we could clearly articulate what the goals of the project really were.

Ted was the main user of the current version of ARS, but he wasn't our primary persona. Although we would make operating the program easier for Ted, we would have failed in our job if that was all we accomplished. Instead, we were making the help-desk system directly accessible to Leo. Formerly, if Leo needed help, he had to telephone Ted, who would dispatch Alison. The full cast of characters articulated very clearly who the players were. This let us communicate to all the engineers that our goal could only be achieved if Leo, the low-tech marketing wonk, could use the ARS system on his own computer to summon technical help without Ted's intervention.

As soon as we could explain this situation in terms of personas, the team members immediately understood that they needed to deemphasize Ted and concentrate all of their efforts on Leo. Ted occupies a role we call a *negative persona*. His existence helps us to understand whom we are *not* designing for.

⌘

We know that we have isolated a persona when we have discovered a person whose goals are unique. It isn't necessary that all of the persona's goals be different, but that its set of objectives is clearly different from everyone else's. Raul, who assembles lawnmowers on an assembly line, has different goals from Cicely, his production supervisor. Cicely wants to improve overall productivity and avoid accidents. Raul wants to get a reasonable quantity of work done without making any embarrassing mistakes. Although they share practical goals, their motivations are quite different. Raul wants stability. Cicely wants a promotion. Clearly, their goals are sufficiently different to demand the establishment of two separate personas.

Primary Personas

Every cast of characters has at least one primary persona. The primary persona is the individual who is the main focus of the design. To be primary, a persona is someone who *must* be satisfied but who cannot be satisfied with an interface designed for any other persona. An interface always exists for a primary persona. In the Remedy ARS example, Leo Pierce was the primary persona.

Identifying the primary persona or personas is a vital step in the development of a cast of characters. In my experience, each primary persona requires a separate and unique interface. If we identify two primary personas, we will end up designing two interfaces. If we identify three primary personas, we will end up designing three interfaces. If we identify four primary personas, we know that we have a big problem.

If we find more than three primary personas, it means that our problem set is too large and that we are trying to accomplish too much at one time. We create personas to narrow down the spectrum of users for whom we design. It follows that if the number of personas grows too much, we are defeating the purpose of creating personas in the first place.

The cast of characters is not just a convenient phrase; it becomes a physical—as well as logical—design tool. After winnowing down the population, we typically end up with anywhere from three to seven useful personas. We assemble all of them on a single sheet of paper containing their names, pictures, job descriptions, goals, and often telltale quotes. This one-page document becomes a ubiquitous part of our process. We print out copies of the cast of characters and distribute it at every meeting, whether or not the client is present. Every designer at all of our brainstorming meetings and all of our detailed design meetings has a cast-of-characters document in front of him at all times. When clients attend these meetings, extra copies are printed and presented to them. Every deliverable document that we create and give to our clients has a cast-of-characters page in it. Our goal is to make the personas unavoidable. They are so important that we cram them down everyone's throat.

It does no good to have good design and not express it in terms of the user personas. It is simply too easy to slip back into speaking about "the user" and lose the hard-won focus on specific archetypal users.

Case Study: Sony Trans Com's P@ssport

In 1997, Sony Trans Com approached us with a remarkable design problem. Sony Trans Com is Sony Corporation's Irvine, California, division, responsible for the design and manufacture of in-flight entertainment (IFE) systems. In-flight entertainment—movies, TV shows, and video games in commercial aircraft—is a large and lucrative business. Sony Trans Com had developed a new generation of technology that brought a new level of capability to airline passengers. The most impressive capability of the new system, called P@ssport, was true video-on-demand (VOD). VOD lets Tricia in seat 23A begin watching *When Harry Met Sally* 10 minutes after takeoff, and it lets Anna in seat 16C start the same movie 45 minutes later—and either passenger can pause or rewind the show without affecting the other.

P@ssport pushed the envelope of IFE well beyond the current technical state of the art. Each seat back contained a video screen and a Pentium computer running Windows 95. In the front of the plane was a powerful array of computers with copious memory for content. A fiber-optic cable connected each seat to the array, with connector boxes placed every few rows throughout the plane, making the system blindingly fast and breathtakingly powerful.

Sony had worked on this system for months before it asked us to help design the interaction. Although the engineers were making good progress, their designers were at an impasse. Just about anybody could occupy an airline seat, so they were trying to accommodate everyone from the total computer novice to the computer expert. They had no idea how to please all those constituencies. Neither did we, but we had our powerful design techniques, including personas, and were confident that we could solve the problem.

The Conventional Solution

Sony Trans Com had already designed and built a prototype of the P@ssport system with a conventional interface. It was very consistent with the program's internal structure—that is, it was very implementation model. Basically, it consisted of a deep hierarchical tree of screens through which the user had to navigate, making decisions at each screen. The evident shortcomings of this prototype are what prompted Sony to approach me.

Each screen represented another layer in the hierarchy, and it required six of them to examine each movie selection.

It was a classic example of what I call *uninformed consent*. At each step, the user is required to make a choice, the scope and consequences of which are unknown. At the first screen the user must choose an entertainment type: music, movies, games, shopping, and so on. Selecting "Video" makes all the other choices disappear, and the next screen demands that the user choose the category of film. The screens keep coming until, at the sixth level down, the user can see a brief preview of the movie and then choose to watch it or not. If she decides to pass, it's six clicks and six screens back up to the top, and then six clicks back down to view the next one. Whew!

Because P@ssport runs on a screen in each seat back, every user is within arm's length of the screen. It was instantly obvious that a touch screen was a great, natural solution, rather than using a handheld remote controller. But Sony rejected the idea anyway. Sony realized that—with six levels down and six levels up for each selection—it would take several dozen taps for the typical user to select entertainment. It realized that the person sitting in front would be enraged by all the tapping on the back of his or her head. In a classic example of what Po Bronson means when he says engineers will keep fixing what's not broken until it is broken, Sony discarded the touch-screen idea and reverted to a handheld controller tied to the seat with a short wire. It threw the baby out with the bathwater. The engineers regretted the decision but saw it as inevitable in light of their schedule constraints.

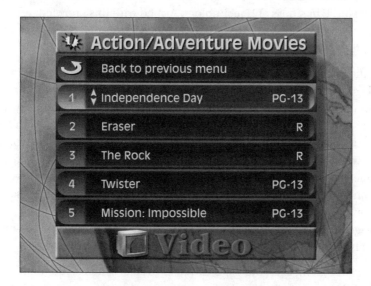

The six-screen interface was a classic example of implementation-model design, accurately reflecting the internal choices of the software. Each decision screen offered up very little context or supporting information, so the user never felt oriented, which made navigation a big problem. Each time the user drilled down into another layer, she lost the current context. After she committed to "Video" she was no longer able to select—or even see—the "Games" option. At each step of the way, the program was ignorant of the bigger picture, so it kept the user similarly ignorant. The user had to choose "Video" without knowing which or how many movies were available. She then had to choose a single category of movie, again without knowing what those categories meant. Is *True Lies* an adventure, a romance, or a comedy? When she is finally shown movie titles, she is bereft of information. Hmmm, *Eraser*, wasn't that an art film about a mild-mannered schoolteacher?

But even while still in the prototype stage, the interface had beautiful 3D graphics, very artistic icons, and a map-and-globe metaphoric theme—all the trappings of a good interface without the substance. It's what we call "painting the corpse."

Personas

As always, our design process began with a thorough investigation phase, consisting mostly of interviews, beginning inside Sony. We listened to most of the people working on the product, including the project manager, the development manager, a couple of the engineers, the product marketing manager, and the content manager. These interviews gave us a good idea of what Sony Trans Com wanted to accomplish with the product. It also gave us some historical perspective on past IFE business and technology. Armed with this knowledge, we shifted our interviewing process to the field. We listened to lots of airline personnel, particularly flight attendants from several airlines.

During the interview process, our design team kept inventing new personas. Every time a flight attendant would tell us a new story, we'd add another persona, until we had about 30. The more we listened, the more we learned, and eventually the similarities among the personas became apparent. As we found personas with common goals, we could collapse them into one. Eventually we narrowed the persona population down to 10; four passengers and six airline employees. As you might imagine, the airline employees with formally described jobs and responsibilities were pretty easy to understand and design for. The tough nut was the passenger persona. Each of the four passenger personas was an archetype in its own way, representing a broad segment of users, but you can't design an interface for four personas. You have to find the one common denominator. Here are the final four:

> *Chuck Burgermeister*, business traveler. A 100,000-mile-club member who flew somewhere practically every week. Chuck's vast experience with flying meant that he had little tolerance for complex, time-consuming interfaces, or interfaces that condescend to novices.
>
> *Ethan Scott*, 9-year-old boy. He was travelling unescorted for the first time. Ethan wanted to play games, games, and more games.
>
> *Marie Dubois*, bilingual business traveler. English was her second language. She liked to browse the shopping, as well as the entertainment selections.
>
> *Clevis McCloud*, crotchety septuagenarian. An aging but still spry Texan, slightly embarrassed about the touch of arthritis in his hands. He was the only one of the four passenger personas who didn't own a computer or know how to use one.

PASSENGERS

 Clevis McCloud
Age: 65, World Odyssey
Class

 Marie Dubois
Age: 31, Odyssey Club
Class

 Chuck Burgermeister
Age: 54, Odyssey Gold
Class

 Ethan Scott
Age: 9, World Odyssey
Class

ODYSSEY AIRLINES CREW

 Brent Covington
Age: 37, Purser

 Amanda Kent
Age: 28, Flight attendant

 Jean-Paul Duroc
Age: 33, Interpreter

 Molly Springer
Age: 41, Content renewal
specialist

 Mel "Hoppy" Hopper
Age: 51, Mechanic

 James A. Tattersall
Age: 47, Pilot

Our interface had to satisfy Chuck, Ethan, Marie, and Clevis while not making any one of them *unhappy.* But that didn't mean that we had to make all four of them exceptionally happy. Ethan knows that wanting to play games, games, games is something special, so he doesn't mind pressing an extra few buttons to obtain exactly what he wants, as long as he *can* obtain it. Chuck knows that his vast experience has earned him some shortcuts, but he is willing to put a little extra effort into learning and remembering those special commands.

Clevis turned out to be our common denominator. Clevis didn't have or want a computer. His motto was, "You can't teach an old dog new tricks." He wasn't stupid or lazy, just not an apologist for the antics of high technology. We knew that if we put a caption bar and close box on the screen, we would instantly lose Clevis. This meant that all computer-like interfaces were out of the question. We also knew that with his arthritis, no complex manipulation would be acceptable. He should be able to operate the system with the ball of his hand.

Any solution that focused on Chuck, Marie, or Ethan would be unacceptable to Clevis. Clevis would be scared and confused by Chuck's shortcuts and Marie's language-selection options. Ethan's twitch games would just get in Clevis's way. Yet a solution that made Clevis, the crotchety old Luddite, happy would be perfectly acceptable to Chuck, Ethan, and Marie, as long as their special needs were accommodated somewhere in the interface.

Chuck and Marie were old hands at flying, so they could find their way around any system, as long as it didn't involve a lot of time-consuming training screens for new users. We knew that if we made the system very simple and visual, it wouldn't involve a lot of interaction overhead, and Chuck and Marie wouldn't be offended. Ethan was easier, because we knew that he would quickly and aggressively explore the system to find out where everything was. As long as his games weren't hidden away somewhere, he'd be happy.

Throughout the entire design project, Clevis was our touchstone. His image became our battle standard. We knew that to make Clevis happy would mean that we would make any and every airplane customer happy. He was our primary persona, and we designed the system for him and him alone.

Designing for Clevis

Clevis had no experience with computers and no patience for the typical attitude of delayed gratification that most programs have. The solution to Clevis's navigation problem was simple: He could not and would not "navigate," so there could be only one screen. The solution to Clevis's reluctance to explore the interface meant that the product had to be very generous with information. We were parsimonious with choices but copious with information.

We turned the screen into a horizontally scrolling panoply of movie posters and album covers. We created a large, rotating knob—which we call a "data wheel"— that Clevis could spin like a station selector on a radio. This was an actual knob on the bezel of the screen, not an image of a knob drawn in pixels. As Clevis spins the data wheel, the posters scroll smoothly by, moving right if the knob is turned clockwise and left if it's turned counterclockwise.

Clevis views the posters going by, like strolling down Broadway peering into store windows. He never has to choose—or even think about—what category a movie is in. Because there was no tree of choices to traverse, we reinstated the touch screen without requiring woodpecker-like tapping. When Clevis sees a movie poster that interests him, he taps it once and immediately sees and hears a brief preview, along with written reviews, cast, crew, and pricing information. Clevis can then tap to watch the movie or tap to resume his leisurely stroll down Movie Street.

The scrolling movie posters are arranged in a manner we call a *monocline grouping*—a single layer of information organized into groups. We often replace interface hierarchies with them. The top of your desk is likely organized in a monocline grouping, as are your bookshelves and your bedroom drawers. People, including Clevis, Marie, Ethan, and Chuck, very quickly and easily grasp monocline groupings. Monocline grouping changes the "category" of movie from a *necessary choice* that must be made in advance into a *helpful attribute*. Clevis can peruse movie posters and see what category any given movie belongs to without committing to it. It also neatly solves the problem of selecting which category something is in. The movie *True Lies*, for example, is an action film, a star vehicle, an adventure, an effects showcase, a romance, and a comedy. A hierarchy would force it into just one of those categories, but in a monocline grouping, it can easily have all of them as attributes.

After Clevis scrolls through the movie posters, the images seamlessly change, first to album covers and then to game posters. There are few enough selections that Clevis can merely spin the knob and bring everything into view. The knob is large enough, and its motion coarse enough, that even Clevis, with his large, hard, oil-field hands with their touch of arthritis can still rotate it with ease. A navigation bar across the bottom of the screen informs Clevis that there are several broad categories of entertainment, and a small indicator on the bar moves to point to his place in the spectrum of choices.

The Sony programmers fell into the three-number trap of 0, 1, and infinity. The P@ssport system can handle, in practical terms, about three dozen movies. From a programmer's point of view, 36—being greater than either 0 or 1—is the same as infinity, and the idea of presenting an *infinity* of movies seemed problematic, so they divided them up into categories. But Clevis enjoys scrolling through the three dozen choices. Even if there were a few hundred movies, he'd still enjoy the leisurely browsing, remembering movies he had seen and anticipating seeing those he hadn't.

A lot of the value of the solution was in the posters, which convey significant information about each movie: the stars, the plot, the attitude. The engineers saw this but were concerned that offering up movie posters would create extra work for the content providers. When we broached the idea to some movie vendors, they reacted in just the opposite way. They were ecstatic at having the opportunity to get their posters into the interface. After all, they had spent hundreds of thousands of dollars to have experts produce a poster that conveyed, most informatively and concisely, as much information as possible about a film and appealed to the broadest audience. Why not put that to use on the airplane? They considered it a great new opportunity to produce bitmaps for the product.

Although we designed the passenger interface for our one primary passenger persona, we made certain to provide for the needs of the secondary passenger personas. Chuck Burgermeister, the frequent flyer, will want some shortcuts, and those are built into the interface so that Clevis won't even notice them. If Chuck wants to move between categories of entertainment more quickly than the data wheel allows, all he has to do is touch the navigation bar at the bottom of the screen. The program immediately jump-scrolls to that part of the monocline grouping without forcing Chuck to scroll there. Clevis never even needs to know about this ever-present idiom, yet it is very easy to discover and learn, and more-experienced travelers like Chuck and Marie will quickly pick up the trick, either from their own exploring or from watching others.

Unlike images on a screen, physical knobs and controls invite manipulation. When Clevis first sees the data wheel, he can easily intuit from its shape and orientation how to work it. Although Clevis cannot intuit its behavior, all it takes is a single, small turning, and its behavior and effects are instantly clear because an equal motion of the movie posters on the screen instantly echoes any motion of the wheel. More probably, Clevis will see some other passenger spin the wheel and see the image scroll in direct proportion. The one-to-one relationship between wheel and screen is instantly understood, and Clevis has learned how to use the system in an instant.

⌘

I've only described the interface we designed for Clevis McCloud, the passenger. We also designed two other large interfaces, one each for the other two primary personas: Amanda Kent, the flight attendant, and Mel "Hoppy" Hopper, the mechanic. Their goals are quite different from Clevis's.

After safety, Amanda must focus on ensuring that each passenger has the best experience possible. Her interface must provide control over all in-flight operations. For example, if Chuck in seat 24C wants to move because Clevis in 24B has fallen asleep and is snoring loudly, Amanda must be able to transfer Chuck's account and his half-viewed movie to 19D, the empty seat that he moves to.

Hoppy's main requirement is to assess rapidly the state of the system. He determines what is malfunctioning, how serious it is, and what he can do to fix it.

Both Amanda and Hoppy use the same screen at the flight attendant's station, but their interfaces are dramatically different because their goals are different.

⌘

If you want to design software-based products that make people happy, you have to know who those people are with some precision. That is the role that personas play. The next step is designing the product to be as powerful as possible, and for that, you need to know more about the user's goals.

10

DESIGNING FOR POWER

Goal-Directed design starts with the definition of user personas and their goals. In the last chapter, I described personas at length. In this chapter, I will give similar treatment to goals, showing how they can be identified and put to use as a potent design tool. The two are inseparable, like the obverse sides of a coin. A persona exists to achieve his goals, and the goals exist to give meaning to a persona.

Goals Are the Reason Why We Perform Tasks

Before the digital age confronted us with cognitive friction, design was mostly an aesthetic thing, and one person's opinion on the quality of a given design was as good as anyone else's. Cognitive friction comes with interaction, and interaction is only necessary if there is a purpose, a goal. In this new light, the nature of design changes. The aesthetic component isn't lessened in any way. It is merely diluted by the larger demands of achieving the user's goals. This means that, unlike in earlier times, the quality of design isn't so much a matter of opinion and is much more amenable to systematic analysis. In other words, in the bright light of a user's goals, we can learn quite directly what design would suit the purpose, regardless of anyone's opinion or, for that matter, of aesthetic quality.

"Good interaction design" has meaning only in the context of a person actually using it for some purpose. You cannot have purposes without people. The two are inseparable. That is why the two key elements of our design process are goals and personas—purposes and people.

What's more, the most important goals are personal ones, held only by the individual. Some real person is interacting with your product, not some abstract corporation, so you must regard people's personal goals as higher than the corporation's. Your users will do their best to achieve the business's goals, but only after their own personal ones are achieved. The most important personal goal is to retain one's dignity: to not feel stupid.

The essence of good interaction design is to devise interactions that let users achieve their practical goals without violating their personal goals.

Tasks Are Not Goals

Goals are not the same things as tasks. A goal is an end condition, whereas a task is an intermediate process needed to achieve the goal. It is very important not to confuse tasks with goals, but it is easy to mix them up.

If my goal is to laze in the hammock reading the Sunday paper, I first have to mow the lawn. My task is mowing; my goal is resting. If I could recruit someone else to mow the lawn, I could achieve my goal without having to do the mowing.

There is an easy way to tell the difference between tasks and goals. Tasks change as technology changes, but goals have the pleasant property of remaining very stable. For example, to travel from St. Louis to San Francisco, my goals are speed, comfort, and safety. Heading for the California gold fields in 1850, I would have made the journey in my new, high-tech Conestoga wagon. In the interest of safety, I would have brought my Winchester rifle. Heading from St. Louis to the Silicon Valley in 1999, I would make the journey in a new, high-tech Boeing 777. In the interest of safety, I would leave my Winchester rifle at home. My goals remain unchanged, but the tasks have so changed with the technology that they are in direct opposition.

This same pattern of directly opposing goals and tasks is easy to find. When the president desires peace overseas, he sends troops armed with guns, planes, and bombs. His task is war. His goal is peace. When a corporate lawyer wants to avoid conflict with a colleague, she argues with him over clauses in the contract. Her goal is accord, but her task is argument.

The goal is a steady thing. The tasks are transient. That is one reason why designing for tasks doesn't always suit, but designing for goals always does.

Programmers Do Task-Directed Design

Too many developers approach design by asking, "What are the tasks?" This may get the job done, but it won't come close to producing the best solution possible, and it won't satisfy the user at all. Designing from tasks instead of goals is one of the main causes of frustrating and ineffective interaction. Asking, "What are the user's goals?" lets us see through the confusion and create more appropriate and satisfactory designs.

Boiled down to its essence, computer programming is the creation of a detailed, step-by-step description of procedures. A procedure, of course, is a recipe for accomplishing a task. Good programmers, of necessity, see things procedurally, or task-wise. Ultimately, the tasks must get done to achieve the business goals, but there are different emphases and different sequences of doing them. Only some sequences satisfy the user's personal goals.

Goal-Directed Design

When interaction designers analyze goals to solve problems, they typically find very different—and much better—solutions.

Imagine Jennifer, an office manager in a small company. Her goal is to make her office run smoothly. Of course, she doesn't want to feel stupid or make mistakes, either. Toward those ends, she must make her computer network run smoothly. She must set it up properly, monitor its performance, and modify its configuration periodically to maintain its peak performance. In Jennifer's mind, her job is a seamless blending of these three *tasks*, contributing to her one *goal* of smooth running. From Jennifer's point of view, there is really no difference among the three tasks. She doesn't sense a big difference between initial setup and subsequent reconfiguration of the network.

Imagine Clancy, a software engineer, who must write the software that Jennifer uses. In Clancy's *Homo logicus* mind, Jennifer's software performs three tasks—three functions—and each will be implemented in a different chunk of software. It seems natural to Clancy that each function also has its own chunk of interface. It's only logical. Clancy is considering an interface with a hierarchical list of system components in the left-side pane, and—when a component in that list is selected—its details are shown in the right-side pane. This interface has the advantage of being approved by Microsoft, and it makes sense to programmers. The user will have to click on lots of system components to find out what is happening in the system, but all the necessary information is there *for the asking*.

Imagine Wayne, an interaction designer, who is charged with making both Jennifer and Clancy happy. In Wayne's designing mind, he knows that the software must represent itself to Jennifer in a way that most closely approximates her goals while ensuring that all of the necessary functions are present. (Jennifer is a primary persona.) Wayne also knows that he cannot specify anything that would create unreasonable or impossible effort for Clancy.

Wayne sees that Jennifer has only a single goal—smooth running—so he designs the interface so Jennifer can see at a glance that things are running smoothly. If some bottleneck occurs, Jennifer's interface clearly shows that *one* trouble spot in a prominent, visual way and lets her investigate and fix the problem by directly interacting with the onscreen representation of the troubled area. Wayne knows that—to Jennifer—there is no difference between monitoring the system and modifying it, and the interface reflects that perception. The only time that Jennifer ever has to ask about a component in her system is when she has already learned that there is a good reason for her to do so.

From Clancy's point of view, the code to show the performance of a component and the code to configure that component are two separate procedures. They have no connection in task-think. But in goal-think, they are intimately bound. Jennifer would never choose to reconfigure a component unless she were first apprised of a reason to reconfigure it by seeing a reduction in its performance. Further, Jennifer would always want to carefully monitor that component's performance level while she reconfigured it.

Designing for the user persona's goals clearly shows us an alternative way to think about delivering functionality. It frequently provides dramatically better ways to solve prosaic design problems. Here are some examples.

Goal-Directed Television News

On one of our projects, a client was working on an ensemble of applications that supported the creation of a television news show. From the engineer's task viewpoint, news shows are built the way bridges are built: one piece at a time. But we determined that the newscaster's goal wasn't to "build" a news show over time, but rather, it was to always *have* a news show that got better over time. Each news show is really a fluid and organic beast that begins and ends life fully grown.

In the news business, anything can happen, so the newscaster wants to always have a fallback position. His goal is to always have a reasonable, broadcastable show. The evening news show begins in the morning as a complete, ready-to-broadcast entity—22 full minutes (not including commercials)—and it always exists in a state of completion. Each story segment has a time allowance, and the segments always combine to total 22 minutes. Like a blurry image slowly coming into focus, the boundaries of the show never change, but the contents become sharper and more precise. From 10:00 a.m. on, the news show could be broadcast if need be, but it will be at its best sometime around 5:00 p.m.

Each news show consists of 20 to 30 news stories blocked out with cues, video clips, remotes, and studio presentations. As the morning progresses, the priority of each story shifts, and the presentation order and allotted time change to reflect the judgment of the news director. During the early afternoon, a breaking story might demand attention, altering the order of the other stories and probably even bumping some of them off the program entirely. The reporters and news director will be tweaking and changing the script up until the last second—sometimes into the broadcast itself.

The software engineers, looking at the problem from a task and procedure point of view, had created an application that allowed a news show to be built story segment by story segment. It was very logical, very reasonable, but very wrong. The news show wasn't a complete thing until immediately before broadcast, and a change to a single segment disrupted all of the other segments, leaving the show unbroadcastable until it was patched together again.

For our design work, we sketched an application that began with a ready-for-prime-time news show and allowed the reporters and news director to constantly tweak it, just as they worked in a manual world. But unlike the manual method, our design brought the power of the computer to bear. For example, if a segment were pulled at the last minute, the time allotted to it would be automatically distributed to the remaining stories in a weighted allocation scheme.

Goal-Directed Classroom Management

In another design project, we were asked to design a classroom-management system for elementary-school teachers. The engineers had provided facilities for testing students, tracking performance, and accessing a database of lesson plans. From a task point of view, things seemed adequate. We looked—metaphorically speaking—deep into the teacher's eyes to determine what the typical primary-school teacher really wanted and came up with a surprising answer.

We learned that teachers feel isolated in their classrooms and crave feedback on how they are doing. In order to improve, a teacher needs a way to measure her own performance. This simple need is not obvious when you decompose the teaching process into its component tasks. That human need is easily visible when you examine goals. In our design, we provided a facility that tracked the teacher's achievements from semester to semester and also from room to room. With this tool, the teachers had a better sense of continuity and progress, and their confidence in their work grew.

Personal and Practical Goals

Earlier in this chapter, I stated that the essence of good interaction design is to let users achieve their practical goals without violating their personal goals. *Homo logicus*, and their apologists, usually find it embarrassing to look too closely at personal goals, so they avoid it. However, the distinction between personal goals and practical goals is critical to success.

I'll use my colleague Ted as an example. He just sent me email complaining about his new television set. He spent an unpleasant hour reading the manual so he could properly set all of the TV's various parameters. He suggested to me that the TV should have provided an on-screen dialog box to step him through the procedure instead of forcing him to read the manual. His solution is fine as far as it goes, but—he is not a designer—he naturally tackled the problem the old mechanical-age way: by focusing on tasks. The on-screen dialogs would simpli-fy the task of setting parameters, but—by examining his goals instead—we use a different approach, which gives us a remarkably better solution.

We start by assessing Ted's goals, and it's always best to start at the top. Obviously, we know that Ted wants to watch TV. He just paid lots of money for a new set, so just as obviously, he wants to be able to take advantage of all of the set's nifty new features. These practical goals are directly related to the task of setting up a new TV set.

But we must never forget that Ted is a person and, as such, he has strong per-sonal feelings that can also be expressed as goals. Ted does not want his new pos-session to humiliate him; he does not want to be made to feel stupid. Ted does not want to make mistakes. He wants to have a feeling of accomplishment, the sooner the better. He wants to have some fun. These personal goals are vital. From an interaction designer's point of view, they are more important than Ted's practical goals.

Ted's complaint wasn't that he couldn't watch his new TV, or that he paid too much for it, or that he couldn't take advantage of all of those nifty new features. *He complained because the TV set made him feel stupid.* He didn't say it using those exact words because just saying "It made me feel stupid" makes one feel stupid, but that was clearly his meaning. While interacting with it, he accidental-ly made mistakes. It took him more than an hour after he plugged it in to have any sense of accomplishment. The parameter-setting process wasn't fun.

While meeting Ted's practical goals, the product's interaction violated Ted's most important personal goals. The specific qualities that make Ted's new TV set a classic example of a new, high-tech, dancing bearware product are not the way it achieves his practical goals, but the way it *fails* to achieve his personal goals.

Armed with the knowledge that Ted's personal goals are sacred, here's how we would design a very different interface for the TV. First, to quickly give him a sense of accomplishment, we must make certain that the TV works well the instant it is plugged in. It doesn't have to do *everything*, but it has to do *something* and do it well. Clearly, putting Ted through the parameter-setting process first fails this instant-gratification test. The software engineers see all parameters as equal, so they lump them together. But we can easily assume some parameter settings, letting the TV do the basic stuff, and delay the need for other, advanced feature parameters until later. We have to unlump the parameters. This is not a technical problem, just a simple reshuffling of interaction priorities.

Our design now fits the definition of a success: Ted could take the TV out of its box, plug it into the wall, and immediately relax in his easy chair to channel surf contentedly, having achieved most of his practical goals without violating any of his personal goals.

Notice that although he doesn't have to achieve *all* of his practical goals at once, he must never find *any* of his personal goals violated. This difference also illustrates the complementary notions of *designing for* and *providing for*. The interaction-design solution must provide ways for Ted to achieve all of his practical goals, but the design must strongly emphasize ways for Ted to achieve his personal goals.

The Principle of Commensurate Effort

Of course, after a while, Ted's desire to fully achieve the practical goal of taking advantage of all those nifty new features would begin to assert itself. But by then he would have spent many happy hours with his new set, would be familiar with it, and would be willing to invest more effort. It would now be harder for the set to humiliate him, his tolerance for its interaction would be greater, and he would have a more precise understanding of exactly what he wants it to do.

It is a proven human trait that people react emotionally to computers (more on this later in the chapter). Because people interact with computers, they naturally regard them as somewhat human. Ted is willing to put more effort into configuring his TV because he feels that the TV has put effort into making *him* feel good.

I call this phenomenon the Principle of Commensurate Effort. People are willing to put effort into tasks because they feel that it is a fair exchange between equals. In other words, users are willing to invest extra effort because they know they will get extra rewards for it.

Personal Goals

Let's look at goals in more detail. I've already introduced two types of goals—personal and practical—but there are also corporate and false goals. Personal goals are simple, universal and, well, personal. Paradoxically, this makes them difficult for many people to talk about, especially in the context of impersonal business.

> **PERSONAL GOALS**
> Not feel stupid
> Not make mistakes
> Get an adequate amount of work done
> Have fun (or at least not be too bored)

Apologists, in general, are very troubled with "not feel stupid." They are proud, intelligent people, and they thrive on confronting complex situations and mastering them. Hmm, sounds a lot like high-tech, Silicon Valley entrepreneurs to me. For example, as a courtesy, after writing down Ted's new-TV story, I sent it to him (he's an accomplished, independent, high-tech entrepreneur), and he replied:

> I wouldn't say I'm made to feel stupid grappling with the 40-page manual. It's more a situation of wanting to be spared the aggravation of spending time on unwanted tasks—indeed, on learning things that might have to be *relearned* again later. (Will a power outage, for example, require reprogramming, with reference to the manual again?)

Ted is an apologist. To even say the S-word impugns his ability to master the TV set in spite of its difficulty. He'll admit to aggravation, time wasting, or needless redundancy, but not to even the appearance of stupidity, which is why I am reluctant to substitute another word. I use "stupid" precisely because it *is* so difficult for competent, intelligent, hard-charging, type-A, Silicon Valley software gurus to say it. As they do say, the first step to fixing the problem is admitting that one exists.

Personal goals are always true and operate to varying extents for everyone. Personal goals always take precedence over any other goals, although—precisely because they are personal—they are rarely discussed. When software makes users feel stupid, their self-esteem droops and their effectiveness plummets, regardless of their other goals. Any system that violates personal goals will ultimately fail, regardless of how well it achieves other goals.

Corporate Goals

Businesses have their own requirements for software, and they are as high level as the personal goals of the individual. "To increase our profit" is pretty fundamental to the board of directors or the stockholders. The designer uses these goals to stay focused on the bigger issues and to avoid getting distracted by tasks or other false goals.

CORPORATE GOALS
Increase our profit
Increase our market share
Defeat our competition
Hire more people
Offer more products or services
Go public

Psychologists who study the workplace have a term, *hygienic factors*, which Saul Gellerman[1] defines as "prerequisites for effective motivation but powerless to motivate by themselves." The lights in your office, for example, are hygienic factors. You don't go to work because the lights are nice, but if there were no lights at all, you wouldn't bother showing up.

I have adapted this term as *hygienic goals*, which I define as goals prerequisite for effective functioning but powerless to motivate by themselves. All of the corporate and practical goals shown in the list are hygienic. From the corporation's point of view they are important goals, but the corporation isn't doing the work; people are, and their personal goals are dominant.

There is a close parallel between corporate and personal goals: Both are the highest expressions of goals for their respective owners. Neither can be slighted. Software that fails to achieve either one will fail.

Practical Goals

Practical goals bridge the gap between the objectives of the company and the objectives of the individual user. The corporation wants everyone working hard to maximize the corporate bottom line. The practical goal of handling the client's demands connects the corporate goal of higher profits with the user's personal goal of being productive.

PRACTICAL GOALS
Avoid meetings
Handle the client's demands
Record the client's order
Create a numerical model of the business

Practical goals have more appeal than the touchy-feely personal goals, especially to sober businesspeople and nerdy programmers. True to their nature, they

---

[1] *Saul W. Gellerman,* Motivation and Productivity; *Amacom, New York, 1963, ISBN 0-8144-5084-9.*

create software that—although it admirably fulfills the practical goals—fails utterly to satisfy the individual user. A task-based interface can provoke users to make mistakes and obstruct their ability to be personally productive, making them feel bad about themselves and the software.

Of course your software has to have the features built into it to accomplish the goals of the business. The user must perform the tasks necessary to handle clients' demands and process orders, but these are only hygienic, because offering these features without addressing the user's personal goals will fail. If the user fails to achieve her own personal goals, she cannot effectively achieve the company's. It is a simple fact of human nature that happy, satisfied workers are more effective ones. This is truer than ever in the modern information economy, in which the true assets of a company are human and not mechanical. On the other hand, if your software ignores practical goals and serves *only* the user's goals, you will have just designed a computer game.

False Goals

Most of the software-based products we use every day are created with false goals in mind. Many of these goals ease the task of software creation, which is a programmer's goal, and this is why they get promoted at the expense of the software's user. Other false goals have to do with tasks, features, and tools. They are means to ends, but not ends in themselves, and *goals are always ends.*

> **FALSE GOALS**
> Save memory
> Save keystrokes
> Run in a browser
> Be easy to learn
> Safeguard data integrity
> Speed up data entry
> Increase program-execution efficiency
> Use cool technology or features
> Increase graphic beauty
> Maintain consistency across platforms

A target like "safeguarding data integrity" isn't a goal for a personal mailing-list program the same way it might be for a program that calculates shuttle orbits. A target like "saving memory" isn't very important for personal-computer database-query programs because downloads are small and computers are big. Even a target like "being easy to learn" isn't always a primary goal. For example, a fighter pilot who found it easy to learn to use her weapons systems, but then found them slow and cumbersome to operate, would be at a distinct disadvantage in an aerial dogfight.

Her goal is to emerge from combat victorious, not to have an easy time in flight instruction.

Since the invention of the microprocessor, the computer revolution has surfed a wave of new technology. Any company that ignores new technical ideas is doomed. But don't confuse these techniques with goals. It might be a software company's *task* to use new technology, but it is never a user's *goal* to do so. As a user, I don't care if I get my job done with hierarchical databases, relational databases, object-oriented databases, flat-file systems, or black magic. All I care about is getting my job done swiftly with a modicum of ease and dignity.

For example, in 1996 the Visioneer Company carved out a big share of the desktop-scanner market from well-entrenched competitors. Visioneer accomplished this remarkable feat with an old-fashioned black-and-white scanner, while its competition could scan either gray-scale or full color. But Visioneer's product included Goal-Directed software that allowed users to easily view and manage their scanned images, while the others' software merely dumped the scans into the complicated file system.

Computers Are Human, Too

Clifford Nass and Byron Reeves, two professors at Stanford University, study people's responses to computers. By cleverly repurposing classic experiments in social psychology, they observed some remarkable behavior. They have published their findings in a book entitled *The Media Equation.*[2] They have demonstrated conclusively that humans react to computers in the same way that they react to other humans.

Nass and Reeves say that "people are not evolved to twentieth-century technology," and that "modern media now engage old brains.... Consequently, any medium that is close enough will get human treatment, even though people know it's foolish and even though they likely will deny it afterward." To our human minds, computers behave less like rocks and trees than they do like humans, so we unconsciously treat them like people, even when we "believe it is not reasonable to do so."

In other words, humans have special instincts that tell them how to behave around other sentient beings, and as soon as *any* object exhibits sufficient cognitive friction, those instincts kick in and we react as though we were interacting with another sentient human being. This reaction is unconscious and unavoidable, and it applies to everyone. With deep and amusing irony, Nass and Reeves used as test subjects many computer-science grad students skilled enough to

---

[2] *Byron Reeves and Clifford Nass,* The Media Equation; How People Treat Computers, Television, and New Media Like Real People and Places, *Cambridge University Press, 1996, ISBN 1-57586-052-X.*

have coded up the test programs themselves. These subjects were highly educat-ed, mature, and rational individuals, and they all strongly denied being emo-tionally affected by cognitive friction, even though the objective evidence was incontrovertible.

Harvard cognitive neuroscientist Steven Pinker corroborates this thesis in his remarkable book, *How the Mind Works.* He says, "People hold many beliefs that are at odds with their experience but were true in the environment in which we evolved, and they pursue goals that subvert their own well-being but were adap-tive in that environment."[3]

Designing for Politeness

One important implication of the research is remarkably profound: If we want users to like our software, we should design it to behave like a likeable person. If we want users to be productive with our software, we should design it to behave like a good human work mate. Simple, huh?

Nass and Reeves say that software should be "polite" because this is a universal human behavioral trait. (Which actions are considered polite might vary from culture to culture, but the trait is present in all cultures.) Our high-cognitive-friction products should follow this simple lead and also be polite. Many high-tech products interpret politeness to mean that it's okay to behave rudely as long as they say "please" and "thank you," but that is emphatically not what politeness is all about.

---

[3] *Steven Pinker,* How the Mind Works, *W.W. Norton & Company, 1997, ISBN 0-393-04535-8. I absolutely love this wonderful, eye-opening, literate, amusing, readable book.*

If the software is stingy with information, obscures its process, forces the user to hunt around for common functions, and is quick to blame the user for its own failings, the user will dislike the software and have an unpleasant experience. This will happen regardless of "please" and "thank you"—regardless, too, of how cute, representational, visually metaphoric, content-filled, or anthropomorphic the software is.

On the other hand, if the interaction is respectful, generous, and helpful, the user will like the software and have a pleasant experience. Again, this will happen regardless of the composition of the interface; a green-screen command-line interface will be well liked if it can deliver on these other points.

What Is Polite?

What exactly does it mean for software to be friendly or polite? What does it mean for software to behave more like humans? Used-car salesmen wear handsome clothes, smile broadly, and are filled with impressive information, but does that make them likeable? Humans are error prone, slow, and impulsive, but it doesn't follow that software with *those* traits is good. Human beings have many other qualities that are present only conditionally but that make them well suited to the service role. Software is always in the service role.[4]

Most good software engineers are at a disadvantage in the politeness realm. Robert X. Cringely says that programmers

> …are expressive and precise in the extreme but only when they feel like it. They look the way they do as a deliberate statement about personal priorities, not because they're lazy. Their mode of communication is so precise that they can seem almost unable to communicate. Call a nerd Mike when he calls himself Michael and he likely won't answer, since you couldn't possibly be referring to him.[5]

You can see how the concept of "politeness" or even "humanness" can be a stumbling block when we ask programmers to be the interpreters of such fuzzy concepts. They struggle with the idea of making computers behave more like humans, because they see humans as weak and imperfect computing devices.

I asked my friend Keith Pleas, who is well known in the engineering community as an articulate, expert programmer sensitive to user-interface issues, about making software more human. Keith interpreted adding "humanness" as adding imprecision to the interaction. He replied:

---

[4] *Games are a notable exception to this rule. Many games just wouldn't be fun unless facts were hidden, processes were obscured, and goals were unclear.*

[5] *Robert X. Cringely,* Accidental Empires, How the Boys of Silicon Valley Make Their Millions, Battle Foreign Competition, and Still Can't Get a Date, *Addison-Wesley, 1992, ISBN: 0-201-57032-7.*

> Would a computer "lie" to you? Would a computer say you have "about $500" in your checking account? Would a computer give you a different answer than it just gave someone else? If we enhance the humanness, some of the computer-ness will be reduced, at least in comparison.

Keith's response is natural from the programmer's point of view. True, the computer would never give you an approximate bank balance, but then the computer wouldn't differentiate between taking one tenth of a second to say you have "about $500" in your account, versus taking 17 minutes to say you have "exactly $503.47." A really polite, more-human program would immediately say you have "about $500" and then inform you it will give you a more precise figure in a few additional minutes. Now it would be *your* choice whether to invest more time for additional precision. This is an application of the principle of commensurate effort; if you want more information you will sympathize with the need to spend more time.

What Makes Software Polite?

Humans have many wonderful characteristics that make them "polite" but whose definitions are fuzzy and imprecise. Nass and Reeves say that the "four basic principles that constitute the rules for polite interaction [are] quality, quantity, relevance, and clarity." Those are good but a little too vague to be helpful. Here is my list of what improves the quality of interaction, either with a human or a high-tech, software-based product rich in cognitive friction.

> Polite software is interested in me
> Polite software is deferential to me
> Polite software is forthcoming
> Polite software has common sense
> Polite software anticipates my needs
> Polite software is responsive
> Polite software is taciturn about its personal problems
> Polite software is well informed
> Polite software is perceptive
> Polite software is self-confident
> Polite software stays focused
> Polite software is fudgable
> Polite software gives instant gratification
> Polite software is trustworthy

Polite Software Is Interested in Me

A friend would ask about me and be interested in who I am and what I like. He would remember my likes and dislikes so he could please me in the future. Any supportive service provider would make an effort to learn to recognize the face and name of her customers. Some people appreciate being greeted by name and some don't, but everyone appreciates being treated according to his own personal tastes.

Most software doesn't know or care who is using it. In fact, none of the *personal* software on my *personal* computer seems to remember either me or anything about me. This is true in spite of the fact that it is constantly, repetitively, and exclusively used by me. Larry Keeley jokes that the automatic-flush urinal in an airport bathroom is more aware of his presence than his desktop computer is.

Every bit of my PC's personal software should work hard to remember my work habits, and particularly, everything that I say to it. To the programmer writing the program, it's a just-in-time information world, so whenever the program needs some tidbit of information, it simply demands that the user provide it. But the thoughtless program then discards that tidbit, assuming that it can merely ask for it again if it ever needs it. Not only is the computer better suited to doing the remembering, but it is impolite for it to forget.

For example, there are 11 people named Dave in my email program's name-and-address directory. I rarely communicate with most of them, but they include my best friend Dave Carlick, to whom I send email all of the time. When I create a new email and type an ambiguous "Dave" in the TO: block, I expect the program to have learned from my past behavior that I mean Dave Carlick. If I want to send something to another Dave—David Fore, for example—I'll type in "Dave F," "D4," "David Fore" or something else to indicate my out-of-the-ordinary choice. Instead, the program behaves stupidly, always putting up a dialog box and making me choose which of the 11 Daves I mean. The program just doesn't care about me and treats me like a stranger even though I'm the only human it knows.

Polite Software Is Deferential to Me

Any good service person defers to her client. She understands the person she is serving is the boss, and whatever the boss wants, the boss should get. When a restaurant host shows me to a table in a restaurant, I consider his choice of table to be a suggestion, not an order. If I politely demur and choose another table in an otherwise empty restaurant, I expect to be accommodated immediately. If the host refuses, I am likely to walk out and choose another restaurant where *my* desires take precedence over the host's.

Impolite software supervises the assumed-to-be-incompetent human's actions. It's okay for the software to express its *opinion* that I'm making a mistake, but it is not okay for it to judge my actions. Likewise, it is all right for software to *suggest* that I cannot "submit" my entry until I've entered my Social Security number, but if I go ahead and "submit" without it anyway, I expect the software to do as it is told. (The very word *submit* and the concept it stands for are a reversal of the deferential role. The software should submit to the user, and any program that proffers a Submit button is, ipso facto, impolite. Take notice, most every active site on the World Wide Web.)

Polite Software Is Forthcoming

At the airport, if I ask an airline employee at which gate I can find Flight 79, I would expect him not only to answer my question, but also to volunteer the extremely useful collateral information that Flight 79 is 20 minutes late.

If I order food at a restaurant, it should be obvious that I also want a knife, fork, and spoon, a glass of water, salt, pepper, and a napkin.

Most software won't do this. Instead, it only narrowly answers the precise questions we ask it, and it is typically not very forthcoming about other information even if it is clearly related to my goals. When I tell my word processor to print my document, it never tells me that the paper supply is low or that 40 other documents are queued up before me, but a helpful human would.

Polite Software Has Common Sense

Although any good restaurant will happily let you tour its kitchen, the hostess's simple common sense directs you to the dining room instead when you first walk in the front door. Most software-based products don't seem to differentiate between kitchen and dining room, putting controls for constantly used functions adjacent to never-used controls. You can commonly find menus offering simple, harmless functions along with deadly, irreversible ejector-seat-lever functions that should only be used by trained professionals. It's like seating you at a dining table right next to the grill.

Offering inappropriate functions in inappropriate places is a hallmark of software-based products. The panic button on my car's remote keyless entry is a fine example of this lack of common sense. The earlier "about $500" example is a good illustration of putting common sense to work in an interface.

There are numerous horror stories of customers permanently offended by irrationally rational computer systems that repeatedly sent them checks for $0.00 or bills for $8,943,702,624.23. Most of the customer-service nightmares have gone away through the judicious isolation of customers from computer systems, but most employees still have to interact with computers. The employees are paid for doing so, so they tend not to complain too loudly, and they typically have no one to complain to—the customer-service department is normally not for them.

Polite Software Anticipates My Needs

My assistant knows that I will require a hotel room when I travel to another city to a conference. She knows this even though I don't explicitly tell her so. She knows that I like a quiet, nonsmoking room, too, and will request one for me without any mention on my part. She anticipates my needs.

My Web browser spends most of its time idling while I peruse various Web sites. It could so easily anticipate my needs and prepare for them instead of just wasting time and effort. Why can't it use that idle time to preload links that are visible? Chances are good that I will soon ask the browser to examine one or more of those links. It is easy to abort an unwanted request, but always time consuming to wait for a request to be filled. If the program were to anticipate my desires by getting prepared for my requests during the time it would otherwise be idling, waiting for my commands, it could be much more responsive without needing a faster Internet connection.

Polite Software Is Responsive

When I am dining in a restaurant, I expect the waiter to respond appropriately to my nonverbal cues. When I am deeply engaged in intense conversation with my tablemates, I expect the waiter to attend to other duties. It would be highly inappropriate for the waiter to interrupt our discussion to say, "Hello, my name is Raul, and I'll be your waitperson for the evening." On the other hand, when our table conversation has ended and I am swiveling my head and trying to make eye contact with Raul, I expect him to hustle over to my table to see what I want.

My computer normally runs in a video mode that gives me 1024×768 pixels onscreen. When I do presentations, I am required to change temporarily to 800×600-pixel mode to accommodate the lower resolution of my video projector. Many of the programs that I run, including Windows 2000, react to the lowered resolution by changing their window size, shape, and placement on the screen. However, I invariably and quickly change my computer back to 1024×768-pixel mode. But the windows that changed to accommodate the lower resolution don't automatically change back to their previous settings for the higher-resolution screen. The information is there, but the program just doesn't care about responding to my obvious needs.

Polite Software Is Taciturn About Its Personal Problems

In saloons, salons, and psychiatrists' offices, the barkeep, hairdresser, and doctor are expected to keep mum about their problems and to show a reasonable interest in yours. It might be unfair to be so one-sided, but that's the nature of the service business. Software, too, should keep quiet about its problems and show interest in mine. Because computers don't have egos or tender sensibilities, they should be perfect for the role of confidant—but they typically behave the opposite way.

Software is always whining at me with confirmation dialog boxes and bragging to me with unnecessary little status bars. I don't want or need to know how hard the computer is working. I am not interested in the program's crisis of confidence about whether to purge its recycle bin. I don't want to hear its whining about not being sure where to put a file on disk. I don't need to hear the modem whistling or see information about the computer's data-transfer rates and its loading sequence, any more than I need information about the bartender's divorce, the hairdresser's broken-down car, or the doctor's alimony payments.

Two issues are lurking here. Not only should the software keep quiet about its problems, but it should also have the intelligence, confidence, and authority to fix its problems on its own.

Polite Software Is Well Informed

On the other hand, we all need more information about what is going on. That same barkeep helps me out by posting his prices in plain sight on the wall and also writing on the chalkboard what time the pregame party begins on Saturday morning, along with who's playing and the current Vegas spread.

Shopkeepers need to keep their customers informed of issues that might affect them. I don't want my butcher to tell me on November 21 that he is out of Thanksgiving turkeys. I want to know well in advance that the supply is limited and that I need to place my order early.

When I search a topic on the Web using a typical search engine, I never know when link rot will make the engine's findings useless. I'll click on the URL of something I'd like to see, only to get a nasty "404 Link Not Found" error message. Why can't the engine periodically check each link to see if it still exists? If it has rotted away, the useless entry can be purged from the index so I won't waste my time waiting for it.

Programs constantly offer me choices that, for some reason, are not currently available. The program should know this and not put them in front of me.

Polite Software Is Perceptive

The concierge at a hotel I frequent in New York noticed my interest in Broadway shows. Now, whenever I visit, the concierge—without my asking—puts a handy listing of the current Broadway shows in my room. She was perceptive enough to notice my interest, and this allows her to anticipate my desires and provide me with information I want before I even think about it. It takes very little effort for the concierge to exploit the value of her acute perceptions, yet it draws me back to this hotel again and again.

Whenever I use an application, I always maximize it to use the entire available screen. I then use the Windows taskbar to change from one program to another. But the applications I run don't seem to notice this fact, especially new ones. I frequently have to tell them to maximize themselves even though they should be able to see that my preference is clear and unequivocal. Other users keep their applications in smaller windows so they can see icons on their desktop. This is just as easy for software to spot and anticipate.

Polite Software Is Self-Confident

I expect the service people with whom I interact to have courage and confidence. If they see me emerge from the men's room with my fly unzipped, I want someone to tell me quickly, clearly, and unobtrusively before I walk into the ballroom to give my speech. It takes some courage to do this, but it is courage appreciated. Likewise, if my assistant can't book me the flight I want, I expect him to confidently book something very close to the one I want without bothering me with details.

If I tell the computer to discard a file, I don't want it to come back to me and ask, "Are you sure?" Of course I'm sure, otherwise I wouldn't have asked. I want it to have the courage of its convictions and go ahead and delete the file.

On the other hand, if the computer has any suspicion that I might be wrong (which, of course, is always), it should anticipate my changing my mind and be fully prepared to undelete the file. In either case, the product should have confidence in its own actions and not weasel, whine, and pass the responsibility off onto me.

I have often worked on a document for a long time, clicked the Print button, and then gone to get a cup of coffee while it prints out. Then I return to find a mindless and fearful dialog box quivering in the middle of the screen asking me, "Are you sure you want to print?" This insecurity is infuriating and the antithesis of polite human behavior.

Polite Software Stays Focused

When I order salad in a good restaurant, they bring me a good salad. In a bad restaurant, I get the third degree along with it: "Spinach, Caesar, or mixed greens? Onions? Croutons? Grated cheese? Parmesan or Romano? Full serving or dinner size? French, Italian, oil and vinegar, or Thousand Island? Dressing on the side? Served before or after the main course?" Even the most demanding gourmet just doesn't care that much about the salad to be subjected to such a grilling, but interactive systems behave this way all of the time. Adobe's Photoshop program is notorious for peppering the user with lots of obnoxious and unnecessary little questions, each one in a separate dialog box.

Impolite software asks lots of annoying questions. Choices are generally not all that desirable, and being offered them is not a benefit but an ordeal.

Choices can be offered in different ways, too. They can be offered in the way that we window-shop. We peer in the window at our leisure, considering, choosing, or ignoring the goods offered to us. Alternatively, choices can be forced on us like a hostile interrogation by a customs officer at a border crossing—*"Do you have anything to declare?"*—with the full knowledge that we can dissemble as much as we like, but the consequences for getting caught can be more than just embarrassing. We don't know the consequences of the question. Will we be searched or not? If we know that a search is unavoidable, we would never lie. If we know there will be no search, we would be tempted to smuggle in that extra carton of Marlboros.

Polite Software Is Fudgable

When manual information-processing systems are translated into computerized systems, something is always lost in the process. Manual systems are typically computerized to increase their capacity, not to change their functionality. But manual systems are typically very flexible, which is not a function that can easily be isolated. An automated order-entry system can handle millions more orders than a human clerk can, but the human clerk has the ability to *work* the system.

In an automated system, the ability to *work* the system disappears. There is almost never a way to jigger the functioning to give or take slight advantages.

In a manual system, when the clerk's friend from the sales force calls on the phone and explains that getting the order processed speedily means additional business, the clerk can expedite that one order. When another order comes in with some critical information missing, the clerk can go ahead and process it, remembering to acquire and record the information later. Typically, this flexibility is absent in computerized systems.

In computerized systems, there are only two states—nonexistence and full compliance—and no intermediate states are recognized or accepted. In any manual system, there is an important but paradoxical state—unspoken, undocumented, but widely relied upon—of *suspense*, wherein a transaction can be accepted while still not being fully processed. The human operator creates that state in his head, on his desk, or in his back pocket.

For example, a digital system needs both customer and order information before it can post an invoice. The human clerk can go ahead and post an order in advance of detailed customer information, but the computerized system will reject the transaction, unwilling to allow the invoice to be entered without it.

I call this human ability to take actions out of sequence or before prerequisites are satisfied *fudgability*. It is typically one of the first casualties when systems are computerized, and its absence is a key contributor to the inhumanity of digital systems. It is a natural result of implementation model. The programmers don't see any reason to create intermediate states because the computer has no need for them. Yet there are strong human needs to be able to bend the system slightly.

One of the big benefits of a fudgable system is the reduction of mistakes. Much bigger, more-permanent mistakes are avoided by allowing many small, temporary mistakes into the system and entrusting and helping the human to correct them before they cause problems downstream. Paradoxically, most of the hard-edged rules enforced by computer systems are imposed to prevent just such mistakes. These inflexible rules cast the human and the software as adversaries, and because the human is prevented from fudging to prevent big mistakes, he soon stops caring about protecting the software from really colossal problems. When inflexible rules are imposed on flexible humans, both sides lose. It is invariably bad for business to prevent humans from doing what they want, and the computer system usually ends up having to digest invalid data anyway.

⌘

Fudgability is one of the few human-politeness traits that can be difficult to build into a computer system. Fudgability demands a much more capable interface. In order to be fudgable, systems have to reveal their process to the moderately skilled observer. The clerk cannot move a form to the top of the queue unless the queue, its size, its ends, the form, and its position can be easily seen. Then the tools for pulling a form out of the electronic stack and placing it on the top must be present. These have to be made as visible as they are in a manual system, where it can be as simple as moving a sheet of paper. Physically, fudgability requires extra facilities to hold records in suspense, but an undo facility has very similar requirements. The real problem is that it admits the potential for fraud and abuse.

Fudging the system can be construed as fraud. It is technically a violation of the rules. In the manual world, fudging is tacit and winked at. It is assumed to be a very temporary, very special case, and the fudger will tidy up all such accounts before leaving for the night, vacation, or another job. Certainly, all such examples are cleaned up before the auditors are allowed in. If this process of temporary rule suspension were well known, it might encourage people to use the technique to the point of abuse.

Especially if the fudging has been documented in detail in the company manual, investing it with respectability, those with weaker characters might see in it a way to avoid doing accurate and complete work, or they might see in it a way to defraud the company of money. It is not fiscally responsible for the company to support fudging.

But fudgability has a powerful effect on the way users regard the system. All of the reasons for not having a fudgable system are very rational and logically defensible (probably legally defensible, too). Unfortunately, the idealized state of affairs that they describe is simply not an accurate description of the way the world works. Everyone in all areas of business uses the fudgability of manual systems to keep the wheels of business—of life—greased and turning easily. It is vital that automated systems be imbued with this quality despite the obstacles.

The saving grace with respect to abuse is that the computer also has the power to audit all of the user's actions easily, recording them in detail for any outside observer. The principle is a simple one: Let the user do whatever he wants, but keep very detailed records of those actions so that full accountability is easy.

Polite Software Gives Instant Gratification

Computer programming is all about deferred gratification. Computers do nothing until you've put enormous effort into first writing a program. Software engineers slowly internalize this principle of deferred gratification, and they tend to write programs that behave in the same way. Programs make users enter all possible information before they do even the tiniest bit of work. If another human behaved that way, you'd actively dislike him.

We can make our software significantly more polite by ensuring that it works for, and provides information to, the user without demanding a lot of up-front effort. Ted's TV should let him watch programs before it makes him configure parameters.

Polite Software Is Trustworthy

Friends establish trust with one another by being dependable and by a willingness to give of themselves. When computers behave erratically and are reluctant to work for users, no trust is generated. Whereas I trust the bank teller because she smiles at me and knows my name, I always count my cash at the ATM because I simply don't trust the obtuse machine.

⌘

Our software-based products irritate us because they aren't polite, not because they lack features. As the preceding list of polite-software characteristics shows, polite software is usually no harder to build than impolite software. It simply means that someone has to envision interaction that emulates the qualities of a sensitive and caring friend. None of these characteristics is at odds with the other, more obviously pragmatic goals of business computing. Behaving more human can be the most pragmatic of all.

Case Study: Elemental Drumbeat

One of our more interesting design projects was for a small start-up company in San Diego named Elemental Software. Its product, Drumbeat, is an authoring tool for creating dynamic, database-backed Web sites.

The cast of characters we developed for Elemental was indispensable, even though it consisted of only two very simply defined personas lacking even last names.[6] By creating these two personas and understanding their goals, we gained radical insight that changed the entire design philosophy of the product.

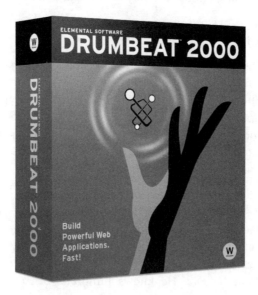

From the beginning, Elemental had set its sights high. Elemental wanted to create a program that was far more powerful than any other competitor's. It also wanted to make its program easier to use than any other. These goals were not at all incompatible. Most of the trouble we had arose because Elemental had acquired an existing product from another company, and we had to build on top of an existing code base. There was constant confusion between what we wanted and what we already had.

The existing product had some powerful features, but it had been constructed with a muddy user vision. None of the features was easy to use, and the effect was

---

[6] *Actually, the full cast of characters had more than two personas, but Betsy and Ernie stole the show.*

a not-very-powerful product. Ed Forman, the new VP of development, took a gamble by bringing in Cooper Interaction Design. He was himself new enough that he hadn't fully earned the trust of his new programming staff, and our presence could have ignited revolution. Ed was an excellent champion, however, and he gave us considerable time with his team to get to know them and to let them hear about our methods.

The Investigation

For our investigation, we interviewed several people, primarily Webmasters. As we proceeded, we saw a clear pattern emerge. The world of Web authoring was neatly divided into two camps. Of course, we defined a representative persona for each camp, and these two became the keys that unlocked the entire Drumbeat puzzle, though not in the way we anticipated.

Within just a few days of starting, we were able to name and roughly describe our two Web builders, named Betsy and Ernie.

Betsy is an artist. She wears black and drinks espresso. She used to be a graphic artist but got bitten by the Web bug, and now she creates screen layouts instead of page layouts. She has read enough books to teach herself how to build nice-looking—but simple and static—Web pages. She has mastered the basics of HTML, but she knows—and cares—nothing of programming. Betsy's own Web site is a model of cool hipness, with subdued typography, swathes of asymmetrical pastels, and quotes from Patti Smith and Esther Dyson.

Every time Betsy needs some advanced processing, she must appeal to Ernie. Ernie is a new-age programmer geek. He loves computers, computer games, computer languages, and computer equipment. Compared to older programmers, he's still kind of lightweight: He doesn't know C, C++, or assembler language, but he is an incredibly facile user of hacker tools such as CGI, Perl, JavaScript, and Visual Basic. He knows hundreds of ActiveX controls and JavaBeans. He can assemble a significant amount of functionality from complex components in just a few days that would have taken a C programmer four years to build back in the 1980s. Ernie's own Web site is a random collection of *Star Trek*iana and *Simpsons* quotations. It uses garish red text on a black background, eight different typefaces, blinking text, streaming audio, jitterbugging icons, Submit buttons, and links to the coolest *Quake* sites.

It was quickly apparent to us that the Elemental team had, without a clear vision of Betsy and Ernie, been developing a program that tried to make them both happy. The result was a fuzzy concoction of powerful and complex features in a graphic presentation. They'd say, "Look what new cool thing the user can do now!" Their "user" was elastic, and they didn't have any idea of his goals. The programmers at Elemental were generally sympathetic to Betsy but, being temperamentally more akin to Ernie, their product had naturally tended toward Ernie's needs.

After we introduced them, the entire company immediately recognized both personas as extremely familiar archetypes and seized on them as useful user definitions.

Who Serves Whom

Visual tools for constructing Web sites was (and still is) a hot marketplace, so there were plenty of competing products, but for the first time our client could assess itself and its competitors relative to Betsy and Ernie.

The competitive market had also split along the Betsy/Ernie division. On one hand, several other Web-authoring-tool companies were writing cool new tools for Ernie. They were all complex and hard to use but let Ernie create powerful, dynamic, and sophisticated Web sites for corporate clients.

On the other hand, some other Web-authoring-tool companies were writing cool new tools for Betsy. They were all simple, visual, and easy to use, but they were all weak as kittens. They could only be used to build static sites with weak functionality, completely disconnected from any outside databases.

After we could see the landscape through the Betsy/Ernie lens, it was clear to everyone that the big opportunity was to provide Betsy with a tool giving her far more power than she was used to. This would give Elemental a desirable product in an uncrowded part of the marketplace. The programmers soon adopted "Betsy" as their rallying cry and focused their efforts on helping her.

This was a good starting point, but as we proceeded with our design efforts, we looked more closely at Betsy's goals and discovered an interesting thing.

In the old world of simple, static, first-generation Web sites, Betsy was independent. She could design *and build* a Web site for a client without any help from Ernie. Because it was just Betsy doing what she was experienced with, she could tell a prospective client how much work was involved, what it would cost, and when it would be done. She could confidently expect to deliver on her promises. That independence and self-determination was what attracted her to the Web in the first place and what convinced her to give up her day job and become an entrepreneur.

As the Web evolved, it rapidly became more powerful, but it also became much harder to build sites. Web sites were now increasingly dynamic, had more functionality, and directly accessed databases. Betsy couldn't do this level of geeky, programmer stuff. Besides, it wasn't that much fun for her, and she didn't *want* to learn. That's when she met Ernie, who could solve all of these technical problems for her. He loved all of this geeky stuff.

But Betsy found that she was now dependent on Ernie to deliver a finished product to her client. For every new Web site she created, at some unavoidable point during the process she had to find Ernie and get him to install the database access and the dynamic page-composition code. She could no longer deliver a finished Web site without using Ernie, and he wasn't anywhere near as punctual as she was. She could no longer give her clients a due date and have confidence that she would deliver. Ernie's randomness upset her business. A somewhat different picture of Betsy's goals began to emerge.

Although Betsy still wanted to build a cool, powerful, dynamic Web site, that was not her most important goal. What had been a hygienic goal, and one that she had taken for granted, was her independence, but as soon as it was gone, it became dominant. Her most important goal was to be independent again, liberated from Ernie. She wanted to be able to strike up a relationship with a client, and then design, create, and deliver a beautiful, powerful, dynamic, database-backed Web site *without ever having to wait while Ernie puzzled out some technical problem.*

Our original vision had been to make Betsy's Web-building tool even more powerful while remaining easy to use. Although this was still very desirable, it merely delayed the time when Betsy would have to seek Ernie's help and wouldn't meet her most important goal. To succeed with Betsy, we had to design Drumbeat so that it would allow her to complete projects all alone.

Ernie wasn't all that happy working with Betsy, either. He needed to get all of his work approved by Betsy, and she was always nagging him about a pixel here and a pixel there—stuff he considered immaterial. She demanded that he rework things five or six times, making irrelevant (to him) changes before she was satisfied. He wanted to be independent of Betsy as much as she wanted to be free of him.

The Design

We were now able to make a very clear and simple case. Instead of delaying Betsy's need for Ernie, we had to put up an impenetrable wall between them, granting independence to both of them. Betsy still needed the functions that Ernie created, and, after all, Betsy was a great source of work and revenue for Ernie, so there still needed to be commerce between them, but their jobs had to be fully disentangled.

This meant that the wall between them had to be a common standard—an interface—for creating and using functional modules. It had to give Ernie a programmer's interface, so his code could be connected to, and it had to give Betsy a Webmaster's interface, so she could create her sites. The Drumbeat program would be the common, neutral ground for both of them. Ernie would write powerful, flexible modules and publish them by using Drumbeat's functional interface. Betsy would use those modules by using Drumbeat's visual programming interface.

Betsy could now create dynamic, database-backed Web sites using published modules, yet never meet their author. Ernie could write, publish, and sell functional code, without ever having to change background colors. By freeing them from each other, we leveraged Betsy's design-and-production skills and also leveraged Ernie's programming skill.

Ernie now finds himself in the role of tool builder instead of custom programmer. He creates plug-compatible code modules that can dynamically become part of Betsy's toolkit. His modules have a wider audience because he can sell them to many other Betsies, who can in turn use them in a variety of other sites.

This is an interesting case in which the interaction design had significant effect on both the internal structures of the program and the way it was marketed. It is a good example of how design affects the inside while specifying only the outside.

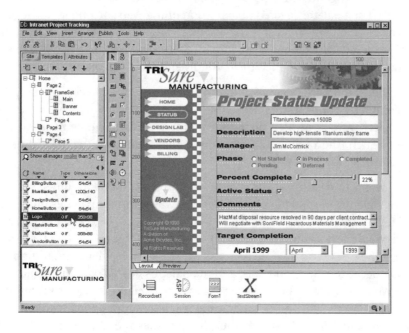

Pushback

The Elemental software engineers were reluctant at first. They thought our solution wouldn't work because they imagined several edge cases in which Betsy would still need Ernie's special talents. "You can't take Ernie totally out of the loop," they said, because Betsy might want to do something very special or difficult.

Well, we thought, that is true, but only in a few cases. In most cases, she would be independent, whereas currently she was *never* independent. For those few edge cases, she would merely be back to the status quo ante of depending on Ernie. This would certainly not make things worse, and in most cases things would be a lot better.

Because Betsy's independence is important to her, she will be willing to make commensurate sacrifices to get it. Because Drumbeat allows her to build Web sites from start to finish completely without Ernie, she is very willing to make minor compromises in her design to take advantage of Ernie's canned routines.[7] This is not a big sacrifice because not that many clients have demands that are out of the ordinary. If she ever gets the commission to build the intranet for Wal-Mart or the online reservation system for Hilton Hotels, she will certainly need to bring in sophisticated programming talent to help her with those gargantuan tasks, but not for most of her clients.

Other Issues

The original program had many small floating palettes containing various drawing tools. Each palette covered up a portion of the Web site under construction. Everyone at Elemental had somehow acquired the idea that users really *liked* to move these palette windows to and fro on their screens as they worked. In every demonstration of the product, they proudly showed them off.

Every one on our design team found the floating palettes intrusive, complicated, and completely unnecessary. Sure, the tools were needed, but we knew there were better ways to present them. Every time we said anything negative about them, though, the programmers—and product managers—would tell us how everyone used them a lot.

As we began to watch real Betsies use the product, we soon understood why floating palettes were so popular. The original design made palettes indispensable. Most of the tools on each palette were rarely used, but each palette had at least a couple very useful, very frequently used tools. This meant that Betsy needed *all* of the palettes to do even a very simple task. Each palette was unnecessarily large because of its extra tools, and the palettes floated over the visual image of the Web site under construction, so, as she worked on the site, she continually had to move the palettes out of her way. An alternative option let her lock the palettes to one side of the screen, but that just meant that Betsy had to repeatedly scroll her work to bring the current part into view. Betsy was stuck between a rock and a hard interaction. She could either spend lots of time unnecessarily scrolling the Web site, or she could spend equal time unnecessarily repositioning the palettes. We call forced, unnecessary actions such as this one *excise*, and the original program was filled with it.

---

[7] *Creating Web sites is programming, and Betsy finds herself under the irresistible influence of code reuse.*

To solve the problem, we knew that the only tools that should be kept around were those that were used very frequently, and any tools kept around were better off if they stayed in one place. Betsy would be confused if they moved around.

By a simple process of reorganizing the palettes so that they contained only frequently used functions, we made them much smaller. We then fixed them onto the screen in static locations. They now became an almost unnoticed part of the interface. This is a good example of how Goal-Directed design actually reduces the amount of interface code needed.

⌘

Both the product and the design have been successful. As the implementation of the version based on our design neared completion, Elemental was able to raise a significant amount of venture capital thanks, at least in part, to the innovations in its interaction. Since its release, Drumbeat has been widely hailed by the industry press. This quote from *PC Magazine* is representative:

> Drumbeat is a unique and impressive product that automates more advanced Web site features than anything else on the market. It lets non-programmers get the job done with drag-and-drop ease. You can build gigantic, professional-level Web sites, optionally using Active Server Pages, without writing a line of code.

The product has been successful, despite the fact that many other Web-site-building programs preceded it to market.

⌘

As you have seen, looking at things through the lens of the user's goals can give us a unique and powerful perspective that opens up new opportunities for creative design. This is the core of Goal-Directed design.

11

DESIGNING FOR PEOPLE

In previous chapters, I described personas and emphasized the importance of goals over tasks. Only after we know our user personas and their goals can we begin to examine tasks with confidence that they won't distort the design process. We call our tool for incorporating tasks *scenarios*. A scenario is a concise description of a persona using a software-based product to achieve a goal. In this chapter, I'll describe scenarios in more detail, along with a few other useful design tools. I'll follow with a case study of how some of these tools, particularly scenarios, work in the real world.

Scenarios

As the design work becomes more detailed, scenarios become more and more effective. We play our personas through these scenarios, like actors reading a script, to test the validity of our design and our assumptions. Not surprisingly, our scenario process has been described as very like method acting, in which the actor must inhabit the character, knowing what he knows and feeling his feelings. We try to think the way our persona thinks. We forget our own education, ability, training, and tools, and imagine ourselves as having *his* background instead. Because we are designers and not actors, this can be difficult without some specific context and detail, so scenarios are very useful. Knowing that Betsy is trying to create a Web site for an insurance company, for example, we can more easily inhabit her character. This is not as strange as it might sound. After all, programmers inhabit the personalities of their computers. It is common for a programmer to describe the actions of the computer in the first person—to say, "I access the database, then I store the records in my cache." Although she says "I," she is not doing a thing: The computer is doing the work, but by assuming the character of the computer, she can more easily sympathize with the system's needs as she codes.

Scenarios are constructed from the information gathered during our initial investigation phase. Typically, in both interviews and direct observation of users, we learn a lot about their tasks. Goals are stable and permanent, but tasks are fluid, changeable, and often unnecessary in computerized systems. As we develop scenarios, we need to seek out and eliminate tasks whose only justification is historical.

Effective scenarios need to be complete in breadth more than in depth. In other words, it is more important that the scenario is described from start to finish than that it cover each step in exhaustive detail.

It is important to develop only those scenarios that will further the design effort and not to get lost in edge cases. We develop only two types of scenarios, although there might be more than one of each kind. The scenario types are daily use and necessary use.

Daily-Use Scenarios

Daily-use scenarios are the most useful and important. These are the main actions that the user will perform, typically with the greatest frequency. In a bug-tracking application, for example, looking up bugs and filling out newly reported bug forms are typical daily-use scenarios. Any tech-support person performs these two tasks numerous times each day.

In general, most users only have a very limited repertoire of daily-use scenarios. One or two is typical. More than three is rare.

Daily-use scenarios need the most robust interaction support. New users must master them quickly, so they need to be supported by good, built-in pedagogy. That is, instructions for use should be written right on the program. However, because the programs are used so often, no users will remain dependent on that pedagogy for long. They will rapidly demand shortcuts. In addition, as users become very experienced, they will want to customize daily-use interaction so that it conforms to their individual work styles and preferences.

Necessary-Use Scenarios

Necessary-use scenarios include all actions that *must* be performed, but that are not performed frequently. Purging databases and making exceptional requests might fall into this category. Necessary-use interactions also demand robust pedagogy. However, the user won't ever graduate from them to parallel interaction idioms such as keyboard equivalents. Because of the infrequent use, any user will be willing to conform to the program's way of doing things and won't require customization. This excuses the development team from providing the same level of finish that a daily-use scenario would require. It is like the difference between the luxurious finish on the inside of your new Jaguar and the rough metal finish of the car's engine compartment.

Although most products have a small repertoire of necessary-use scenarios, it will typically be larger than the set of daily-use scenarios.

Edge-Case Scenario

Of course, there is a third type of scenario: the edge case. Programmers will naturally emphasize edge cases, but they can largely be ignored during the product's design. This doesn't mean that the function can be omitted from the program, but it does mean that the interaction needed for them can be designed roughly and pushed way into the background of the interface. Although the *code* may succeed or fail in its ability to handle edge cases, the *product* will succeed or fail in its ability to handle daily use and necessary cases.

If a user performs a task frequently, its interaction must be well crafted. Likewise, if a task is necessary but performed infrequently, its interaction, although designed with different objectives, must still be well designed. Tasks that are neither necessary nor frequent simply don't require careful design. Time and money are never available in unlimited quantities, so this is the place to conserve our resources safely and concentrate them where they do the most good. We must provide for all scenarios, but we need to design only for those that are important or that will occur frequently.

⌘

Personas, goals, and scenarios are the heavy hitters in our design corner. Before moving on to a scenario case study, I'd like to mention a few other useful design concepts: inflecting the interface, perpetual intermediates, vocabulary, brainstorming, and lateral thinking.

Inflecting the Interface

You can always make an interaction easier, simply by removing functions and making the product less powerful. Occasionally that is an appropriate tactic, but not usually. The more-difficult design problem demands ease of use without sacrificing functions and power. This is difficult to achieve, but by no means impossible. All it requires is a technique I call *inflecting the interface*.

Even though a program must deliver lots of functions, not all of them are needed everywhere, by all users, or at all times. For any given use scenario, the user persona will need to use only a small subset of controls and data, although that set might change over time or with the particular problem under study. The interface can be simplified dramatically by placing the controls and data needed for the daily-use scenarios prominently in the interface and moving all others to secondary locations, out of normal sight.

The interfaces of most big programs are offered up like a Chinese-restaurant menu in which hundreds of choices cover page after page. This may be desirable for choosing dinner, but it just gets in the way in high-tech products.

In Microsoft Word, for example, the default toolbar has icons for opening, closing, and printing the current document. These tasks are performed with reasonable frequency, and their presence is appropriate. However, adjacent to them are icons for generating a schematic map of the document and for inserting spreadsheets. Microsoft put those icons in the prime space so we will appreciate how powerful Word is. Unfortunately, most users never need those functions, and if they do, they don't need them on a regular basis. They simply do not belong on the toolbar, an interface idiom primarily for frequently used functions.

Perpetual Intermediates

Typically, our most powerful tools help us to understand, visualize, and inhabit the personalities of our users. One mental model that we use routinely is called *perpetual intermediates*. Most users are neither beginners nor experts; instead they are perpetual intermediates. Remember Rupak, Shannon, Dexter, and Roberto from the discussion of skill levels in Chapter 9? Although their backgrounds vary widely, all four of them are perpetual intermediates.

The experience of people using interactive systems—as in most things—tends to follow the classic bell curve of statistical distribution. For any silicon-based product, if we graph the number of users against their particular skill levels, there will be a few beginners on the left side, a few experts on the right, and a preponderance of intermediate users in the center.

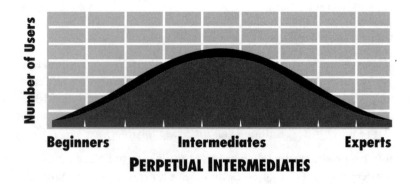

PERPETUAL INTERMEDIATES

But statistics don't tell the whole story. This is a snapshot frozen in time, and although most people—the intermediates—tend to stay in that category for a long time, the people on the extreme ends of the curve—the beginners and experts—are always changing. The difficulty of maintaining a high level of expertise means that experts come and go rapidly. Beginners, on the left side of the curve, change even more rapidly.

Although *everybody* spends some minimum time as a beginner, *nobody* remains in that state for long. That's because nobody *likes* to be a beginner, and it is never a goal. People don't like to be incompetent, and beginners—by definition—are incompetent. Conversely, learning and improving is natural, rewarding, and lots of fun, so beginners become intermediates very quickly. For example, it's fun to learn tennis, but those first few hours or days, when you can't return shots and are hitting balls over the fence, are frustrating. After you have learned basic racket control and aren't spending all of your time chasing lost balls, you really move forward. That state of beginnerhood is plainly not fun to be in, and everybody quickly passes through it to some semblance of intermediate adequacy. If, after a few days, you still find yourself whacking balls around the tennis court at random, you will abandon tennis and take up fly-fishing or stamp collecting.

The occupants of the beginner end of the curve will either migrate into the center bulge of intermediates, or they will drop off the graph altogether and find some activity in which they *can* migrate into intermediacy. However, the population of the graph's center is very stable. When people achieve an adequate level of experience and ability, they generally stay there forever. Particularly with high-cognitive-friction products, users take no joy in learning them, so they learn just the minimum and then stop. Only *Homo logicus* find learning complex systems to be fun.

Now let's contrast our bell curve with the way that software is written. All programmers qualify as experts because they have to explore every obscure case and unlikely situation to create program code to handle them. Their natural tendency to design self-referentially means that they write implementation-model code that gives every possible option equal emphasis in the interaction. If you graph the suitability of use of the typical implementation-model product, it rises high on the right side for experts. The intermediate users don't get much attention.

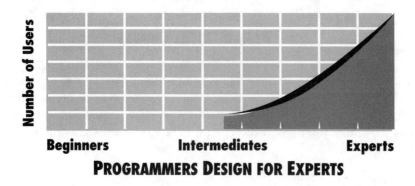

PROGRAMMERS DESIGN FOR EXPERTS

Inside a company, sales, marketing, and management are always showing off the product to customers, reporters, partners, and investors who are unfamiliar with the product. Of necessity, these professionals are constantly exposed to beginners, and their view of the user community is strongly biased toward this problematic group. All of these influential players naturally lobby for bending the interface to serve beginners. They want to see training wheels attached to the product to help out the struggling beginner. Our graph of the product's interaction suitability now rises high on the left side for beginners.

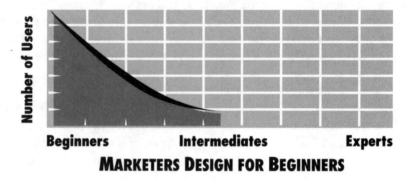

MARKETERS DESIGN FOR BEGINNERS

Superimposing the two graphs makes it clear that not only are the two strongest influences on interaction design antipodal, but they are both largely beside the point. The programmers demand interaction suitable only for experts, and the marketers demand interaction suitable only for beginners, but the largest, most stable, and most important group of users is the perpetual intermediates, who are ignored.

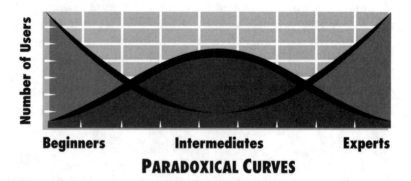

PARADOXICAL CURVES

This discontinuity between developers' perception of users and of their true nature results in added cognitive friction. You can easily see this in most internal corporate software and most mass-marketed software-based products. To use them successfully, you need to be a computer programmer, while simultaneously they have a profusion of such artifacts as wizards and on-line help for beginners. These features are merely welded-on training wheels. Wizards and help tend to get users out of scrapes without actually enlightening them as to how to avoid such scrapes in the future. Experts never use them, and beginners quickly desire to discard these embarrassing reminders of their ignorance. But the perpetual intermediates are perpetually stuck with them.

⌘

Armed with the Goal-Directed design tools of personas, goals, scenarios, perpetual intermediates, interface inflecting, and others, we can assault a client's design problem with confidence. We know that even the most intractable issues will eventually yield to our process.

"Pretend It's Magic"

Each engineer views his product in different terms, but—because he programs—he rarely views it in terms of a specific user (at least not to the level of specificity that I find useful). In our brainstorming sessions, we cut through all of the constraints and expectations. We begin our design from a blank slate, but with careful attention to our personas and their goals. We often use a creative-thinking exercise we call "pretend it's magic," in which we act through a scenario with a "magic computer" that has no constraints at all.

This exercise increases the contrast between tasks and goals. When technology changes, tasks usually change, but goals remain constant. By imagining a magic technology, we force all tasks to change, thus highlighting the goals. Although we imagine things to be magic, the process is a very straightforward mental exercise. Sometimes the correct answer appears to the designers in a flash of insight, but just as often it comes as a result of long discussion and study.

Vocabulary

During the design process, and particularly during brainstorming, I place a unique emphasis on creating and using a detailed and precise vocabulary. I believe that the technical nuance of designing interactive products is so important that a single misconstrued word can derail an entire project. I have seen different members of a client team use common words such as *button* or *dialog* for dramatically different things. I recall a client meeting in which 10 highly paid professionals wrangled for two hours over a disagreement that existed only because the various parties knew different definitions for the same words.

If you don't have words to express an idea, it is nearly impossible to communicate it. Certainly it is impossible to analyze and decompose the idea at a level of technical detail sufficient to implement it in C# or Java.

When the words are fuzzy, the programmers reflexively retreat to the most precise method of articulation available: source code. Although there is nothing more precise than code, there is also nothing more permanent or resistant to change. So the situation frequently crops up in which nomenclature confusion drives programmers to begin coding prematurely, and that code becomes the de facto design, regardless of its appropriateness or correctness.

When there are insufficient or imprecisely defined terms, people's thinking grows more conservative. Without a robust and precise set of terms, new ideas can't be defended well, so they are discarded prematurely.

The terms we select are not those that will be plastered on the outside of the box. We use our vocabulary internally, so we don't care about the marketing palatability of the words. They need only to be precise. Later on, the marketing department will come up with appropriate words that can be used on the buying public. The Logitech ScanBank, for example, was originally called the "shuffler," which was perfectly adequate for us to use in the design process and was never intended for public consumption.

During one project, our own design staff was deadlocked on a problem. As we argued back and forth, it became evident that some of us were using terms differently from others. Our discussion lacked effectiveness because we didn't have a common vocabulary. I insisted that we break down the components of our design into their atomic pieces—which we could all agree upon—and assign them completely new, unrelated names. For no particular reason, I chose the names of Alaskan mountain ranges. We named the four primary chunks of the product St. Elias, Brooks, Alaska, and Wrangell. We all had a good laugh at the incongruity of our new terms, but then we proceeded to achieve instant consensus and move our design process forward very quickly.

Breaking Through with Language

Primarily, using a robust vocabulary makes our communications more effective. However, developing a strong nomenclature sometimes has another—very important—use. Occasionally we find that certain terms have become ossified in a client team's culture. A phrase like Microsoft's "Embrace the Internet" is a good example. It can attain an almost religious significance and be treated with a kind of awe. This awe leads to an inability to deconstruct its meaning and reexamine it in light of new design imperatives. Does it mean embrace browsers, or HTML, or just TCP/IP? The sacred words are the fence around the shrine. It doesn't further our design effort much if we trample our client's sacred beliefs in the process. So we break processes, tasks, and software down into well-defined, discrete chunks and assign them new names that are utterly nonmnemonic. These new names are also typically humorous, too, and the levity helps to break through everyone's serious mien.

Reality Bats Last

The typical engineering process begins with a recitation of the constraints and limitations. The catechism of things "we cannot do" is stated often and forcefully enough to become doctrine, regardless of its truth. Interaction designers must keep a healthy suspicion of all assumptions about what cannot be done. Time and again, we find ways around such assumed limitations merely because we refuse to accept them at face value.

Of course, sometimes those limits are real, and we cannot get around them, but there is great value in trying anyway. Even if we cannot finesse a constraint, our journey down the dead-end path might shed light on some previously hidden opportunity. This process is based on the "lateral thinking" work of Edward de Bono.[1]

Programmers are princes of the practical. Their pragmatism leaves them little patience for improbable thinking. However, this strength can also be a weakness because sometimes a practical process can't solve the problem. When engineers invent, they arrive at their solution through a succession of practical, possible steps. Because of this, their solution will always be a derivative of the old, beginning solution, which is often not good enough.

Instead, we merely assume that all things are possible and design from there. By sidestepping all those assumed restrictions, we can see goals and personas with more clarity, and we can imagine solutions that could not have been arrived at conventionally.

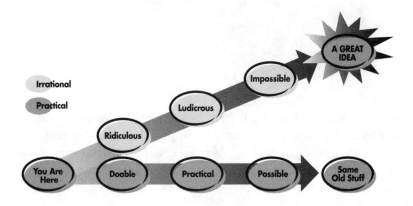

---

[1] *Edward de Bono,* Lateral Thinking, Creativity Step by Step, *1970, Harper & Row, New York, New York, ISBN: 0-06-090325-2.*

Engineers are uncomfortable stepping away from their firm foundation of rationality and prefer to cling to their assumed limitations. Because they *know* that we will eventually confront those constraints, they feel responsible to defend them. They call this "playing devil's advocate." Although I appreciate their concern, the constraints of reality are the one thing that needs no help. *Reality never needs an advocate*, because it can never be denied. It is always true that reality bats last. Knowing that reality will always get its turn at bat, we know that regardless of what we imagine or design, it will never become real if it is not possible. Only someone without skin in the game would design something unbuildable. What's more, we very often find that constraints are illusory and self-imposed. You cannot see that until you step around them.

Case Study: Logitech ScanMan

Our "pretend it's magic" design tool was particularly effective in one large design project. The scanner division of the Logitech Corporation in Fremont, California, retained us to help design the software for a whole new generation of desktop scanners for the home and small-office markets.

Logitech's new scanner device, code-named "Peacock," uses a new generation of scanning technology and connects to the computer with the USB port. About the size of a rolled-up newspaper, this inexpensive product is small and unobtrusive enough to sit handily on your desktop. You can insert any one-page document into its slot, and a small motor pulls it through to the other side, scanning the image as it goes.

Logitech's company philosophy has long centered on small, auxiliary hardware components given a premium value by the software that accompanies them. This certainly sounds good when viewed from Logitech's engineering point of view. But it's not such a good approach for the user. It isn't goal directed.

Logitech assumed that numerous software features added value to the hardware device. After all—went the thinking—adding features in software is a lot cheaper than adding features in hardware. This reasoning examines the cost-benefit equation from the manufacturer's point of view rather than from the user's.

The predecessor to the Peacock product overflowed with features, and each member of the Peacock team—marketers, product managers, programmers, and senior managers—had pet features that he advocated aggressively at strategy meetings. But if there was ever a product that called out for a featurectomy, it was Peacock.

We rarely find it necessary to eliminate features to smooth out a product's inter- action. However, in the case of Peacock, the widely held idea that Logitech added value with lots of software features was erroneous. Our personas and scenarios made it very clear the product's interface was overburdened with unneeded, unwanted, and unused features.

As usual, we began our process by creating our cast of characters. Here's how we arrived at them.

The scanner had a street price of around $150. For a consumer product, it was quite powerful, with a high resolution and color, but still not in the league of pro- fessional, flatbed scanners that typically sold for $800 to $1,000.[2] It was clear to everyone that the main marketplace for this product was the user in a small office or home office, called SOHO by demographers.

Malcolm, the Web-Warrior

We created the persona of Malcolm, the Web-warrior, to represent the SOHO user. He is a young man who has started a small consulting business at home cre- ating Web sites. He isn't very technical, nor is he a graphic artist, but he is famil- iar with computers and knows that fast-loading, simple images are better than lush—but slow-to-download—graphics. The Peacock scanner allows him to get medium-resolution images into his Web sites easily without unreasonable expense or complication.

Chad Marchetti, Boy

The Peacock scanner also had significant appeal to people with home comput- ers who scanned in pictures and documents for personal, rather than business, use. To represent the home user, we invented the persona of Chad Marchetti, a 10-year-old boy who uses the scanner to make his homework projects look bet- ter with color images.

---

[2] *As usual, time and the plummeting prices of silicon have changed the scanner landscape con- siderably. This was all true in January 1997.*

Magnum, DPI

We knew that professional graphic artists would demand thousand-dollar flatbed scanners, so we deemphasized that market segment. However, we also knew we couldn't ignore that market altogether because "from tiny acorns mighty oaks grow." A young, freelance graphic artist just breaking into the business wouldn't have any cash to spare, and Peacock would get him through his first year or two until he could afford an industrial-strength product, but only if he could squeeze sufficient performance from Peacock.

To represent our acorn, we defined a persona named Magnum, DPI. (His name is a play on words using the old Tom Selleck TV show *Magnum, P.I.* and the acronym for dots-per-inch, the common measure of the resolution of a digitized image.) Magnum might not represent a large user segment, but he is certainly an influential one. All of his home-computer-user friends ask his advice when it comes to graphics software and peripherals. In another year, he'll be able to buy a flatbed scanner, but until then, he'll make do with his Peacock.

Neither Malcolm nor Chad knows much about image manipulation. Malcolm is too focused on other things, such as building Web sites and making money. Chad is too focused on other things, such as not losing his pictures in the file system. Neither sees much reason to twiddle with pixels. They both want to scan images in, crop them to size, and then place them in documents they are using. The documents, not the images, are the end result. We found that they shared three significant goals:

> They don't want to manage scanners, resolutions, or settings.
> They want to find their scanned images quickly and easily.
> They want to get their scanned images into other documents in other programs quickly and easily.

Magnum, DPI is a different breed of cat: He *does* know about resolutions and he *is* comfortable with various image-manipulation settings. Knowing this, you might assume that adding such features would benefit Magnum. However, Magnum already owns Adobe Photoshop. This powerful, complicated, and expensive image-manipulation program is his primary tool, and he knows it inside and out.[3] Whenever he has any task to do, regardless of how small, he uses Photoshop. Any attempt that Peacock might make to duplicate the functionality and power of Photoshop would be feeble. Like Pee Wee Herman stepping into the ring with George Foreman, Peacock wouldn't last a round with the champ. We shouldn't even bother putting effort into something that won't be used and can only embarrass us.

---

[3] *I would love to give this powerful, complicated program an interaction redesign! Note: At least a half-dozen people who previewed this manuscript underlined this footnote and added a comment like "You and me both!" or "Please do!"*

However, two out of three of Magnum's goals are identical to Chad's and Malcolm's: He wants to find his images easily, and he wants to get his images into another program (Photoshop) easily.

The only setting that Magnum might make during the actual scan is specifying the physical resolution of the scan in dots per inch. In older, slower scanners, there was always some speed advantage to be had by scanning at a faster, lower resolution, so Magnum saved time with the setting. The new Peacock scanner is much faster, and its maximum density is a healthy 200 DPI. In full color, this takes only about 20 seconds for an 8 1/2- by 11-inch sheet of paper. There just isn't any advantage to having Magnum spend 10 seconds changing a setting that only saves him 5 seconds of scan time, yielding a lower-quality scan for his trouble. Why would anyone—even Magnum—want to lower the DPI setting if the scan speed was sufficiently brisk at maximum resolution? This insight allowed us to see that the goals of all three users were happily in accord, and we could make our users happy and still dispense with almost all of the features.

Playing "Pretend It's Magic"

During brainstorming, we played "pretend it's magic." We found that Chad was quite content getting images into his computer without even using a scanner. This exercise showed that the one thing that Chad—and Malcolm and Magnum—didn't want was to manage scanner hardware. From this perspective, it was easy to see that the only thing he wanted to manage was the scanned image after it has been entered into his computer. He doesn't care if the image is scanned in with black magic, but after it's inside the computer, he needs to be able to find it, crop it, and put it into his other programs.

Most competing scanner products—and Peacock's predecessor—just dump the images—and the user—into the Windows file system, letting them use the conventional hierarchical display to store, manage, and retrieve their scanned images. That file system is really very hard to use and unhelpful.

The file system requires Chad to create a name for his new scanned image and then choose a place in the file system hierarchy for storing it. When Chad wants to find that image again, he has to remember what he named it and where he put it. It just so happens that remembering such trivia is something that Chad, being human, isn't very good at. The computer, having a hard disk, happens to be superbly well suited to remembering such trivia, but it doesn't bother. Instead, it forces Chad to do the work of remembering the name and place.

In our design, the scanner software never forces Chad to name and place his incoming images. Instead, it quietly takes the image in and manages its storage for Chad. When he comes back at some future date looking for the image, in addition to simply recognizing it in a thumbnail, he can recall it by any one of a number of its attributes, such as when it was scanned, how big it is, whether it includes text, or whether he exported the image into some other program.

Instead of letting Chad and Magnum control the hardware by fiddling with various scanner settings, we concentrated instead on three more-important things:

We eliminated all scanner-management interface idioms.
We made it impossible to lose scanned images in the file system.
We made it trivially easy to put scanned images into documents in other programs.

We looked at all the available image-manipulation functions and decided that there were only three indispensable ones. The rest could be omitted or would be performed later in other, better-suited programs, such as Photoshop. The three functions were:

Crop: Clipping the sides of the image
Resize: Changing the size of the image
Reorient: Turning the image onto its side or back

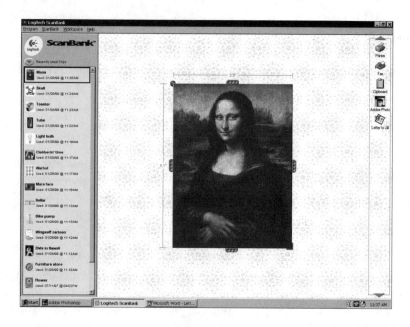

Our suite of functions was very small, but they were necessary and would be used frequently, so we decided to make them of an extremely high quality and very easy to use. The net savings in coding many fewer functions gave the programming team the necessary time to put more effort into these three.

World-Class Cropping

All computerized cropping tools I've ever seen work in the same inappropriate way. The user clicks and drags a rectangle with the mouse. The point where the click occurs is the upper-left corner of the cropping rectangle, and the point where the drag ends is the lower-right corner of the rectangle. Everything outside this rectangle is permanently discarded, and what is left inside it becomes the new image. This method is quick, simple, and easy to program and to explain. Heavyweight graphics program Photoshop uses it, for example. Nevertheless, it has severe drawbacks. Mainly, the drag-rectangle method is hard to control, and it has to be done perfectly in one smooth motion. It's all too easy to get three sides of the crop rectangle correct, and then to find it nearly impossible to correct the fourth side without disturbing one or more of the other three. Also, the permanent nature of the crop means the program cannot accommodate two different crops of the same image.

Our crop-tool solution solved both of these significant problems in simple, easy-to-learn, and easy-to-understand ways. Each of the four sides of the scanned image has its own permanently visible crop handle. This handle offers clear affordances for direct manipulation. All Chad needs to do is click and drag on a handle to receive immediate and proportional visual feedback of the consequences of his action. As the crop handle moves in, the outside part of the image is shown in a ghostly gray. This makes it clear that the image is being cropped but also hints that the cropping is not permanent. Chad can just as easily drag the crop handle back out, once again revealing the original image in full color.

As Chad moves one crop handle, he instantly sees that the four sides are independent and that moving one doesn't affect the others. He can adjust and fine-tune the cropping as many times as he likes. This is a very different sensation from using more traditional cropping tools, in which the act of cropping is modal and permanent, and must be done perfectly in a single motion. Very few computer users have the manual dexterity to perform this action well. Chad certainly doesn't. What's more, the nature of cropping is visual and typically iterative. Even fine artists will take a few tries before they settle on a final crop. Older tools simply didn't support this behavior. The crop tool we provided for Logitech did it quite admirably.

Even after Chad settled on a crop setting, the crop function was not permanent. The current crop settings were merely considered attributes of the image, which was always stored as a complete image. (There was a menu item for making the crop permanent if disk space was at an unusual premium.) This meant that Chad could scan in a photo of his family, crop down to an image of his mother for a homework assignment, and then—three months later—return to that same image and recrop to show only his father for a letter he was writing. Any other scanner program would have forced Chad to scan in the image a second time.

World-Class Image Resize

Resizing an image in most graphics programs entails entering dimensions into a dialog box. The dialog offers great precision and the ability to stretch an image disproportionately, but the precision is rarely needed and out-of-proportionality is rarely wanted. Although the dialog box offers what is not wanted, it doesn't offer what *is* wanted: the ability to see how big or small to make the new image. A resize control should be visual.

Our resize-tool solution is a small, red angle positioned on the bottom-right corner of the scanned image. When the cursor rolls over it, it visually changes very slightly, growing in size by a couple of pixels. This is what I call the *pliant response*, and it hints to Malcolm that the object can be directly manipulated. When Malcolm clicks and drags on the red angle, the image resizes in real time either larger or smaller, depending on the direction that he drags the angle. The image always stays in correct proportion. Disproportional resizing is Magnum's job, and he uses Photoshop for it.

Adding to the utility of the resize control are the dimension lines extending from the sides of the image. These change in real time as Malcolm drags the angle, giving him immediate quantitative feedback about the exact size of the image. A function on the menu allows Malcolm to set the dimensions to show in units of pixels or metric measure, instead of English measure.

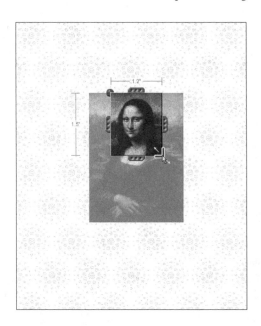

World-Class Image Reorient

The capability to rotate a scanned image is a function typically found in graphics programs. There are three general uses for a rotation function.

⌘ Rotating portions of images to change the composition
⌘ Straightening a picture that was scanned very slightly off the vertical
⌘ Reorienting a sideways or upside-down image to right side up

Most scanner products—including Peacock's predecessor—have a rotation tool that allows its user to perform all three functions. We looked at this power and complexity from Chad's, Malcolm's, and Magnum's points of view and decided to take a very different approach.

We immediately discarded rotate use number one. Only an artist needed it, and none of our users was an artist. Magnum was closest, and he would use Photoshop's powerful rotate function.

Rotate use number two, called *alignment*, cannot work well because of limitations of the technology. Virtually all rastering devices, such as video screens, scanners, and printers, render straight lines that are just one or two degrees off the vertical or horizontal with ugly zigzags called "aliasing" or "the jaggies." After a line has been scanned in with the jaggies, no amount of computer processing can straighten it, and using the typical rotate function to force the line to the vertical creates a dizzying optical illusion that makes for a cure far worse than the disease. As if that weren't bad enough, the software needed to rotate an image just a couple of degrees is extremely complex and sophisticated. Most other scanner products proudly include this less-than-useless function as a fine example of what Po Bronson meant about engineers when he said, "Blindness improves their vision."

If an image is scanned in a degree or two off, it's much faster, better, and easier just to line it up better and scan it in again. The scanner hardware not only facilitates this solution with its precisely aligned rollers and high speed, but it also makes it very hard to align the scan incorrectly in the first place.

Rotate use number three is reorientation. It is easy to inadvertently scan an image in sideways or upside down. It is easy and effective to use software to flip an image 90°, 180°, or 270°, orienting it correctly.

Thus we designed a "reorient" tool instead of a "rotate" tool, and once again we took pains to make it the best of breed. In the upper-left corner of the scanned image is a blue circle, similar to the red resize angle. When the cursor flies over the circle, it visually changes into a slightly larger circle, once again hinting at pliancy.

When Malcolm clicks and drags the circle, a bright-green rectangle appears around the edges of the image. This rectangle, called a *bombsight*, indicates where the image will land when Malcolm releases the mouse button. As the circle is dragged past the corner of the image, the green bombsight snaps to the next cardinal alignment: 90°, 180°, or 270°. Malcolm can easily see in advance the effect his actions will have on the image. He clearly sees that alignment is only allowed on cardinal directions and that free rotation or alignment correction is not available here. All of our personas understand the feature instantly.

World-Class Results

At our client's request, we did some user testing on this product and discovered a remarkable thing. We expected that all the test subjects would be very pleased with our interface and would be able to understand it and use it easily. In this we were not disappointed. What surprised us was that every one of the test subjects expressed the opinion that Peacock was the "most powerful." In literal terms of the number of features, this was far from true. In terms of effective power realized by the user, we had increased it significantly.

When the ScanMan product finally shipped, it generated a stir in Logitech's tech-support department because it received remarkably fewer calls about using it than was normal for a new product.

Bridging Hardware and Software

From an interaction designer's point of view, the divisions between hardware and software are inconsequential because they are inconsequential to a user. The user doesn't care which is more expensive to build. Thus, interaction designers can resolve problems that arise during development of hybrid products.

In the world of engineering, there are hardware engineers who create circuit boards and microchips, and there are software engineers who create program code. Although the fruits of their labor are sold in a common—or hybrid— product, the two factions typically don't work cooperatively. Sometimes they don't even communicate, but instead merely throw completed modules over the fence into the other's backyard.

For historical reasons, hardware engineers dominate most hybrid-product companies, but as the availability of hardware increases to the point of ubiquity, hardware and its engineers assume a less critical role. Conversely, the true value to the user of most products is increasingly due to the unique contributions of the software. This makes for an uneasy truce in most hybrid-product companies.

Hewlett-Packard is a good example of a hybrid-product company dominated by hardware engineers. Its printers are fabulous products with exemplary engineering, but after two decades of refinement, none of my HP printers yet cooperates fully with my computer. They don't bother to tell my computer how much paper is in their feed bins, how much ink is left in their cartridges, or how many print jobs are currently queued up and ready to go. This kind of thoughtless disdain for the human's need for information is the telltale smoking gun of companies dominated by hardware engineers.

Ironically, hardware companies are more experienced at seeking outside help from industrial-design firms to help them make their products more desirable and useful to their users. Software companies tend to go it alone. In any company making hybrid products, when hardware and software engineers don't have designers to mediate between them, the result will be products that fail to please. Most of the examples in Chapter 1, "Riddles for the Information Age," make this clear.

As more and more products are hybrids of hardware and software, the need for a Goal-Directed design increases, because it is agnostic regarding the implementation medium.

3Com Corporation—original maker of the PalmPilot—is a good example of a hybrid-product company where design created a smooth integration between hardware and software. A single tap of the screen and the machine awakens instantly in the exact state it was in when it was last shut down. When hardware is instantaneously responsive to users' actions, it is a clear indicator that the hardware design incorporated the needs of the software. Conversely, my Nikon CoolPix 900 takes seven long seconds to boot up every time I turn it on, and it doesn't even have a disk drive. When hardware is this sluggish, it is clear that the hardware engineers ran the show.

Of course, in the real world of product design, most software companies quite rightly stay out of the hardware world. Designers respect this, even when dedicated hardware would confer significant advantage.

However, if the cost structure of the design problem allows for it, designers should not hesitate to make recommendations about hardware. The Sony P@ssport IFE system in Chapter 9, "Designing for Pleasure," ran on dedicated computers, and the vendor had complete control over all hardware and all software. My designers made several hardware recommendations.

In the Elemental Drumbeat design in Chapter 10, "Designing for Power," the product was destined to run on any vanilla, Wintel desktop computer. My designers stayed well away from any hardware recommendations.

For several client projects, including Logitech's Peacock, my designers were lucky enough to find opportunities to add value with hardware design. Each company had the option of venturing into the world of hybrid solutions, with all of the danger and opportunity that that entails.

Less Is More

Those gadget-obsessed, control-freak programmers love to fill products with gizmos and features, but that tendency is contrary to a fundamental insight about good design. Less is more.

When an interaction designer has done a particularly good job, the user will be quite unaware of the designer's presence. Like service in a world-class restaurant, it should be inconspicuous. When the interaction designer has accomplished something really good, users won't even notice it. In an industry that promotes "coolness" as a design objective, it really gets tiresome to find my way so often obscured by interaction artifacts that have obviously taken some poor programmer lots of time and work. Too bad his efforts didn't go into something effective. Many visual designers think that good design is cool, and occasionally it is, but *no matter how cool your interface is, less of it would be better.*[4] Again, the point is that the less the user sees, the better a job the designer has done. Imagine watching a movie and seeing klieg lights in the corners of the frame or hearing the director yell "Cut!" at the end of a scene. Imagine how intrusive that would be and how it would break the viewer's spell.

Super programmer and software designer Kai Krause is famous for his unique interfaces. Kai has created some of the most powerful and interesting graphical-manipulation software. His products always have breathtakingly beautiful interfaces. They also tend to be inscrutable, kind of like a game. In addition to his programming ability, Kai is a visual designer, and his products reflect the visual designer's willingness to make things obscure—like modern art—for the sake of effect. This works because his user base is other visual designers and hobbyists. It doesn't go over very well outside that world.

⌘

In programming, there is always an infinite variety of ways to solve any given problem. Experienced programmers, as they explore their options searching for the optimum solution, occasionally stumble on a technique that allows them to throw out hundreds—or even thousands—of lines of code. This only happens when the programmer has made a valuable conceptual leap forward. When she can toss out lots of code, her program is getting better. Less code means less complexity, fewer bugs, fewer opportunities for invalid interactions, and easier maintainability.

Interaction designers share this sensation. As they explore their options, they discover places where they can dispense with entire screens or discard large and complex dialog boxes. The designer knows that each element of the user interface is a burden on the user. Each button and icon is one more thing that the user must know about, and must work around, to get to what she really wants. Doing more with less is always better.

If the designer is doing well, she is *removing* interface from a product. She is not designing screen after screen of buttons and gizmos. A product manager from a large software company visited us one day, inquiring about having us redesign a

---

[4] *In my book,* About Face, *I introduce over 50 powerful design axioms. This is one of them.*

product for them. He told us that he expected the interface to have about a dozen dialog boxes. We explained to him our process and then quoted a price for their design. It was about $60,000, if I remember correctly. The manager then exclaimed, "But that's outrageous! It's $5,000 per screen!" I didn't have the heart to tell him that we would probably reduce the dialog box count down to one or two and that the price—when calculated on a per-screen basis—would be a lot higher. He just didn't get it. Paying for design on a per-screen basis is like paying a waiter by the number of trips he makes to each table. A better waiter makes *fewer* trips, and a better designer always creates lots less interface.

Sometimes being an interaction designer can be so frustrating! If, as a designer, you do something really, fundamentally, blockbuster correct, everybody looks at it and says, "Of course! What *other* way would there be?" This is true even if the client has been staring, empty-handed and idea-free, at the problem for months or even years without a clue about solving it. It's also true even if our solution generates millions of dollars for the company. Most really breakthrough conceptual advances are *opaque in foresight and transparent in hindsight*. It is incredibly hard to see breakthroughs in design. You can be trained and prepared, spend hours studying the problem, and still not see the answer. Then someone else comes along and points out a key insight, and the vision clicks into place with the natural obviousness of the wheel. If you shout the solution from the rooftops, others will say, "Of course the wheel is round! What other shape could it possibly be?" This makes it frustratingly hard to show off good design work.

Computer scientist Alan Karp says, "Almost every patent application I have submitted has been rejected as 'obvious.'"

When I say less interface, I don't mean less functionality—although that can sometimes be the case. I mean that the user doesn't have to interact with the program any more than is absolutely necessary to get any particular task accomplished.

⌘

In this chapter and in Chapters 9 and 10, I presented a brief look at our most widely used design tools. They have proven to be very effective in designing products and services ranging from industrial control to enterprise planning to consumer products. In the next chapter, I will examine some other available tools that claim to help create better-designed products.

Part V

Getting Back into the Driver's Seat

12

Desperately Seeking Usability

The explosion of software-based products into the mass market, in either general-purpose computers or appliances, has transformed the user population. Formerly it was a small group of forgiving, technology-loving implementers. Today it is a teeming multitude of impatient, unhappy, nontechnical consumers. Everyone, both inside and outside of the software industry, has heard the users cry in painful frustration and has felt the pressure to *do something*. Many specialties have stepped forward, eager and willing to fill the vacuum. All of them have a good story, most of them have bright credentials, and many of them have stellar client lists. Collectively, though, they have produced more heat than light, and their solutions lack for nothing except desirable software-based products. The result has been widespread confusion about how to really solve the problem of unhappy users. In this chapter, I'll try to dispel some of the confusion, showing where each specialization can be most effective and how it can dovetail with Goal-Directed interaction design.

The Timing

Probably the single most important aspect of design is the sequence of events in the software-construction process. Since the earliest days of software development, the sequence of events has been program, bug test, tweak. First, the programmer writes the program. He then puts it through its paces, looking for any inadvertent errors in its construction. Next, he tweaks the code to correct those errors. Finally, the program is ready to be deployed.

Doesn't Work

It is only natural that the engineers will accept any new discipline more readily if it does not disturb the established order of activities. One method, called *user testing*, that has grown to significant proportions in the industry examines empirically how actual users interact with the product. The main reason why empirical user testing has been widely accepted in the high-tech business is that it fits easily into the existing sequence. Most user testing depends on having a working program to test with, so necessarily it must wait until the program is up and running. This places user testing in the sequence conveniently in parallel to bug testing. The programmers are comfortable with this piggybacking of a new form of testing because it doesn't upset their established sequence.

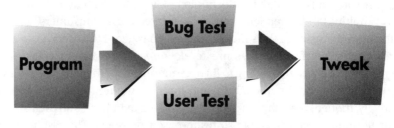

Still Doesn't work

As I've pointed out, writing code is to interaction design as pouring concrete is to building architecture. No matter who does the designing, regardless of the method she might apply, the effect of design will be negligible if the coding is underway. A fundamental premise of bringing design to the software-development process is that it must occur before the programming begins. Obviously, I'm an advocate for Goal-Directed design, but any systematic design process performed in advance of programming will be much more effective than any process that comes afterward.

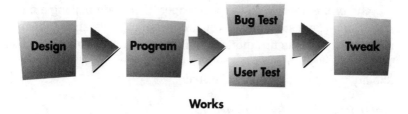

Works

Putting design before programming means fundamental change in the software-development process. Programmers, who are naturally affected by this, see it in vaguely threatening terms. They have heretofore been first and, by implication, most important. If some other discipline comes first, does that mean the other practitioners are more important? This is not true, and I will discuss it in more detail in the next chapter.

In the software world, I have programmed, invented, tested, documented, designed, sold, shipped, and supported, and I can say without doubt that programming is by far the most difficult and demanding task of them all. (I'm referring to *professional* programming of software suitable for commercial release. As a general rule, the complexity of a program increases exponentially relative to its size in lines of code. Although most people write small, 100-line programs in college, and many people write similar-sized programs for their work, the sheer size of commercial applications, which can easily exceed 50,000 lines, pushes their complexity beyond the comprehension of most mortals.) Even if other practices are unclear on this point, the programmers are not, and they know that they, by far, have more skin in the game than anyone else.

The myth of the unpredictable market that I presented in Chapter 3, "Wasting Money," is another reason why the "program, test, tweak" sequence is so well established in the industry. If we can't know what the market will want, why bother wasting time designing up front? Just code it and ship it, and the market will tell us. It will also absolve us from any responsibility for the failure.

These issues notwithstanding, it is absolutely vital that cooler heads implement this change in sequence, putting design in front of programming.

User Testing

Any process based on observation must take the back seat to acts of creation. Programmers create. The usability discipline tacitly hands the reins to the programmers, saying, "You build it, and then I'll test to see how well you have done." But in this fast-moving, high-tech world, after it is built, it ships. Post-facto testing cannot have much influence on the product.

To me, usability methods seem like sandpaper. If you are making a chair, the sandpaper can make it smoother. If you are making a table, the sandpaper can also make it smoother. But no amount of sanding will turn a table into a chair. Yet I see thousands of well-intentioned people diligently sanding away at their tables with usability methods, trying to make chairs.

User Testing Before Programming

It is certainly possible to perform user testing before programming begins, but the nature and value of the process changes dramatically. This kind of testing is similar to the pure research that one would expect to find in a university setting. A colleague at a major software company performed a classic user test that simultaneously demonstrates the strength and weakness of this pre-facto user testing. He wanted to determine the effectiveness of the status bar at the bottom of the screen. He had people use a spreadsheet program to perform some innocuous task, and about every five minutes a message would flash across the status bar saying, "There is a $50 bill taped to the bottom of your chair. Take it!" In a full day of testing with more than a dozen people, nobody claimed the cash.

The insight that users don't pay much attention to what is displayed on the popular-among-programmers status bar is certainly valuable. It doesn't shed much light on the underlying problems, though: What constitutes "status" worth displaying? Should it be displayed at all? Where should it be displayed? Those design problems remain as open as they ever were.

Fitting Usability Testing into the Process

The professional literature is filled with detailed advice on how to perform tests, but it says little about inventing something to test if the product doesn't already exist. In practice, some simulacrum must be created and tested. These generally take the form of either a quickly written prototype program or a "puppet-show" made from paper cutouts or some equivalent, low-tech material.

You can learn a lot about users' reactions from paper puppet-shows, but what gets tested can still be quite inappropriate unless design is done first. Also, the personal presence of the tester inevitably looms large in this form of test, and a word, nod, or glance can easily skew the test's results.

For the most meaningful results, you have to do prohibitively expensive comparison testing by creating two programs to test against each other. Even then, all you learn is that one of the candidates is better than the other. You don't know what is the best you can achieve.

Thoughtful user testing can uncover a designer's incorrect assumptions. Exposing your design work to users and then redesigning iteratively is always better than not doing so. Some new technologies, such as voice recognition, are so untried that the insights provided by basic user testing can be of great value.

Arguably, the most valuable contribution of usability testing is made when programmers are forced to sit behind the one-way mirrors to view typical users struggling with their programs. The programmers are shocked and incredulous, shouting sentiments like, "You are testing mental retards!" Usability testing is a useful whack on the side of the head for recalcitrant software engineers, showing them that there is indeed a problem. It can serve the same purpose for management, too.

To paraphrase the toothpaste people, user testing has been shown to be an effective, decay-preventive technique when used in a conscientiously applied program of Goal-Directed design and regular professional care. The key here is to remember that other factors can have an even greater effect.

Multidisciplinary Teams

The software engineer's resistance to letting anything upset the familiar sequence of events in the development process has led to a lot of tortuous logic on the part of the design community. One widely proposed solution has interaction designed by teams with representatives from many different disciplines.

The hypothesis is that better results can be obtained by working in a team with equal representation from users, programmers, managers, marketers, and usability professionals. In my experience, this "seat at the table" doesn't work. The goals and concerns of the members diverge, and the one constituent whose goals are most relevant—the user—is often the poorest equipped to articulate his concern. What's worse, the programmers—who always have ultimate control over the software-based artifact anyway—inevitably drive the team, usually from the back seat.

The seat-at-the-table solution still fails to put design in front of programming. It is a buzzword-compliant, polycultural, inclusive, multidisciplinary, and democratic approach, but it still fails to address the flawed sequence, which remains as a virulent cause of bad interaction.

Programmers Designing

The first "volunteers" to address the problems of the new nontechnical users were the programmers themselves. That their culture and tools were wholly inadequate to the task was less relevant than that they were the only available candidates for the job. Like the bystander unlucky enough to be near the scene of an accident, programmers were called upon to deliver first aid to interfaces by the simple virtue of their propinquity. Programmers are nothing if not game, and prideful in their competence, so the difficult challenge of designing interaction appealed to them, and they invested considerable effort. This gave rise to the sardonic joke in the industry that says, "Design is what the programmers do in the 20 minutes before they begin coding."

I've shown throughout this book that the programmers' efforts were ill-fated from the beginning. As Po Bronson says, they consider the absence of criticism a compliment, so their assessment of their own performance is unrealistically positive, and many of them insist on continued ownership of the design role. Like mad kings, programmers are unwilling to relinquish territory after it is occupied, even if the occupation is unpleasant, unprofitable, undesired, and untenable.

Regardless of how much you might teach, test, or design, you are a programmer if you program professionally. In the same way that there is no such thing as being a little bit pregnant, there is no such thing as doing a little bit of programming.

Even though many developers remain unconvinced that a significant problem exists ("the users just need to learn more"), others clearly see the frustration and expense caused by wholesale dancing bearware. The good news is that this latter group is gaining strength, and the willingness of most development organizations to seek outside help is growing.

Most programmers are actually pretty good at design, and many of those who are not are humbly aware of their shortcomings and avoid practicing it. The giant caveat is that when programmers design, their effort is almost always based on the unique personality of *Homo logicus*. The end result is a difficult-to-use and inappropriate product that other programmers tend to really like.

How Do You Know?

Many usability professionals believe that you cannot know whether an interaction is good unless you test it. That's why they are constantly asking, "How do you know?" But I have noticed something very curious. When they ask, they are not playing devil's advocate. They are asking for the simple reason that they really *don't* know good design when they see it.

At least four large companies that I work with have a long history with usability professionals. The companies decided to invest in usability. They hired professionals who built their labs, performed their studies, identified likely problem areas, and made a series of guesses about how to improve things. The programmers diligently made changes to their programs, *and not much happened*, except that the programmers had worked a lot harder. After a few cycles of this, the programmers simply gave up, and so did most of the managers. They could see that it was very expensive and time consuming, yet it wasn't solving the fundamental problem.

Interaction designers rely on their experience, training, and judgment to make an accurate evaluation. They have principles, idioms, and tools for every situation, and they triangulate these tools with other sources of information. How does a radiologist know that someone needs surgery from examining an X-ray? X-rays are so difficult to read that it is hard for a layperson to imagine reading one, but trained doctors do it all the time. How does a judge know whether a defendant is guilty? How does an investor know that now is the time to buy? These professionals might not be right all of the time, but they don't guess.

I have seen well-respected usability professionals blandly take potshots into the dark. They developed sophisticated tests to isolate users' reactions to existing software, and then they studied the tabulated results to find interactive rough spots. When their rigorous, scientific method uncovered a problem area, they would lapse into the most amateurish babbling about solutions: "Well, I guess we could move this control over to this dialog box," or "I suppose that if we added a button here the user could have better control."

It is fine to say, "I don't know" but very self-defeating to guess at answers. What's worst is that any gazing off into space and guessing will cause programmers—the ones with skin in the game—to quietly write you off as a quack.

Style Guides

The partnership of designer Shelley Evenson and scientist John Rheinfrank at Xerox's Palo Alto Research Center in the 1980s yielded some important ideas about visual communications. They created a consistent visual vocabulary, called a "visual design language," for all Xerox photocopiers: green for originals, blue for supplies, red for service areas. Similar nontextual cues are very useful in high-cognitive-friction interfaces, and they are communicated in a "style guide," a book of examples and use suggestions.

Many software engineers and development managers who are frustrated by user-interaction problems would love to have a style guide that tells them what interface their product needs. Many corporations have developed interface style guides for all of their internal software, and several software vendors have them for independent vendors who write compatible software.

Although style guides can help, they really don't address Goal-Directed interaction design problems. These need to be treated on a case-by-case basis. Users with different goals use the various applications, and each product's interaction must address the appropriate goals. A common visual language and consistent controls can help, but they alone don't solve the problem.

Conflict of Interest

If Bill Gates publicly demanded that all vendors other than Microsoft stop innovating in interaction design, those vendors would hoot him from the stage. Yet, Microsoft's interface style guide does just that, and it is one of the company's most potent competitive levers in the industry.

Both Microsoft and Apple sell interface style guides and promote their power and usefulness, and—at first glance—those companies would seem to be the most authoritative sources. However, the platform vendor is in a vicious conflict of interest, and its motivations cannot really be trusted.

Both platform makers use a quiet form of coercion to ensure compliance. If an independent software developer doesn't follow the style guide's recommendations, the vendor won't let the developer claim to be "platform compliant," an important marketing position. Thus, most makers of desktop software are eager to follow their vendors' recommendations.

By insisting that their independent developer communities follow the stated guidelines, however, these companies surreptitiously suppress innovation from the application community.

Meanwhile the platform vendors are free to experiment, evolve, and innovate as much as they desire. They are under no compulsion to follow their own style guides. Of course, no company more flagrantly and frequently violates those guidebooks than Microsoft and Apple.

I'm not advocating that we ignore style guides and give in to interface chaos. I'm merely saying that we should regard the style guide in the way a senator regards a lobbyist, not in the way a motorist obeys a state trooper. The legislator knows that the lobbyist has an axe to grind—that the lobbyist is not a disinterested third party.

Focus Groups

Many industries have discovered the value of focus groups for learning what customers like and don't like about various products. However useful focus groups are for gaining insight into what customers think about most consumer goods, they are troublesome when used in the software business. The biggest problem is simply that most people, even professional software users, are ignorant of what software is and what it can and cannot do. So when a focus group participant asks for a feature, the request is made from a shortsighted point of view. The user is asking for what he or she thinks is likely, possible, and reasonable. To consciously ask for something unlikely, impossible, or unreasonable would be to voluntarily seem stupid, and people don't willingly do that.

Stanford University scientists Nass and Reeves have studied people's reactions to computers, and they see conclusive evidence that people's own evaluation of their reactions to computers is unreliable. They say, "Many popular methods, especially focus group techniques, rely heavily on the assumption that people can be introspective about [interactive] experiences. This is an assumption that we think is frequently wrong."

Larry Keeley says that "users will reject new ideas if you ask them." This makes focus-group techniques suspect for any significantly innovative products. Today, most software-based products are sufficiently innovative to be un-focus-groupable.

Focus groups can be effective for some product categories, but it is a mistake to trust them for a reliable evaluation of high-cognitive-friction products.

Visual Design

In *About Face*, I showed why it wasn't the graphical nature of the graphical user interface (GUI) that made it the dominant form of computer interaction. Rather, it was the tightly restricted interaction vocabulary of the new interfaces that made them so much better than their green-screen predecessors. Good visual design can be an important contributor to the quality of any interface, but many people in the industry still credit it with value that it simply doesn't have.

I was a judge one year in a contest for the design and construction of in-house application software.[1] One of the top prize winners was a program that managed ticket sales at an annual aviation-enthusiast's convention in Wisconsin. The point-of-sale terminal—the beating-heart of the system—was decidedly non-graphic, showing only a simple textual display that was singularly stiff, rectilinear, and aesthetically primitive. Yet the program was a clear winner because the design paid close attention to the peculiar needs of the all-volunteer sales staff at the convention. These volunteers had a mission-critical but simple job to do, and they had to do it rapidly and with minimal training. GUIs are superb tools for showing managers the big picture of how their business is doing, but the users of this point-of-sale system had no such need because each successive customer who appeared at the head of the line was different and disassociated from every other customer in line. Seeing the big picture wasn't part of the requirement. A simple textual screen was entirely sufficient to make the product an award winner. This lesson is lost on many practitioners.

One of the characteristics of GUIs is their ability to display rich bitmapped graphics. It is feasible to have program interfaces that are as visually lush as the game *Myst*. Consequently, there are numerous visual designers and graphic

---

[1] *The seven-year-old contest, held at COMDEX industry conferences, was called Windows World Open and was sponsored by Microsoft, Computerworld, and Ziff-Davis Events.*

artists out there who will gladly put attractive bitmapped graphics on the face of your program. But graphic artists rarely address the underlying interaction.

This interface is one of those useless eye-candy programs given away free with new computers and worth every penny you pay for it. Its purpose has something to do with running the phone or the CD-ROM, I'm not exactly sure which. The interface is undeniably beautiful, particularly if you are a gadget-loving technophile, but its use is inscrutable. It is an example of what we call "painting the corpse." The programmers took an interface that was unusable because of deep behavioral design flaws and put a sexy visual cover on it.

Hardware vendors seem to be particularly enamored of this approach—remember, this came free with my new computer. I suspect it is because the interface is so metaphorically faithful to a vision of cool hardware.

We often see products that *look* really good—whose aesthetics are superb—but whose functionality or whose interactivity isn't adequate. That is not because the product wasn't designed, but because it was designed by an aesthetic, visual designer rather than by an interaction designer with the tools to master cognitive friction.

Industrial Design

Another profession whose expertise is sought for help is industrial design. This older, well-established profession is skilled at creating objects in three dimensions that fit your vision, your body, and—especially—your hands. In general, industrial designers do excellent work, and their sins are those of omission rather than commission. Industrial designers are trained to create buttons, knobs, and controls that are easy to feel, manipulate, and see. However, they are not specifically trained to satisfy the demands of cognitive friction, or to work with software engineers. Like the buttons in the remote keyless entry system described in Chapter 2, "Cognitive Friction," the buttons are instantaneously recognizable as buttons, even by feel. Their physical use is intuitive, but their logical use—their metause—remains as unclear as ever.

The five remote-control devices on my coffee table, taken individually, are nice enough, but collectively they make my home-entertainment system largely unusable. Although they are sensuously curved and attractive to look at, you are hopelessly lost when you need to change the channel or mute the audio in the dark. The industrial designers who designed them satisfied the demands placed on them by the equipment vendors, but they did not satisfy the interaction needs of the user.

It is easy to see why product managers can mistake industrial design for interaction design. Industrial designers also deal with the interface between people and high-technology artifacts. They also make it easy for people to use these high-tech contraptions. The fact that the buttons are easy to find and press doesn't mean that the user will know which button is the right one to press. That is a problem of cognitive friction, not of industrial design.

Cool New Technology

There is one final pretender to the throne of interaction design, and that is technology itself. Microsoft, in particular, is touting this false panacea. Microsoft says that interfaces will be easy to use as soon as it can perfect voice recognition and handwriting recognition. I think this is silly. Each new technology merely makes it possible to frustrate users with faster and more-powerful systems.

A key to better interaction is to reduce the uncertainty between computers and users. Natural-language processing can never do that because meanings are so vague in human conversation. So much of our communication is based on nuance, gesture, and inflection that although it might be a year or two before computers can recognize our words, it might be decades—if ever—before computers can effectively interpret our meaning.

Voice-recognition technology will certainly prove to be useful for many products. I think it is foolishly optimistic to think that a new technology will be any better at rescuing us than any of the others were. Technology requires design to be a complete solution for real users, regardless of the combination of technologies we use.

Iteration

It is a commonly accepted truth about software development that the way to get good interaction is to iterate. The devotion to usability testing at most universities and many large software-development companies—particularly Microsoft—led to the spread of this idea. And, yes, iteration is an important element of good design: Keep working on it until it's right. However, many product developers have interpreted this to mean that you can dispense with design and merely iterate across random thrusts in the dark.

In 1986, Microsoft rushed version one of Windows to market, and it was so pathetic, it deservedly became the laughingstock of the industry. Six months later, Microsoft shipped version 1.03, which fixed some bugs. A year later, Microsoft shipped 1.1, and then version 2.0.[2] Each iteration of the product tried to solve the problems created by the previous version. Finally, four years after the first version shipped, Microsoft shipped Windows 3.0, and the industry stopped laughing. Few companies in the industry have pockets deep enough, or the tenacity, to ignore public humiliation for four years to finally get it right. One side effect of this is that the industry sees its de facto leader staggering blindly about until it does get it right, and the industry makes the obvious assumption that that is the correct way to do things.

But shipping all of those interim versions was very expensive. If Microsoft could have arrived at the quality of Windows 3.0 without shipping a couple of those intermediate releases, it could have saved millions in development and support dollars, earning additional millions in sales much earlier in the product's life (not to mention saving their customers billions of dollars and many headaches). Accepting as true that multiple versions are inevitable is an extremely expensive capitulation of good sense.

Microsoft's strategy is based on simple attrition. In military terms, attrition means that you might be evenly matched with your enemy in quality—or even somewhat inferior—but you have so many soldiers and guns that you merely trade down until your opponent cannot field any more regiments. In software terms, it means shipping a bad product—a real dancing bear—then listening to your clients moan and complain. You tweak what they dislike and ship an updated version. After three or four versions, the overt pain suffered by the users subsides and the quality of the product reaches some acceptable minimum, aided by broad functionality, and does not improve thereafter. Iteration never creates great products.

The attrition strategy is not only expensive and time-consuming, but it is a hateful one because it is abusive of people who use computer technology. Unfortunately, it is working pretty well for Microsoft. Time after time, it has shipped half-baked, ill-conceived, poorly built, undesigned products to the sneers and derision of industry observers, both partial and impartial. But while the industry

---

[2] *Microsoft's version-numbering logic is nonexistent. There were at least four major releases of Windows before Windows 3.0. Windows 3.1 was a dramatically different and improved version, with many major changes, and it clearly should have been called Windows 4.0. I'm sure that Microsoft marketing people called it 3.1 instead because they didn't want to squander the market equity already earned by "version three."*

pundits jeer, Microsoft continues to support its first efforts with 2nd, 3rd, 4th, 5th, and 11th versions. Such products as Windows, ActiveX, Word, Access, Windows NT, and many others have eventually emerged as Goliaths in their respective markets.

The attrition strategy only works if you have a rock-solid brand name, lots of time, the nerves of a poker player, and vast quantities of money. So far, no other players in the computer industry have exhibited those qualities in equal measure to Microsoft.

The real problem with Microsoft's spectacular commercial success is that many smaller companies attempt to emulate its success by emulating its attrition strategy. This is often quite unsuccessful in the long term, as Web browser maker Netscape has shown, but it continues the legacy of abusing end users.

It is quite possible to beat the attrition player, but not by using a matching strategy. After all, regardless of who you are, Microsoft has more money than you do. Instead, you must strike Microsoft hard where it is weakest—in its development process, which puts programming in front of interaction design. Microsoft is doubly handicapped in that it has many people at the company with the title of "designer" who do design-related things. As shown by the excerpts from Fred Moody's book in Chapter 8, "An Obsolete Culture," the Microsoft culture has already made a place at the table for ineffective, after-the-fact design. Any company willing to do *real* interaction design can beat Microsoft.

13

A MANAGED PROCESS

I believe that most managers in the business of creating software-based products don't really have a clear understanding of how to identify the best, most successful products or how to make them. Lacking this awareness, managers take counsel of their fears, but after they do so, they are riding a tiger. Although they are moving rapidly, they are not in control, and if they let go they will only be eaten. In this chapter, I will examine the technical manager's dilemma and show how design can be just the tool for taming the tiger.

Who Really Has the Most Influence?

How can you know whose advice to follow and whose to ignore? I see executives behaving like car-chasing dogs in the middle of a busy intersection, barking furiously and trying to run in all directions at once. Top management says, "Make it look like Outlook 98." Marketing says, "Match the competition." Sales says, "This customer wants that feature." The programmers say, "Stay consistent with our last version." Who are you to believe?

Product-development managers try their best to say yes to all of these constituents. Programmers have disproportional influence because of their ownership of the code, so their goals tend to be met regardless. However, the one group whose needs always seem to take precedence over others' is the customers. After all, although each constituency is standing there demanding action, the customer is the only one *who is also holding a check*. No businessperson can fail to be influenced by that!

The Customer-Driven Death Spiral

If you take that check, you begin the transformation into a "customer-driven" company. Although this has a nice ring to it and is widely used, it is a mistake. It puts you squarely on the back of the tiger. Throughout the 1980s, IBM prided itself on being a customer-driven company, and it let its customers drive it right off the top of the mountain. IBM virtually owned the computer business back then—to a much greater extent than Microsoft does now—yet it is just one of the pack today—still large, but a follower and not a leader.

Usually, a new company bases its first product on some technological advance. That first product is designed according to the inside vision of how things should be done. At this stage, what customers the company might have are only loosely committed and will offer only desultory guidance. After the new product is finally delivered, though, the customers become more self-interested because they are investing time and energy into the product. Inevitably, they have requests for changes and additions.

There is a big difference between *listening to* and *following* your customers. Listening is good. It means applying your own filter to what you have heard. Following is bad. It means merely doing what your customers tell you to do. This lets the tiger decide where you will go.

After the vendor begins to let its customers dictate what features the product will have, a very serious, but almost unnoticeable, change transforms the vendor. The vendor ceases to be a *product* company, inventing things to sell to its customers, and becomes a *service* company, performing jobs on demand for its customers. Everyone inside the company is sensitive to this subtle shift in power, and they correctly respond to it by promoting the demands of the client above all others.

Today, many enterprise-software companies, such as Oracle and SAP—which experienced explosive growth in the early 1990s as their modern, client-server architecture replaced the older, mainframe software—are reliving IBM's customer-driven nightmare. After introducing their new technology, these so-called enterprise resource planning (ERP) companies started listening to their customers. They began to add features that their customers requested, without fitting them into a larger, longer-term plan.

I have heard managers tell me that no change whatsoever is made to their product unless a customer demands it. Each customer does business in a slightly different way, and each one asks the ERP company to make changes and add features to accommodate its particular methods. In a misguided effort to be helpful, the eagerly listening, blindly following, customer-driven vendor complies.

You are a single vendor, but you will have dozens or hundreds of customers. If you respond to them all (or to the biggest ones), who is reconciling their conflicting demands?

Many of the high-tech managers I know have backgrounds in engineering and are often former programmers. At the least, they have acquired their positions because they are very knowledgeable about and sympathetic to programmers. As I showed in Chapters 7, "Homo Logicus," and 8, "An Obsolete Culture," programmers look to functions and features for answers. When customers bring requests for features in one hand and a check in the other, technical managers find the combination irresistible. This is one more reason why so many product-development organizations use feature-list negotiation to manage themselves. They are riding the tiger, and deadline management assures that they will ride at a dizzying pace.

Conceptual Integrity Is a Core Competence

After you take that check, you are handing over the reins of your product-development shop. The customer might have money, but it lacks two vital things: It doesn't have your best, long-term interests at heart, and it doesn't know how to design your product.

Customer-driven products don't have a coherent design. They lack what software guru Frederick Brooks calls "conceptual integrity," a single-minded vision of a program which, he goes on to say, is the most important ingredient for success. Lacking conceptual integrity, two things happen: The customers take control of your product's design, and you abdicate control of your product's design. The customers, no matter how well meaning they might be, don't have the ability to think of your product as a single, conceptual whole. Having a clear vision is a core competence, and most companies are hard pressed to focus sufficiently on their *own* business, let alone yours. Even while they are shouting conflicting orders at you, they are expecting *you* to select the right ones to obey.

When you are customer driven, your product mutates from one release to the next, instead of growing in an orderly manner. The product ends up filled with mismatched parts and random features and becomes what product developer John Zicker calls a "dog's breakfast." Each customer has to pick its way through your product, finding the features it likes and avoiding the features it doesn't, but *all* of them find the going gets tougher with each new release. Some well-known companies have products that are so incredibly complicated that it takes months of training to do even the simplest tasks. Entire businesses spring up to train, install, configure, and maintain these monsters. Although customers might purchase a dog's breakfast, there is little love for the product. It has no desirability, which, as I showed in Chapter 5, "Customer Disloyalty," makes it—and you—very vulnerable to competition.

A Faustian Bargain

One way to look at this shift from a vision-driven company to a customer-driven company is as a shift from a product company to a service company. David Maister's remarkable book, *Managing the Professional Service Firm*,[1] talks about the problem of being customer driven in the different context of a service provider: a consultant. Of course, because the service business is very different, he uses very different terms. He speaks of selling his problem-solving *expertise* versus selling his past *experience*. He refers to them as "brains" and "gray hair," respectively.

Selling brains is difficult. Anyone who will hire you for your brains must trust you to a high degree, because they are expecting you to do something that you have not yet demonstrated competence in. Selling gray hair is easier. A potential client can see that since you have solved this same problem before, you can solve it again for them.

Most consultants start out selling brains to their colleagues—that is, people who already have an established trust. When the consultant solves the client's problem, she begins building a reputation, and more clients appear at the door. These clients will be progressively more removed and will have progressively less trust in the consultant at the outset. So they will ask the consultant to do gray-hair jobs. After all, your experience attracted the new client, and it is the kind of assignment that a client will give to an unproven vendor.

After a consultant establishes her reputation, her gray-hair clientele grows, and she finds herself making more and easier money by applying her experience. After all, she is doing the kind of work that she has already done many times.

As your business gradually shifts from a brains business to a gray-hair business, the very qualities that make you valuable as a consultant begin to wane. You fall off the cutting edge. The service you offer is not one of brilliant problem solving, but one of pedestrian task execution. Your desirability as a consultant shrinks, and your own clients begin assigning you ever-more-demeaning, low-level tasks. They begin to court other consultants who are farther out on the cutting edge— those who use their brains more.

It's the customer-driven death spiral all over again, but this time from a service perspective.

---

[1] *David Maister,* Managing the Professional Service Firm, *1997, Free Press, New York, New York, ISBN 0-684-83431-6.*

The lesson is that if you become customer driven, you accept easy money in the short term, but you cease to grow, and you resign any hold on the future. You give up your role as a leader.

Everyone colludes in this game. Customers are very comfortable with it. The new ones approach you and say, "Put this one feature into your product, and then I'll buy it." This is a test to see whether you are a compliant service organization. The sales force puts a lot of effort into such a big sale, and adding one little feature seems like such a small price to pay for establishing a relationship with a new customer. Revenue beckons.

The solution that Maister proposes is obvious: Do more brains projects. In the service context, you have to convince your current gray-hair clients to give you brains work, and he goes on at length on how to do that. He says it means turning down the easy money of gray-hair projects to get harder and less-profitable brains projects from existing clients. Translating Maister's solution into the product business, we find that whereas all customer requests are gray-hair jobs, the brains jobs are all internally driven assignments. In other words, it's *your* responsibility as a product manager to keep yourself on the cutting edge and avoid the customer-driven death spiral. You have to look inside yourself for answers, the same way you did when you first started.

It means taking a longer view, taking responsibility, taking time, and taking control.

Taking a Longer View

In order to maintain your competitive edge, you have to put short-term gain into perspective. You must ensure that your people understand that when you focus exclusively on short-term gains, you start a time bomb ticking. You must avoid doing this despite the short-term expense.

Taking the longer view means walking away from some very lucrative deals. This is hard to do but necessary for your survival in the long term. In my experience, you rarely actually lose those deals. If you have the confidence to walk away from a client proffering money, that client will likely gain increased trust in you and reevaluate what they are asking of you. Still, you must be willing to walk.

Taking Responsibility

You have to establish the balance early on. You can't say, "I'll just use short-term tactics for two years and then switch to long term." You have to balance both from day one. You can always postpone short-term thinking, but you can never postpone long-term thinking.

This is all about corporate culture, and it is hard to introduce the long view to an established short-view culture. It is risky to step back from the lucrative precipice of being customer driven. You will draw fire. Take heart that you are doing the right thing.

Taking Time

Many high-tech companies have a policy of shipping a new release of their software every year. Some ship even more frequently than that. This means that their main body of programmers is working on an annual cycle, and that any work must go from conception to design to programming to testing to market within that year. This is too fast to do really innovative design, so most companies try to overlap design with programming. As I've described at length already, when you overlap design and programming, what you get is programming.

Taking Control

Above all, high-tech development managers have to seize control of their development process away from the rampant tiger. You have to get off of the beast and take the inevitable thrashing. If you survive it, you can then begin to rebuild your process so that you balance brains and gray-hair work and keep your edge for the future.

Finding Bedrock

Most companies do very careful planning and thinking on the financial and operational side of the business. On the product side, they imagine that using feature lists is equally rigorous planning, but it is emphatically not. Software development is simply too hard, too expensive, and too difficult to do without careful planning and thinking. In the context of software development, "careful planning" can only mean interaction design, which, as has been established, is quite neglected.

One of the collateral benefits of Goal-Directed design is the cast of characters: the list of specific types of users. This document offers significant help in determining how you should react to your customer's demands for features. You first assess which user persona the new feature would service, and then decide whether or not it is one of your primary personas. If it is, you can seriously consider it. If it is not, you will drop another step farther back from the leading edge, regardless how much money you will get. If a customer walked into your office and offered you $100,000 to throw out your accounting system or set fire to your filing cabinets, would you do it?

Knowing Where to Cut

When a company is customer driven, this is a clear symptom that the product managers believe in the myth of the unpredictable market. They really don't know whether or not a feature is good or bad, necessary or unnecessary. They turn control over to the customer because, well, why not? *They* certainly don't know. If the customer says, "Add a left-handed monkey-wrench feature," the product manager figures the customer must know something. The manager believes that it might be the magic feature that will make the product a big success.

The flip side of this is that the product manager doesn't have a clue about what features to *cut* either. When external forces constrict the schedule, the manager has to cut features, but he has no idea which features are vital and which are mere gravy.

Letting nondesigners cut features is like letting anyone cut wires in an airplane. The cutting is random, or based on some unrelated quality such as the color of the insulation or the distance from your seat—you might or might not cut important wires. One moment you are disabling the reading light in seat 22A, and the next moment the engines quit. But letting designers cut features is like letting the airplane's designer cut wires: He will avoid the ones that are needed for flight and disable all of the nonessential equipment first.

Making Movies

Making movies is exorbitantly expensive, just like writing software. Moviemakers have been making films in Hollywood longer than we've been creating software in Silicon Valley, and we can learn something from them. The actual filming of a movie is the really expensive part. All of those cameras, sets, technicians, and actors can cost many thousands of dollars every day. Good moviemakers keep tight controls on this production phase by investing in detailed advance planning. By putting time and money into creating detailed storyboards and shooting schedules, they save orders of magnitude more money and time during filming.

The process of getting a film made can be broken into three major phases: preproduction, production, and postproduction. In the preproduction phase, the producers have the script written and polished, design sets and costumes, hire the cast and crew, and raise funds. During the production phase, the lights glare, the cameras roll, the directors shout orders, and the actors emote. During the postproduction phase, the film is edited, the soundtrack is recorded, and the marketing campaign is assembled. These phases correspond quite closely to the software-construction process.

During the preproduction phase, the managers do the interaction design for the product, hire the programmers, and raise funds. During the production phase, the CRTs glow, the compilers roll, the managers shout directives, and the programmers emit code. During the postproduction phase, the code is debugged, the documentation is written, and the marketing campaign is assembled.

	Pre-production	Production	Post-production
Film	Write script, storyboard, production design, casting, raise money	Cameras roll, directors yell "cut", lights glare, actors emote, technicians tech	Editing, soundtrack, marketing
Software	Interaction design, storyboard, screen sketch, hire programmers, raise money	Programmers code, managers fetch pizza, designers solve minor interaction problems	Debugging, documentation, marketing

Take Time to Save Time

The significant aspect of this tripartite structure is that the purpose of the pre-production phase is *to minimize the duration of the production phase.* It is excruciatingly expensive to put a film crew to work, and shaving just a few days off a long shooting schedule can pay for weeks of additional pre- or postproduction work. A contemporary film will spend a year or more in preproduction, and then a couple of months in intense filming, and then many more months in postproduction.

What's more, as our films get increasingly technical (what do you get when you cross a film with a computer?), more and more of the production work simply cannot be done without meticulous advance planning. If your leading actor must have a light-saber duel with a computer-generated alien, he must have an imaginary fight with just a blue-screen background, so his every action must be first choreographed down to the slightest step and glance.

Moviemakers know that they only get one chance to do it right, so they never skip the preproduction effort. In the world of software engineering, many managers believe that they can just fix it in the next release, so the pressure for advance planning is reduced. That's an awfully expensive assumption.

It is just as complicated to make modern software as it is to make modern films, yet most development processes seem to ignore that fact. Most development teams that I have seen spend a few days or weeks (at most) in planning and design, and then anywhere between 6 and 18 months programming, and then just a couple more months of debugging, testing, and documentation. I suspect that we have a lot to learn from filmmakers. If we spent more time in preproduction—in design—we could cut our expensive programming time considerably.

The moviemaking preproduction phase is the one in which the least money is spent. It doesn't cost much to create a detailed storyboard of an expensive chase scene filled with explosions and special effects. To make dramatic changes all it takes is an eraser, a pencil, and some time. Getting all of the details right on paper will save millions when the camera is rolling and the cars are filled with stuntmen and explosives. Preproduction is an investment in time that saves cash and increases the likelihood of eventual success.

If the director changes his mind and wants to blow up a helicopter instead of a railroad train, it is simple, cheap, and easy to do in preproduction. To make that kind of change during filming would be ridiculous. Filmmakers know this, so they take their time to get it right during preproduction and then proceed as planned during production.

Why do we approach software construction with such a different mindset? We put so little time and effort into advance planning. Instead, we fill up the white-board, create the spreadsheet of one-line feature names, and then send those incredibly expensive programmers out into no-man's-land to code. Just like film-makers, we know how expensive it is to make changes during coding, yet we don't bother to invest the time and effort in the planning process. Instead we hire the programmers, let them start coding, and then plead that we can't make changes now because the expensive coding is underway.

For existing products, the cycle is even more skewed. An annual feature upgrade to an already shipping product might have *no* calendar time allocated to it for preproduction design work. Instead, the product manager simply maintains a list of features requested by customers, and it is just annually, unceremoniously handed to the programmers for coding.

Just as in the preproduction phase in filmmaking, adding a thorough product-design phase to the software-development process will yield enormous benefits. By creating a detailed paper plan for the product, we eliminate the vast uncer-tainties of programming, along with significantly reducing the risks normally attributed to releasing software-based products.

The Deal

Management must make a commitment to bringing design in before program-ming begins. Analogously speaking, interaction design is architecture, not inte-rior design. Interaction design determines where the concrete for the foundation will be poured as much as it determines which fabric will be most appropriate for the window treatments. This commitment must extend to giving the interaction designers the moral authority to dictate the shape and constitution of the prod-uct to the programmers. This will involve significant cultural upheaval, but the programmers will be happier after the change, and you will benefit from short-ened programming time and an immensely superior product.

In exchange for this power, the interaction-design community must make two commitments of its own. First, interaction designers need to get some skin in the game. They need to stop standing on the sidelines giving advice to the program-mers, while passively letting them take full responsibility for the success of the products. It is not good enough merely to have the right ideas. You have got to get those right ideas applied to practice, and the only time that is going to happen is when the interaction designers put themselves in harm's way. The programmers do it every time they write a line of code.

The second commitment that interaction designers must make is to put their design in writing.

Document Design to Get It Built

One of the really tough lessons that I have learned over the years is that good, even great, design is meaningless unless it gets built. And it will never get built unless it is described at length, with precision and detail, in terms that make sense to the programmers who must build it. It has to be in writing, in exhaustive detail, with supporting evidence and examples. It has to be printed and bound in multiple copies. It must be presented personally to the development team, with the VP of development standing there nodding his head and smiling. Better if it's the CEO.

The designers need to write, storyboard, animate, and sketch their solutions with sufficient completeness and detail that programmers can treat the solutions like blueprints and actually write code from them. Enough situations must be described in detail to give the developers confidence that the solution is robust enough to survive implementation.

The written design is like a written battle plan. Everyone knows his part and what the critical and timely issues are. Everyone can move in synchrony and harmony to create a product that is targeted at a specific user.

Programmers rely on a persuasive technique called "passive-aggressive." Instead of forcing a confrontation that must decide an issue, they avoid attention and quietly take—or don't take—action. It's like a passenger steering a canoe by sur-reptitiously leaning to one side or another. One of my favorite business axioms, "If it isn't on paper it doesn't exist," is truer than ever in the world of software design. Anything left unwritten is more than likely to be misconstrued or ignored because the motivations of the programmers are so divergent from the motiva-tions of the users. It's not enough *not* to specify a dialog box, but the designer must explicitly state where the programmer is *not* to voluntarily insert an extra dialog box. To a programmer, dialog boxes are good things, and he feels like he is doing the user a favor to toss in a couple of extra ones in his spare time. To users, dialog boxes are hateful things that sap their energy and derail productivity.

Interaction designers, like architects, deliver a set of blueprints that describe the product to be built. But although the similarity between blueprints and software design documents is very close, they have great differences, too. Blueprints have a lot of leverage. A single line on paper can indicate a wall of 100,000 bricks. When interaction is involved, most of the leverage shrinks away. It might take a 100-page document to describe the behavior of 100 pages of code. With only a small dose of facetiousness, I say that *a sufficiently detailed specification is indistinguishable from the code that implements it.* In a perfect world, developers will grant designers a year to design and then give the programmers three months to code. In *this* world, the numbers are reversed.

What this means is that the design document must, of necessity, omit some things. As well as knowing what is good design, the designer must know what is important. The interaction designer must decide which parts of the program *must* be designed, and which parts can be left to the indigenous solutions of the programmers.

All of my design documents are organized in the "spiral" method of a newspaper. The headline of a news story tells the entire tale. Then the first paragraph tells the story again with a bit more detail. Then the next three paragraphs tell the story once again, this time with more information. Then the remainder of the article, which might take several columns, tells the entire story in complete detail. This allows the reader to take what she wants without drowning in unnecessary detail.

Design Affects the Code

Many people have the mistaken assumption that what interaction designers do, and that what needs to be done, is user-interface design. Interface design is certainly *part* of what needs to be done, but it holds only a secondary role in the process of design, much like packaging does in retail sales. Interface design is what is done after both the purpose and behavior of the interactive product are already established. But a bad product in beautiful and imaginative wrappings is still a bad product.

When experts are called in to do interface design, they are often summoned only after the product is already substantially built. The opportunity for significant design has passed, and the designer's efforts—no matter how heroic—have relatively limited impact.

Interaction design can have a dramatic effect on the actual implementation process, although this does not mean that the design is explicit about implementation issues. For example, the programmers might be expecting the designers to specify how an important dialog box should look to the user. However, interaction designers might wish to replace that dialog box with another idiom, such as a toolbar. But the designers are not concerned with how either dialogs or toolbars are actually coded.

Because the interaction designer might have a large effect on what does and does not get built, while studiously avoiding details of *how* things get built, we think of design as a product-definition process. Essentially, interaction designers determine the inside of the product by describing the outside of it. The interaction with the user is specified with great detail and precision, and the implementation issues are left to the programmer.

Design Documents Benefit Programmers

In Chapter 3, "Wasting Money," I asked the question, "What does 'done' look like?" The central purpose of the documents produced by the interaction designer is to answer that question. In general terms, a written design document is a robust mechanism for controlling the actual coding. It acts like the script and storyboard of a movie, making it clear to everyone how it will work, what is involved to build it and to use it, and when construction on it is done. The coding portion of development is typically the most uncontrollable and most fraught with risk, so not knowing when it is done is quite costly.

A clear, written design helps upper management understand precisely what it is building so it can create a more tightly focused business. Management will have a stronger message to deliver to investors, partners, employees, and colleagues. This ensures that all of the company's efforts work toward the same objective.

Programmers want strong and intelligent leadership. After all, they are strong and intelligent, and would obviously wish to be led by their equals, not their inferiors. Jerry Weinberg claims that everyone knows that "bad managers are easier to find than good programmers." This gives the good programmer more leverage over the manager than the manager has over the programmer, despite his nominal authority in the corporate hierarchy.

Product managers are weak if they cannot articulate with precision and conviction exactly what it is they are building. Typically, management expresses what it wants only in the vague terms of deadline management and too-specific feature-list negotiation. Only the programmers know with any precision what the actual product will look like, so they have more control over the project than the manager has.

I've worked with programmers who loathed the presence of an outside design firm. They know that my job is to "design," and they know that design is the creative, fun part of *their* job. After they have the opportunity to work with us, however, they realize that not only do we not detract from their job, but we also enhance it.

Recently, I attended an acrimonious meeting where some client programmers were invited without being briefed on our role. One gray-bearded programmer, named Fred, was particularly conspicuous. Throughout the meeting, whenever we presented some new idea or different way of offering up information to the user, he would attack us. He was highly intelligent and articulate, and he had a particularly stentorian voice. Every time we revealed another slide showing how the interaction would change, he would roll his eyes, smile condescendingly, and then make some remark about how we "didn't realize what large feats of magic" we were demanding from him and his team. At each step, he indicated that our design decisions made his job harder rather than easier.

Finally, at the conclusion of the meeting, as everyone streamed out of the room, our team was able to speak with Fred privately. We explained to him that our charter was to make the program easier and more powerful *for end users*, and that we were fully aware that our design decisions would entail significant additional thinking at the program level. We insisted that our concerns were only for the end user. All of a sudden a look of astonishment burst onto Fred's face. He exclaimed, "You are providing me with a *significant technical challenge!*" His entire attitude changed as he realized that we brought to him the grail of all programmers: a difficult problem worth solving.

Far from threatening him, we were bringing to him that which he most coveted: a chance to prove himself yet again as the cleverest, smartest, most skilled programmer around. His attitude changed when he realized that we took away only the messy human side of the program that he disliked, leaving him master of the clean, algorithmic internal part of the software. We became his benefactors instead of his nemeses.

Design Documents Benefit Marketing

In most noncomputerized businesses, marketing professionals own the product-definition step. In the software business, the marketers have been shunted out of the process. All they have to work with are requests for features. If they demand fixes, the programmers will merely fling the restrictive schedule back in their faces, asking, "How can I fix it if you won't give me time?" The marketing manager dares not give up precious time because not only will the schedule slip, but then everyone will see that the schedule is really just a sham, and the programmers will then proceed to abuse it with impunity in the future. Marketers know that a feature list is a very weak mechanism, and they often agitate for more involvement in the definition process. Unfortunately, marketers seem unable to provide direction that the developers find meaningful or useful.

One of the most important benefits of a strong design process—and the rigorous documentation that is part of it—is the power it makes available to marketers. The marketers describe to the designers the unfilled need or desire they hope to satisfy. The interaction designers then study potential users to determine their goals and to create a cast of characters. The crisply defined user personas are an important part of the written design documentation, and they become a focal point for marketing efforts. Even though the programmer works only with code, the design personas inform that code. Even though the marketer works with channels, target markets, media, and resellers, the design personas inform them. At last, the programmer and the marketer have a common ground.

In effect, interaction designers act as a go-between for marketing professionals. A designer is a person who can translate from marketese to programese. When marketers have a vague concern, they can describe it to the designers, who will work with them to develop the thought in terms of a persona. From there, the designer can translate it into a specification for interaction. What's more, the marketer can now see his input is being addressed and can be confident that he won't be handed raw technology and instructed to find a buyer for it.

The development of user personas is typically very familiar to marketing professionals. They often do a similar exercise, determining the product's buyer personas. These personas are determined by examining distribution channels and demographics rather than user goals and scenarios, so they are usually different from the designers' personas, but the user personas are always very helpful to the marketing experts in developing their own plans. Marketers can clearly express to the *buyer* how the product will help her *users*.

Design Documents Help Documenters and Tech Support

Any technical writer will tell you that good design eliminates the need for prodigious quantities of documentation. Fewer complex interactions mean fewer long explanations. The documentation writers can invest more time in writing at a higher level. Instead of devoting their efforts to leading users by the hand through the swamps of confusing interface, they can elevate their aspirations and put their efforts into taking users into more-beneficial areas of solving the problems of the application domain. Instead of discussing where files are stored in an inventory system, for example, the documentation can more profitably discuss inventory-leveling processes.

The same applies to technical support. The better the design is, the fewer calls come from the field. As the Peacock design described in the last chapter showed, a written design will cause a dramatic reduction in the need for technical support.

Design Documents Help Managers

Of all the constituencies, development management is the one interaction design helps the most. By describing what will be created well in advance of any programming, the entire process of development becomes faster, better informed, less risky, and less expensive. The entire process of development becomes more effective and is cut loose from being customer-driven.

Above all, design means more predictability. A designed product means that the programming phase will be more predictable. It also means that the success of the product can be more easily predicted and measured. These are the two most risky and expensive aspects of software-based product development. They reduce the cost of production, and they vanquish the myth of the unpredictable market. Ed Forman, the development VP of Elemental's Drumbeat product says, "I measure the value of design services in months of burn rate saved."

Design Documents Benefit the Whole Company

The essence of creating a successful business is to ensure that everyone involved is working to achieve the same goals. Any confusion or discord in objectives dissipates energy twofold. First, you lose the effort of those who are not going in the right direction, and second, their effort is applied against those who are striving in the correct direction. Like one person in a boat rowing in a direction opposite to everyone else, the boat is simply not competitive. In order to succeed, everyone must be rowing in the same direction, and any force that diverts the attention of one incurs a cost by all.

What's more, knowing with precision what you *are* doing helps you avoid wasting effort on things that you are *not* doing. No company has cycles to waste on efforts that are not right on point.

By vanquishing deadline management and feature-list negotiation, a written product description turns the company's attention to product quality, which has the inevitable result of its dramatic improvement. This in turn generates more of that priceless commodity: customer loyalty.

Who Owns Product Quality?

When everyone has responsibility for product quality, nobody is responsible for product quality. It is far too easy to assume that your colleague will solve the quality problem while you work on something else. The programmers are solely responsible for eliminating all bugs from the code. The sales staff is solely responsible for closing deals. The marketers are solely responsible for packaging and positioning. At the present time, though, no one is responsible solely for the quality and appropriateness of the product. Sometimes they lack the tools to locate and solve the problem. Sometimes they lack the skills to communicate the solution. Sometimes they lack the authority to have their solutions implemented.

As we have seen in the previous chapters, coding compromises the programmers' ability to address users' goals. Product managers already have plenty of work to do, and they cannot focus on the details of a product's behavior. Marketers' lack of a technical background weakens their ability to communicate technically, which undermines their credibility with the programmers. Without a thoroughly documented design, there is little hope of getting it implemented properly and effectively.

The central recommendation of this book is that *the interaction designer should be the ultimate owner of product quality.* He must be allowed to determine the content and behavior of the program. He must own the feature list and, in large part, the schedule. This person is the advocate for the user and should have the authority to control all external aspects of the product.

In return for all of this authority, the interaction designers have some very significant responsibilities. Unless designers have a combination of authority and responsibility, programmers will not respect the designers and will retake control of the product. Designers must have skin in the game. The interaction-design team's mandate includes designing a feasible-to-build, easy-to-use, attractive product that allows the user to achieve her practical goals without violating her personal goals. What's more, the interaction designers must describe in exhaustive detail, in writing, a narrative description from which the programmers can reasonably be expected to build the design. The interaction designers must provide marketing with a clear, written description of the users and how the product will satisfy their needs. Most important, the designers accept responsibility for the quality of the final product.

Creating a Design-Friendly Process

In the last chapter, we saw how many of the professionals who have offered to help with interaction design have not succeeded. We have examined usability testers, industrial designers, and others who have tried and failed to solve this problem. Currently, there is no group of any size in the industry that *can* solve it.

As the ranks of interaction designers slowly grow, keep in mind that fostering a design-friendly *process* is more important than hiring the most talented designer. The most important thing is to make a commitment to take time out for design before you code. Finding the most brilliant designer in the world will do no good if the product is going into beta next week.

For example, many software dynasties have been established on the backs of very young, very inexperienced programmers. They were likely given a free hand with programming issues, and the pairing of immense responsibility with immense authority can often be a crucible for creating greatness. The same forces apply in interaction design. If someone is given the responsibility for product quality, *and she is given authority equal to it,* she will often rise to the challenge regardless of her experience. If you take a suitable person and give her full control over the quality and behavior of a product, you will have a much, much better product than if you don't. The problem is with the process, not with the people. Of course, all things being equal, it is always better to get an expert with relevant experience. However, if experts are in short supply or not in the budget, using less-skilled practitioners is better than just letting the programmers run loose.

What does it mean to be a "suitable person?" The most suitable would be someone without an interest in the construction of the product and with the detachment to put himself in the user's place. This could easily be a programmer, but certainly *not* one of the programmers who will have to build this particular program. That imposes too great of a conflict of interest.

Where Interaction Designers Come From

Still, you have to choose someone to do your interaction design. After you start to look for them, you will find frustrated interaction designers already present in almost every high-tech company: technical writers who have programmers coming to them for help thinking things through, product managers with bookshelves full of interface-design books, usability testers who talk about getting involved in development earlier in the process, marketing managers who point out that they purchased the stereo with the fewest buttons, programmers who do very little coding but whom other programmers ask to work with. In fact, after it becomes known within a company that a project will start with a design phase before the coding begins, someone is sure to step forward and ask for the assignment, saying that she *wants* to be the person held responsible for the quality of product.

When you hire full-time designers, good applicants might or might not bill themselves as interaction designers. You need people with a general understanding of technical constraints and a passion for design, but you can find people like that working in many different environments and with widely varied backgrounds. In hiring people for my design studio, I ask people to respond to a design problem as a test because I know that their resumes can vary dramatically. At my studio, I have several designers with backgrounds in technical writing, software project management, tech support, and graphic design. Many of my designers have degrees in the humanities, but I also have designers with degrees in physics, architecture, computer science, and industrial design.

Experience in tech support or documentation provides designers with perspective in thinking about typical users' needs. Software product managers know about the needs and concerns of programmers in the development process. Graphic and industrial designers have a passion for design elegance and skills to produce it. Designers with a humanities education who have worked in high tech combine a knowledge of technology with an ability to articulate their thinking.

Building Design Teams

A discussion of how one organizes and runs a design team could easily fill a book of its own. In this book, I have touched on some design methods in order to make clear what I mean by "design," but I have not attempted to lay out an entire design methodology. However, my experience running teams of designers at my studio suggests a few key principles.

Keep the teams small. In order to progress, the designers need to share the same vision. I assign a team of two or three designers to each product, supported by occasional help and contributions from a few other specialists. In complex projects, the design might reach a point at which the product has a few distinct interfaces. At that point, you can split up the problem and put it into the hands of a few different teams. Before that point, too many cooks spoil the broth.

Insulate the team from managers and programmers. Early in a project, the designers need to talk to the other people working on the product to formulate a clear statement of the problem and define their personas. After that point, they need independence to follow some blind alleys before they reach their best solution, and they need privacy to do that effectively.

Assign a design communicator responsible for documenting the team's work. All team members will contribute to the documentation, but someone needs to own it in order to make it most effective.

Allow the team time to compose its thoughts. Late in the project, when the fundamental problems have already been solved, it is wise to go to your design team for answers to specific questions. Early in the project, the team needs to think things through carefully and present its reasoning as a coherent whole. When my studio does a full framework for a client, we provide a document and present our designs with informal checkpoints as needed. In the first presentation, we frame the problem, present the personas, and articulate the problems that the design must solve. In each successive presentation, we describe the design of the product in greater detail.

With a managed process, centered on design instead of on programming, companies can avoid riding a high-tech tiger. They can know in advance what their users will like and how to provide it to them. They will know when the development process is done, and the various disciplines will have a common, and specific, vision to rally around.

14

POWER AND PLEASURE

For you to realize the full measure of benefit from using interaction design in your business, it has to be baked into the software-development process as an integral part. It cannot be tacked on afterwards, added as an afterthought.

In the last chapter, I wrote that design needs to be written down before the coding begins. However, in the steaming cauldron of product development, the programmers can still simply ignore the design document, regardless of its quality. This is quite likely in the passive-aggressive culture of software engineering, in which the developer treats any design input as advice, to be complied with when possible and as workload permits.

It must be made emphatically clear to everyone on the project that the design is a blueprint that must be followed and is not merely a suggestion. Unless the commitment to design is demonstrated vigorously and publicly, the developers will assume that they alone have the real responsibility for creating a successful product.

There is only one way to communicate this effectively. The company's top management must state unequivocally to all other managers of both design and development that programmers are off the hook. They must make plain that the design team is now responsible for product quality and that the designers have the authority to make the call, subject—of course—to management oversight.

The programmers are welcome to improvise below the surface of the program, but every aspect of the defined user interaction must be assumed to be firm. This is not to say that it cannot be questioned, but it cannot be unilaterally ignored or changed. It cannot be treated as advice that can be selected from or edited.

The design team must have responsibility for everything that comes in contact with the user. This includes all hardware as well as all software. Collateral software such as install programs and supporting products must be considered, too.

This is probably the most radical requirement of successful design and the one that will demand the most cultural adaptation. Later in the chapter, I will discuss the cultural-change issue in more depth. Right now, let's look at an example of a company that smoothly integrated design into its process.

An Example of a Well-Run Project

My design studio completed work on one of our most successful design projects for a small company in the Pacific Northwest called Shared Healthcare Systems Inc. (SHS). It was building software to manage every aspect of long-term health-care facilities.

During our initial meetings, I took pains to explain to SHS the importance of personas and how we use them throughout our design process. To our great pleasure and surprise, the SHS team really embraced the concept. When they showed up for the project kickoff meeting, they brought with them their own cast of characters, with about a dozen personas already defined. We still had to go through our process of investigation and learning about the product domain in order to verify and refine the personas, but the whole issue of communicating the persona tool to the developers and product marketers was completely eliminated.

SHS's business takes it into what Michel Bourque, of Clinidata in Montreal, calls the "clinical vortex." Although doctors' offices were some of the first small businesses to be computerized, it was only the billing part that converted. The facet involving doctor interactions with patients has steadfastly resisted the encroachment of the digital age and is one of the last bastions of the fully noncomputerized world.

Although much of SHS's efforts would be administrative, a large portion of its work would step right into that vortex. We had done some small design projects for other clients in this area but had yet to be given full charge of the entire vortex. We were very excited about working on this big, challenging project.

SHS was excited, too, and it initially told us that the scope of its business was so wide that it really didn't believe that we could ever wrap our heads around it. SHS believed that its business was simply too big to be understood. We took that as a challenge and accepted it willingly.

The project was *big*. We identified *five* primary personas, two more than we had ever found in any previous project. At first we were suspicious of this count, but upon review, we realized that SHS was really tackling a huge segment of the health-care business. Of course, creating software for five primary personas is a project too large to build all at once. SHS realized this, and the product was designed and built in successive phases, one persona at a time.

David West, the VP of development and our contact at SHS, also has the trust and respect of the others in his growing organization. The product-marketing people know that he has their best interests at heart, as do the programmers. They know that he is fair but firm. He is a rock in the middle of the swirling white water of development. His visible commitment to the design process made it possible for the other developers to trust our design work and take it seriously as a specification.

When SHS came to Cooper Interaction Design, its software-development department was arranged along the same functional lines as its legacy product, which was divided into two parts: clinical and financial.

After we conducted our investigation and developed our personas, we quickly realized why the current system was failing to satisfy the caregivers. Apart from significant interaction problems, there was an artificial dividing line between the clinical and financial information subsystems. This necessitated extra paperwork on the user's part to circumvent the data-processing system's shortcomings. Each user was stuck on his own island of data, unable to communicate because of the lack of communication between the two sides of the system.

We recommended a unified resident (patient) record that maintains both clinical and financial resident information in one consolidated database, and a modular user interface that allows each persona to see the specific view of the information that is necessary for his tasks. As a result of this insight, SHS redesigned the database underlying the product. Even more remarkable, it reorganized its software-development staff to conform to the new design! The developers formed into two new groups, one that works with the architecture of the resident record and database, and a second group that works with the persona-specific interfaces. All further software specifications and documents at SHS will use the names of the personas to clearly articulate their function.

The programmers at SHS were wisely delaying the programming process to await the completion of the design. David and the team at SHS know full well the cost of idle programmers, but they also know how much more expensive it is to have the programmers go off and pour the concrete of code in the wrong places.

The programmers worked on some processing in the back end of the system that did not affect the user interaction. They also divided their project up into multiple phases that included a short-term, crash project to get an existing, legacy version of the product functioning at a higher level. This kept the programmers busy without impacting the larger, longer-term strategic project.

As part of the strategy to move forward while waiting, we subdivided the process into several big chunks.

We mutually decided to address only two of the five primary personas in our initial design and to put efforts into the other three later. Again, this allowed us to get in our design licks in advance of programming without idling their developers.

A Companywide Awareness of Design

In most companies, designing the primary product or service is assumed to be a core competence. In the world of high-tech software-based products, it is assumed—wrongly—that product design is a core competence of the engineering staff. Actually, there are two parts to the act of creation: design and programming. It demands a significant cultural change to willingly allow interaction designers to work on the business's essential core alongside the engineers.

At any company, regardless of the business it is in, the employees know that they have certain obligations. For example, in a company that manufactures wire coils for loudspeakers, the production manager knows that, although her job is buying wire from the best and cheapest supplier, she cannot sign a supplier's contract until the company's legal counsel has reviewed it. The production manager doesn't know very much about contract legalities, but she knows that encumbering her company without first bringing in the professionals with specialized skills in the area of contract writing and negotiation is wrong. Even though she is not skilled with contracts—or because of her lack of skill in this area—she knows that the lawyers must be involved.

The receiving clerk at the freight dock—despite being the most junior person on the staff—knows that he is empowered only to sign for prearranged deliveries but that he cannot sign for anything else.

The founder and president of the coil-manufacturing company is also quite aware of the need for legal review at all levels. She isn't formally trained in law, either, and she consults with her counsel before signing any formal documents.

Even though none of these people, from the president down, is skilled in legal issues, they are all fully aware of the importance of legal review. Nobody in the company will make any commitments until the lawyers have had their say. There is a companywide awareness of the need for legal oversight and, when appropriate, intervention.

This companywide awareness is true in other areas as well.

When the coil-winding company needed a new manufacturing building, it hired an outside professional, an architect. Even though the production manager and the president were both well versed in the needs of the production floor, they knew that their understanding of the nuances of worker flow and building construction was sketchy. Nobody in the company would imagine expanding their physical plant without first consulting an architect. The architect translated the needs of the user into terms that could be understood by the builder.

The same is true for advertising. The marketing manager wouldn't think of asking a coil-winder to describe the benefits of the product for the company's brochure or for an acoustic-industry magazine. Everyone in the company, regardless of his or her sophistication, understands that advertising is the purview of professionals and that advertising experts must craft the company's public presence. Of course, those experts can be employees of the company or they can be hired from an outside advertising agency. Either way works just fine.

The analogy isn't perfect because neither architecture nor legal advice is a core competence of a product company. Programming, however, is the creation of a product, and that *is* typically assumed to be a core competence. Given the direct effect on the business, you would expect any company to be even *more* circumspect about turning the reins over to the wrong people than with advertising, architecture, or purchasing.

We have to build awareness across the entire company that interaction design is a realm that requires professional skills and that interactive products cannot be just engineered, but must also be designed in order to succeed in the open market.

Benefits of Change

In the software world, the apologists are so numerous and influential that their rule is waning only slowly. But wane it will. What it takes is a widespread understanding that technology doesn't have to be so dehumanizing. As more and more users of software-based products have interactive experiences that are not humiliating, they will come to lose patience with those that continue to harass and embarrass them. They will boot the dancing bears out of town.

When the users of software-based products were few, they were also the insiders, who knew how difficult software's feats were. As the technology explodes into the mainstream, those who partake of its power are less aware of the greatness of the accomplishment. They are not willing to forgive a product with bad interaction just because building it was difficult.

Following technology seems like a good plan, but it usually brings only boring products that are more-complex derivatives of products that came before them. Interaction design lets you break out of that pattern and create products that do things that have never been done before.

Interaction design makes your product desirable, conferring on it the singular advantage of customer loyalty. After you make a customer happy with your product, he will stick with your company and your brand for a long time. If your product is merely dancing bearware, your customers will be quietly casting their eyes around, looking for easier, friendlier alternatives.

Interaction design can shorten the amount of time that you spend developing your product. Knowing what to do in advance means that you will spend less time blundering about trying to discover by accident the right thing to do.

Getting to the right product is always a matter of iterating. It always takes several tries to get the details right. With interaction design done in advance, the number of iterations it takes can be reduced significantly. There is enormous cost in each new version of a product, so if you can reduce the version count from, say, four to two, there is a lot of time and money to be saved.

Having to make fewer versions and having to throw away less code will make the development process cheaper. Programmers often complain that our designs involve more-complex code, and sometimes this is true. However, there is typically a lot less of it in total. The cost of code doesn't increase much as its difficulty increases, but it becomes a lot more expensive as the *quantity* of it increases. Each extra line of code must be tested, debugged, and supported.

Let Them Eat Cake

I live and work in Silicon Valley, California. Virtually everybody I know is involved in the high-tech industry. We are all affluent, highly educated, and geographically and socially mobile, and we are all very comfortable with computers, cell phones, DVDs, ATMs, and every other software-based product in the middle-class menagerie. When I eat lunch at the Crescent Park Grill or Spago, the people at the next table are always discussing "client/server this" and "Web-based that." It's an exciting place to live, but it isn't representative of the majority of people in this country, let alone around the world. Here in Silicon Valley, it is easy for our estimation of the suitability of high-tech products to be terribly skewed. We forget how hard these products really are to use.

Ten years ago, retail consultant Seymour Merrin said that we have found it easier to convince consumers that software is easy to use than it is to actually *make* it easier to use. Merrin was being cynical, but he was also expressing surprise that we were getting away with such a bold lie. His assertion is as true now as it was then, but with the growth of high tech, we cannot continue on mere cynicism—we need a real solution.

People know that using computers is very hard, but they assume that there are good reasons for the difficulty. Most people assume that things work as well as they possibly can.

Although most users of software-based products outside of the computer industry are extremely frustrated with hard-to-use products, most of the people creating them are satisfied with the status quo. Programmers don't find using computers particularly hard, so they are willing to tolerate things while they play with technology and have fun creating cool new dancing bearware.

For the rest of us, we get the software that we demand, and so far, we have demanded little. Software vendors give us geegaws, gadgets, and features we don't want and never use, yet we buy them anyway. We demand that our programs don't crash, so our programs are exhaustively tested, and they are reasonably reliable. We demand the newest versions right away, so they ship at breakneck speed. But unaware that things could be better, we don't demand that they be powerful and pleasurable, so they are weak and oppressive instead.

Occasionally, consumers hold out the vague and quixotic hope that the next wave of high technology—such as voice recognition—will make software-based products easy to use. This hope is naïve and foolish, and it saddens me how the apologists cruelly fan it.

Computer software is precisely that—soft—and it can be molded into anything that its makers want it to be. They don't make it easy to use because they don't know how, not because it can't be. Rather than admit that embarrassing fact, they claim that it cannot be done for "technical reasons." Computer users, who are not programmers, are forced to agree with the experts and suffer, or to disagree with the experts and—what?—suffer anyway. Not being experts, they are unable to proffer solutions of their own, so they are just regarded as unproductive complainers.

Detroit used to make huge, chrome-encrusted, gas-guzzling cars and proclaim self-righteously that it "only gave the consumer what they wanted." In the gas crisis of the mid-1970s, the Japanese stepped in with conservative, fuel-efficient small cars and dealt Detroit a blow it will never forget. Today, American auto makers show a much greater respect for the consumer's desires, and they will never again make the claim that they know best.

The Japanese seized the high ground of the auto market by giving users something that they didn't even know they wanted. But they knew a good thing when they saw it. In the same way, the high ground of software interaction is currently unoccupied and up for grabs. Microsoft is as vulnerable today as General Motors was in 1974.

The mass market of low-tech consumers will quickly leap on easy-to-use products, as the explosion of the Web attests. The same people who were attracted to the Web because it does a simple thing simply will be attracted to well-designed products that do complex things simply.

Those low-tech consumers outside of enclaves like Silicon Valley won't demand change because they simply cannot become a cohesive group. Sure, they know good stuff when they see it, but they only see it after it has already been built and put on store shelves.

Change will occur only when the people inside business who have influence early in the product life cycle become interested in fixing this problem. Programmers have a conflict of interest, so my appeal is to the ranks of apologists in the heart of the high-technology industry. And if you are in business today, you are in the high-technology industry whether you want to be or not. There is hardly any business left in the world that is not in the process of becoming dependent on information technology or that has not already become so.

None of our current crop of software-based products is capable of delivering power and pleasure to people outside of the techno-smitten minority. The engineering community says merely that users will have to become "computer literate." I believe history will view that phrase in the same way we treat Marie Antoinette's famously condescending "Let them eat cake." The French Revolution gave food to the masses, and the coming design revolution will give technology to the masses.

Changing the Process

The majority of software engineers and technical managers do what they do now because they believe in the process, but they are not dogmatic about it. They are pragmatic enough to change when they see how effective interaction design is. After they see its value, in my experience, they are very willing to integrate it into their development process.

Software engineers have a long history of changing their spots. Sure, they are engineers and will always think like engineers, but they will adopt new—even radical—techniques if they can see their effectiveness clearly demonstrated.

Twenty years ago, it was normal in the programming business for software engineers to test their own code. In fact, it was normal for a programmer to assert that he was the only person who could reliably test his own code, that he was the only person who could know all of its weak spots and its dusty corners that needed probing.

Surprisingly, it was also true that—although they *had* to do it—programmers almost universally hated testing and begrudged the time and effort it demanded. But programmers did the test work required of them because they conscientiously believed in their role in the process as well as the need for aggressive testing.

Slowly, over the last couple of decades, the idea that a corps of professional testers could separate out this part of the programming job and relieve programmers of its responsibility took root in the industry. After initial skepticism, programmers saw the value. The testers—to the enduring astonishment of most programmers—actually *liked* testing. They enjoyed crafting new, ever more diabolical tools for exercising the product, looking for weaknesses and omissions, probing edge cases, and pounding on probable cases. Of course, having products stretched by a trained corps of professional testers was far better than having programmers do it. And the programmers found that a large, unpleasant part of their job not only went away but was now accomplished more reliably, more timely, and with better organization and thoroughness. Contemporary doctrine in software-development circles says that a one-to-one ratio of testers to coders is correct. There isn't a programmer working today who still insists that he is the best person to test his own code.

We will see a similar gradual change occur when design becomes part of the development process. Because of the benefits of adding design, early adopters in this effort will reap those benefits the most.

Software engineers share the goals of the interaction designers: They want the product to be successful. It's just that their tools and terms for measuring that success are dramatically different from those of the designers.

In the absence of any convincing evidence, the programmer will always fall back on her own training, experience, and gut sensibilities. Her guts tell her to provide as many functions as possible. Her experience tells her to not let amateurs disturb the sensitive, difficult, and delicate development process with whims and guesswork. Her training tells her to construct interfaces in her own image.

The interaction designer cannot attack these motivations directly. Developers are too rational to abandon their experience for the opinions of others. The designer must show them a new way of looking at the problem, and he must show them two additional things: that it is effective and that it is compatible with their existing ideas.

Regardless of the strength of the interaction designer's position, it is extremely unlikely that he possesses better knowledge of the program's internals than the programmer. In other words, he cannot possibly take a more accurate look at the problem than from the programmer's point of view. In order to succeed, he must approach the problem from another point of view.

Where interaction designers can approach programmers on an equal basis is in the precision and completeness of the interaction specification. When designers deliver solutions that are compellingly correct, programmers come to trust and depend on them.

⌘

In a 1998 article in *Business Week*,[1] columnist Stephen Wildstrom broached the topic of frustrated computer users. The response from his readership overwhelmed him with its polarized point of view, its quantity, and its vehemence. It caused him to conclude:

> The computer industry has a lot of baffled, frustrated, and unhappy customers. That is a much graver threat to the long-term health of the high-tech sector than the Asian crisis, the Year 2000 bug, or just about anything else.

He reprinted the all-too-familiar cries of pain from the survivors—"My machine makes me think I'm an idiot!"—along with the equally familiar cries of the apologists—"Users don't know what they want, and when they do, they all want something different. And they won't read manuals or learn about programs." He concluded with this interesting observation:

> There's one thing missing from this outpouring. I've heard from engineers, programmers, and usability gurus. But the product planners and marketers who make the key hardware and software design decisions have been conspicuously silent. You folks have a lot of angry customers out there. How are you going to respond?

Indeed, how are you going to respond?

---

[1] Business Week, *October 19, 1998, "They're Mad as Hell Out There," Stephen H. Wildstrom.*

Index

J - K

Alan Cooper

As a software inventor in the mid-70s, Alan got it into his head that there *must* be a better approach to software construction. This new approach would free users from annoying, difficult, and inappropriate software behavior by applying a design and engineering process that focuses on the user first, and silicon second. Using this process, engineering teams could build better products faster by doing it right the first time.

His determination paid off. In 1990 he founded Cooper, a technology product design firm. Today, Cooper's innovative approach to software design is recognized as an industry standard. Over a decade after Cooper opened its doors for business, the San Francisco firm has provided innovative, user-focused solutions for companies such as Abbott Laboratories, Align Technologies, Discover Financial Services, Dolby, Ericsson, Fujitsu, Fujitsu Softek, Hewlett Packard, Informatica, IBM, Logitech, Merck-Medco, Microsoft, Overture, SAP, SHS Healthcare, Sony, Sun Microsystems, the Toro Company, Varian, and VISA. The Cooper team offers training courses for the Goal-Directed® interaction design tools they have invented and perfected over the years, including the revolutionary technique for modeling and simulating users called *personas*, first introduced to the public in 1999 via the first edition of *The Inmates*.

In 1994, Bill Gates presented Alan with a Windows Pioneer Award for his invention of the visual programming concept behind Visual Basic, and in 1998 Alan received the prestigious Software Visionary Award from the Software Developer's Forum. Alan introduced a taxonomy for software design in 1995 with his best-selling first book, *About Face: The Essentials of User Interface Design*. Alan and co-author Robert Reimann published a significantly revised edition, *About Face: The Essentials of Interaction Design*, in 2003.

Alan's wife, Susan Cooper, is President and CEO of Cooper. They have two teenage sons, Scott and Marty, neither of whom is a nerd. In addition to software design, Alan is passionate about general aviation, urban planning, architecture, motor scooters, cooking, model trains, and disc golf, among other things. Please send him email at inmates@cooper.com or visit Cooper's Web site at www.cooper.com.